LEADING
CONSTITUTIONAL
DECISIONS

LEADING CONSTITUTIONAL DECISIONS

CASES ON THE BRITISH NORTH AMERICA ACT

EDITED AND WITH AN INTRODUCTION BY

PETER H. RUSSELL

The Carleton Library No. 23

McClelland and Stewart Limited
Toronto / Montreal

Copyright © McClelland and Stewart Limited, 1965

Reprinted 1968, 1969, 1971, 1975
Revised Edition 1973

The Canadian Publishers
McClelland and Stewart Limited
25 Hollinger Road, Toronto

PRINTED AND BOUND IN CANADA

CONTENTS

PREFACE

This book has been prepared neither for lawyers nor by a lawyer. While the interests of professional lawyers and law students in Canadian constitutional law have been well served by the law reports and legal case books (particularly Professor Laskin's), those not professionally trained in the use of legal materials nor with easy access to such materials have often experienced difficulty in finding a convenient way to the leading judicial decisions on the B.N.A. Act. It is hoped that this collection of cases will increase the facility with which non-professionals – especially students and teachers of Canadian government and politics – can support their study of the Canadian Constitution by direct reference to the judgments of the Judicial Committee of the Privy Council and the Supreme Court of Canada.

A volume of this size can contain only a small sample of the constitutional decisions of the Privy Council and the Supreme Court. This collection is confined to cases which are concerned with the division of legislative powers and furthermore, it contains only a small sampling of the several hundreds of decisions in this area of constitutional law. Even in the twenty-five cases which have been included considerable editing has been required. This is particularly true of the Supreme Court's judgments. Unlike the Privy Council, which delivered only one opinion for each case, the Supreme Court's practice has been to permit all the Justices sitting for a case to write an opinion. To compound an editor's difficulties, no one of the opinions of the majority is designated as the opinion of the Court. At the end of each of the Supreme Court decisions reported in this volume the positions of those Justices whose opinions have not been included, together with the voting of concurring Justices, have been summarized. The criterion which has guided this necessarily extensive process of editing and selection has not been the purely legal significance of the material but its relevancy to the questions most likely to concern students of Canadian government.

The cases have been organized in six parts, each of which focuses on one of the central questions in the judicial interpretation of the B.N.A. Act. Within each section the cases are arranged in chronological order. In some instances cases in one section touch on issues relevant to other sections. Whenever possible these connections have been pointed out in the introductory notes. The symbol ~ has been used throughout the text to indicate material interpolated by the editor.

The following abbreviations have been used in citing and identifying cases:

A.C. (preceded by date) . . . Law Reports, Appeal Cases, House of Lords, since 1890. (e.g. 1891 A.C.)

App. Cas. . . . . Law Reports Appeal Cases, House of Lords, 15 Vols., 1875-1890.

S.C.R. . . . . Canada, Supreme Court Reports.

Privy Council decisions have also been identified by referring to their place in Richard A. Olmsted's three-volume *Canadian Constitutional Decisions of the Judicial Committee of the Privy Council.*

PREFACE TO THE REVISED EDITION

The first edition of *Leading Constitutional Decisions* was based on Privy Council and Supreme Court decisions up to the end of the 1950's. In the 1960's there were even more constitutional cases before the Supreme Court than there had been in the preceding decade. Again there was a marked trend towards challenges to provincial legislation. Of the 39 constitutional cases before the Court during the decade, 28 of them involved attacks on provincial laws. Although in only 7 of these was the provincial legislation invalidated, it is interesting that in all 11 cases involving federal authority, the legislation was upheld.

In the past decade the Supreme Court has attracted much more political attention, particularly in the Province of Quebec, and has consistently been included in the proposals for constitutional reform brought forward by federal and provincial administrations. Some of the cases included and referred to in this second edition give some indication of the politicization of the Supreme Court. The Court's inconsistent responses to the Canadian Bill of Rights (see Part VI) have sharpened public awareness of the Court's role in protecting civil liberties. In the Court's more traditional area of constitutional adjudication on the division of powers its decisions in the *Caloil* and *Chicken and Egg* cases dealing with the Trade and Commerce power (see Part II) as well as its decision in the Offshore Mineral Rights reference (see Parts I and III) involved the Court in important political disputes in Canadian federalism. It is notable that in all three cases the Court's decisions were adverse to claims or interests of the Province of Quebec. This outcome has probably undermined the Court's credibility as a constitutional arbiter in the eyes of Quebec's political elite, a possibility which may have serious implications for the future of Confederation.

The past decade's activity suggests that students of Canadian government and politics have still good reason to give some attention to the leading constitutional decisions of the Supreme Court of Canada.

PETER H. RUSSELL
University of Toronto
June, 1972

INTRODUCTION

JUDICIAL REVIEW AND THE
BRITISH NORTH AMERICA ACT

It is in keeping with the nature of much of Canada's constitutional history that one of the most influential elements in that development – the judicial interpretation of the British North America Act – was accepted at the outset with little awareness of its full significance. The Fathers of Confederation were remarkably insensitive to the problems connected with judicial review under a federal constitution. This, despite the fact that American experience had, by 1867, given every indication of the crucial importance of the Supreme Court in determining the extent of national and state powers. Section 101 of the B.N.A. Act granted to the national Parliament the power to establish a general Court of Appeal for Canada, but nowhere in the Constitution was there explicit recognition of the power of that Court, nor of the Judicial Committee of the Privy Council (the English tribunal which was then the final court of appeal for British colonies), to determine the constitutional validity of federal or provincial legislation. Nor were Canadians ever to witness a case like *Marbury* v. *Madison*, in which Chief Justice Marshall successfully claimed for the United States' Supreme Court the role of arbiter of the Constitution with the power of striking down any act of government, national or local, which in the Court's view violated the terms of the Constitution. Yet it was precisely that power which, from the outset, the Canadian judiciary, without explicit acknowledgment and despite the incompatibility of judicial review with the traditional British practice of parliamentary sovereignty, assumed with respect to the B.N.A. Act.

Educated as we now are by the textbooks of federalism, we are apt to look upon judicial review as a necessary ingredient of a federal state. But to those who accepted judicial review so readily in the 1870's and 1880's, especially to the jurists who manned the Judicial Committee of the Privy Council, the courts' power to pass on the constitutional validity of legislation might have been as much a corollary of imperialism as of federalism. The B.N.A. Act was, after all, an Act of the Imperial Parliament, and according to the Colonial Laws Validity Act Dominion statutes were void if they conflicted with British statutes. No doubt, in time, with the development of Dominion autonomy and the experience of the ambiguities and controversies inherent in the division of powers between national and provincial legislatures, the theoretical underpinning of judicial review has come to turn exclusively on the logic of federalism. Canadians today are perhaps all too ready to accept Roscoe Pound's maxim, "A federal polity is necessarily a legal polity." It is, indeed, ironical that as Canadian federalism has become less dependent on the vagaries of judicial interpretation, Canadians have developed a much keener awareness of the role of the judiciary as the indispensable umpire of the federal system.

Not only were Canadians rather slow to realize the implications of judicial review but, more important, until 1949 their highest court of appeal in constitutional matters was an alien tribunal, the Judicial Committee of the Privy Council. After the Supreme Court of Canada was established in 1875, there was some attempt made, especially by the Liberal Minister of Justice, Edward Blake, to limit, if not abolish, appeals to the Judicial Committee. But these efforts came to naught before the determined opposition of the British law officers and Sir John A. Macdonald's Conservative Party, both of whom looked upon the appeal as an essential link of imperial union. In the twentieth century the agitation to abolish appeals was rekindled, in part by the growing fervour of nationalist opinion, but also, with increasing urgency, by those Canadians who resented what they regarded as the unduly rigid and decentralizing tenor of the Judicial Committee's constitutional adjudication. The enactment of the Statute of Westminster in 1931 opened the way for the Canadian Parliament to abolish appeals to the Privy Council. Although Parliament's power to enact such a law was at first challenged in the courts, it was finally confirmed by the Judicial Committee itself in 1947.[1] It is significant that when the Supreme Court Act was finally amended in 1949 to make the Supreme Court supreme in fact as well as in name, the most serious opposition came not from Anglo-Canadian imperial sentiment but from spokesmen of provincial interests who by this time had come to see that they had a vested interest in the Judicial Committee's line of constitutional interpretation.

There can be no doubt about the supremacy of the Judicial Committee until the abolition of appeals in 1949. In some of its earliest constitutional decisions the Supreme Court did exhibit considerable independence. The Court's initial approach to the Dominion's "trade and commerce" power, as indicated by the

[1] *A.-G. Ontario* v. *A.-G. Canada*, [1947] A.C. 127.

majority's opinions in *Severn* v. *The Queen*[2] and *City of Fredericton* v. *The Queen*,[3] entailed a much broader interpretation of that power than the Privy Council was to accord to it. But within a decade the Court had succumbed to the reality of its subordinate position in the judicial hierarchy and remained, with few exceptions, a "captive court" until its emancipation in 1949. In the words of Professor Laskin, "The task of the Supreme Court was not to interpret the constitution but rather to interpret what the Privy Council said the constitution meant."[4] The Court's own recognition of its subservience to Privy Council decisions was reinforced by the decision of Canadian litigants in some of the most important constitutional cases to by-pass the Supreme Court altogether. If we take the whole range of Privy Council decisions on the Canadian Constitution we find that nearly half of them (77 out of 159) came in cases that were appealed directly from provincial Appeal Courts.[5]

Although the Supreme Court has now become the highest court of appeal, it is unlikely that this development will immediately lead to that Court's striking out on an independent line of constitutional interpretation. In law, it is true, the Supreme Court is not bound by the prior decisions of the Privy Council. As Justice Rand's declaration of independence in the *Farm Products Marketing Act* case indicates, in theory, the Supreme Court is as free as was the Judicial Committee before it to revise or restate constitutional interpretations contained in earlier cases.[6] But it would be unrealistic, in fact, to expect the Supreme Court to show any marked inclination to exercise this newly acquired freedom. The legal profession's concern for consistency and predictability in the law is too ingrained, and the Privy Council's decisions far too extensive and prescriptive, to

[2] *Severn* v. *The Queen*, (1878), 2 S.C.R. 70. See below pp. 65-72.

[3] *City of Fredericton* v. *The Queen*, (1880), 3 S.C.R. 505.

[4] Bora Laskin, "The Supreme Court of Canada: A Final Court of Appeal of and for Canadians" (1951), 29 *Canadian Bar Review*, 1038, at p. 1069.

[5] This enumeration is based on the compilation of cases in *Decisions of the Judicial Committee of the Privy Council Relating to the British North America Act, 1867 and the Canadian Constitution 1867-1954* arranged by Richard A. Olmsted. If we confine our attention to Privy Council decisions which deal with the division of powers in the B.N.A. Act, the total must be reduced by 16 to 143. Over 50 per cent of these (73) were appealed directly from provincial courts.

[6] *Reference re Farm Products Marketing Act (Ont.)*, [1957] S.C.R., 198 at p. 212. See below pp. 101-16.

leave very much scope, at least in the short run, for judicial pioneering. Still, some of the Supreme Court's recent decisions which are included in this book, particularly in relation to the Dominion's general power and "trade and commerce" power, indicate, if not a radical departure from Privy Council precedents, at least a much more pragmatic attitude to the problem of adapting the division of powers in the B.N.A. Act to the requirements of effective policy-making. Also, of course, in the field of civil liberties the Supreme Court has been able to break a great deal of new ground for the simple reason that the Privy Council had never pronounced on the serious issues in this area of constitutional adjudication.

But however independent the Supreme Court may become in the future the Privy Council's constitutional handiwork seems destined to have a lasting effect on the Canadian federal system. The core of that legacy is, above all, a tendency to look upon federalism as "a level of sovereign jurisdictional rivalry."[7] In their anxiety to preserve a division of powers appropriate for "classical federalism" and thereby resist the strongly centralizing tendencies of the plain words of the constitutional text, the Judicial Committee developed an acute sensitivity to the competing claims of the provinces and the Dominion. Despite the emergence of the so-called "co-operative federalism" of modern-day Canada, this atmosphere of competitive jurisdictions has remained an enduring feature of Canada's political landscape. The first question that Canadians are still most likely to ask of any new subject of legislation is, "Does it come under provincial or federal jurisdiction?"

PROBLEMS, PRINCIPLES, AND PROCEDURES OF CONSTITUTIONAL INTERPRETATION

For those who approach the subject of judicial review from the point of view of political science, it is essential to realize that a degree of discretion is inherent in the courts' (particularly the final court of appeal's) function of applying the terms of a federal constitution to the enactments of national and local legislatures. Although the authors of the B.N.A. Act were relatively painstaking in delineating the powers assigned to the two levels of government, the language they used to define those powers was still, of necessity, general and abstract. Phrases such

[7] F. E. Labrie, "Canadian Constitutional Interpretation and Legislative Review" (1949-50), 8 *University of Toronto Law Journal* 298.

as "peace, order and good government," "trade and commerce" and "property and civil rights," which appear in Sections 91 and 92, the vital sections for the division of legislative powers, are obviously replete with ambiguities. Even though some of the other subject-matters of legislation are more precisely described, the list, taken as a whole, could never anticipate the enormous range and complexity of problems which through the course of time have concerned Canadian legislators. These problems have not had the happy knack of manifesting themselves in terms of the neat classifications of the B.N.A. Act, nor indeed have the appropriate legislative responses to them often emerged in a way which brings them clearly under national or provincial heads of power.

Judges, in any case where they are asked to find whether or not a given statute is within the powers granted by the Constitution to the legislature which enacted it, must pronounce upon two related issues. They must, in the first place, define the nature of the subject-matter of the legislation whose constitutionality is questioned. But the determination of this issue will be guided by the court's second and larger decision: the meaning which is attached in this or earlier cases to the legislative categories of the B.N.A. Act. Neither of these issues is likely to be susceptible to a purely mechanical resolution – one which does not force the court to choose among quite closely competing alternatives.

Almost all of the cases included in this book illustrate this fact. The Saumur case is one of the more dramatic examples. In this case the Supreme Court had to decide how to characterize Quebec legislation forbidding the distribution of literature on the streets of the City of Quebec without the permission of the chief of police. Was this merely legislation designed to regulate municipal streets and keep them free from litter, or was it really a cloak for the specific policy of restraining the Jehovah's Witnesses from the dissemination of their ideas and thus a serious curtailment of an important civil liberty? But the answer to this question had to be conditioned by the judges' understanding of the meaning of Sections 91 and 92. Do civil liberties, according to the terms of the B.N.A. Act, constitute a distinct subject-matter of legislation? What matters are embraced by the provinces' power to deal with "property and civil rights"? How is that power related to Paraliament's general power to make laws for the "peace, order and good government of Canada"? On questions such as these rational men can differ. The answers determine not only whether a given piece of legislation stands or falls but also, in the long run, the substantial meaning of the constitutional text. Judicial review in Canada is, in a word, a significant area of policy-making.

In the application of the general terms of any law to particular circumstances there is always some room for judicial discretion. But, as has so often been pointed out, the judicial interpretation of the law of the Constitution, especially that part of it which defines the powers of the state's legislative authorities, has a higher degree of finality than that which is usually associated with the courts' rulings on ordinary statutes or the common law. With the latter, if the elected legislature is opposed to the judicial decision it can reverse or amend it by legislative action; whereas the only direct way of undoing the highest court's interpretation of the Constitution is through the cumbersome process of constitutional amendment. In Canada, especially with respect to those parts of the B.N.A. Act which deal with the division of legislative powers, amending the Constitution is, to say the least, a heroic procedure.

Ironically, the methods of interpretation adopted by the Judicial Committee of the Privy Council in the early stages of its adjudication of the B.N.A. Act denied any fundamental distinction between that Act and any other piece of legislation. Their Lordships decided to apply to the Canadian Constitution the same methods of construction and exposition which are applied to ordinary statutes. While these rules are far from being unambiguously formulated and uniformly applied, they meant as a minimum, when applied to the B.N.A. Act, that resort could not be had to any of the historical materials recording the intentions of the Fathers of Confederation. Thus, in drawing out the meaning of the various sections of the Act and applying its abstract terms to the concrete issues of Canadian life, the Judicial Committee explained its decisions solely in terms of the bare words of the Act and the formal relationship of its different clauses to one another. Professor Kennedy, looking back over more than half a century of judicial review, saw clearly the marks of this narrow, legalistic approach to judicial review. "A complete examination," he wrote, "of all the cases in all the courts in which have arisen problems connected with the B.N.A. Act discloses that, in the overwhelming majority of them, the *ratio desidendi* depended on reasoning entirely divorced from external sources or references. . . ."[8]

Occasionally, statements of the Privy Council did imply

[8] W. P. M. Kennedy, "The British North America Act: Past and Future" (1937), 15 *Canadian Bar Review* 393-4.

recognition of the extraordinary significance attaching to the interpretation of a statute which contained the written constitution of a large state and hence the need to treat it with some sensitivity to the actual milieu in which it originated and in which its terms must take effect. The most famous of these utterances was Lord Sankey's *dictum* in the *Persons* case in which he compared the B.N.A. Act to "a living tree capable of growth and expansion within its natural limits." He went on to advocate a much less literalistic and more liberal approach to judicial review. "Their Lordships," he stated, "do not conceive it to be the duty of this Board – it is certainly not their desire – to cut down the provisions of the Act by a narrow and technical construction, but rather to give it a large and liberal interpretation...."[9] Lord Sankey's "living-tree" doctrine did not, however, herald a revolution in judicial attitudes to constitutional interpretation. The so-called "judicial activism," embraced by an influential wing of the Supreme Court of the United States which looks upon the central challenge of judicial review as that of consciously adapting the terms of the Constitution to the changing needs of society, has never been deliberately taken up by the jurists responsible for the interpretation of the Canadian Constitution. Justice McGillivray of the Alberta Court of Appeals in an abjuration of deliberate judicial statecraft to which most of his Canadian colleagues would probably subscribe, has stated "that none of the observations of Viscount Sankey can be said to provide legal justification for an attempt by Canadian courts to mould and fashion the Canadian Constitution by judicial legislation so as to make it conform according to their views to the requirements of present-day social and economic conditions."[10]

Such avowals of judicial self-restraint, however sincere and typical they may be, cannot conceal the degree of judicial law-making which has, in fact, been inherent in the precedents established by the Privy Council. The plain words of the Act, to which the Privy Council claimed to confine itself in interpreting the Canadian Constitution, do not yield unambiguous meanings. Indeed many of those who have studied Canadian constitutional law closely are convinced that the most obvious interpretation not only of the intentions of those who framed the Act but also of the central terms of the B.N.A. Act itself,

[9] *Henrietta Muir Edwards* v. *A.-G. Canada,* [1930] A.C. 124 at p. 136.

[10] *Kazakewich* v. *Kazakewich* [1937] 1 D.L.R. 548, at p. 567 (Alberta).

especially the introductory paragraph of Section 91, the "trade and commerce" power and the general relationship of Section 91 to Section 92, points to conclusions quite different from those reached by the Privy Council in some of the leading cases which deal with these matters. In a few of these cases the policy considerations which supported the Judicial Committee's reading of the Constitution are quite clearly stated. The *Local Prohibition* case of 1896, which was one of the most decisive cases for the development of Canadian constitutional law, provides what has become perhaps the best known confession of judicial policy-making. Here Lord Watson supported his argument construing the Dominion's general power as subordinate to the enumerated powers of Section 91 and Section 92, with the following words, "To attach any other construction to the general power which, in supplement of its enumerated powers, is conferred upon the Parliament of Canada by s. 91, would, in their Lordships' opinion, not only be contrary to the intendment of the Act, but would practically destroy the autonomy of the provinces."[11] While the judges have rarely been so candid as this, in many other cases, certainly in most of those included in this volume, a vital determinant of the way in which they have interpreted particular terms of the B.N.A. Act or the significance of impugned legislation has been their implicit commitment to a certain view of federalism or some other social or economic value.

— One cannot complain, therefore, that the Judicial Committee failed to introduce into its interpretation of the Constitution values and beliefs extrinsic to the bare words of the Act. On the contrary, the main stream of criticism which has run through much of the Canadian literature on judicial review has been based on objections either to the actual policy preferences of the Privy Council, especially provincial autonomy, which, it is alleged, it read into the B.N.A. Act, or to the abstract and formal manner in which it phrased its judgments. The latter point has perhaps had the greater significance for the long run. More often than not, in the critical cases on the division of powers, the Judicial Committee's argument has turned on the apparently inescapable inference which flowed from some verbal formula or conceptual distinction – the "trenching" and "necessarily incidental" doctrines, the distinction between interprovincial and intra-provincial trade, John Stuart Mill's definition of an

[11] *A.-G. Ontario* v. *A.-G. Canada*, [1896] A.C. 345, at p. 360. See below p. 11.

indirect tax, the concept of a British Empire treaty. Comparing these cases with decisions of the United States' Supreme Court which focus on roughly similar issues, one is struck by the relative lack of thoughtful articulation of the real problems and alternatives inherent in the adaptation of a written Constitution to a dynamic society. This criticism, if well founded, points to much more than a stylistic shortcoming. While, on the one hand, the stringent approach has often had the effect of hiding the real issues and grounds of constitutional adjudication, not only from the Privy Council's public but at times, it would appear, from its own members, on the other hand, the complex formulae and conceptions it has developed have added an elaborate gloss to the B.N.A. Act which has created serious impediments to the effective handling of later cases. There is perhaps no more glaring instance of this than the Judicial Committee's treatment of Section 91 (2), the Dominion's trade and commerce power. Beginning with the *Parsons* case, which excluded from the scope of Section 91 (2) "The power to regulate . . . the contracts of a particular business or trade . . . in a single province,"[12] successive cases have hedged in this power by a long series of semantic provisos. Consequently, over time, the court's main preoccupation when called upon to deal with this question of the division of power in the field of trade and commerce became not that of identifying the economic activities which are inherently extra-provincial in scope, but instead the rather mechanical application of abstract conceptions to the terms of the legislation before the court.

The Supreme Court's accession to the position of final appellate court has not brought about a very perceptible departure from the rigid ways of the English law lords. Some of the Canadian justices, especially Justice Rand, have on occasion been prepared to deliberately analyse the possible effects of a decision concerning the division of powers on the capacity of governmental agencies, national and local, for effectively handling a given problem. The opinion of Justice Locke in the *Johannesson*[13] case is a particularly good example of this tendency, as is Justice Rand's in the *Farm Products Marketing Act*[14] case. But these exercises in self-conscious judicial state-

---

[12] *Citizens Insurance Co.* v. *Parsons*, (1881), 7 App. Cas. 96 at p. 113. See below pp. 79-80.

[13] *Johannesson* v. *West St. Paul*, [1952] 1 S.C.R. 292. See below pp. 62-64.

[14] *Reference re Farm Products Marketing Act (Ont.)*, [1957] S.C.R. 198. See below pp. 106-11.

craft have not led the Canadian Supreme Court generally to the candid acknowledgment of its policy-making role that we now associate with an influential bloc of judges in the United States' Supreme Court.

Such reticence should cause no surprise. In comparing the Canadian Supreme Court's constitutional adjudication with that of the Supreme Court in the United States, we must remember not only that the scope of judicial review is much narrower in Canada (where no constitutional Bill of Rights exists), but also that the Canadian Court, with respect to both its practice and the experience of its members, is much less thoroughly concerned than is its American counterpart with public law issues. In contrast to the Supreme Court of the United States, the Supreme Court of Canada sits at the top of a single judicial hierarchy. In this position it serves as the final court of appeal for every class of law: cases involving the interpretation of the B.N.A. Act comprise only a small fraction of its work. Equally important is the fact that most Canadian Supreme Court judges, like their predecessors on the Privy Council, have spent the bulk of their earlier experience in the private law field. In the United States many of those who have served on the Supreme Court have previously been prominent in public life, as names like Jay, Marshall, Taney, Hughes, Taft, and Warren testify. But in Canada professional competence as a judge or a lawyer is the main criterion of selection to the Supreme Court. Consequently, those appointed to Canada's Supreme Court are likely to bring with them attitudes and techniques not easily adaptable to adjudicating issues of major importance to the nation.

Besides these general constraints which are imposed upon Canada's highest court by the context in which it works, there are more specific constraints which the judges have imposed upon themselves. It would appear that the most important of these is the rule of *stare decisis*, according to which previous decisions are authoritative and binding. Although the Privy Council had stated that in constitutional cases it was not bound by its own decisions, in practice it took the view that "on constitutional questions it must be seldom indeed that the Board would depart from a previous decision which it may be assumed will have been acted upon by governments and subjects."[15] Certainly, it never explicitly overruled a previous decision. The Supreme Court of Canada, as long as it occupied a subordinate position in the judicial hierarchy, was bound by the Privy

[15] *A.-G. Ontario* v. *Canada Temperance Federation*, [1946] A.C. 193 at p. 206. See below p. 55.

Council's decisions, and, in addition, it announced as early as 1909 that aside from "exceptional circumstances" it would consider itself bound by its own previous decisions.[16] Despite the fact that since 1949 the Supreme Court of Canada has possessed the same degree of independence with regard to previous constitutional decisions as the Privy Council, nevertheless, like the Privy Council, it has continued in practice to pay homage to the principle of *stare decisis*. It has not expressly reversed either one of its own or one of the Privy Council's previous decisions.

Many students of judicial review in Canada have urged that however appropriate *stare decisis* might be in most branches of the law, in constitutional law it is not the wisest policy. They would apply to Canadian constitutional law the reasoning which Justice Brandeis urged upon the Supreme Court of the United States: ". . . . in cases involving the Federal Constitution, where correction through legislative action is practically impossible this Court has often overruled its earlier decisions. The Court bows to the lessons of experience and the force of better reasoning, recognizing that the process of trial and error, so fruitful in the physical sciences, is appropriate also in the judicial function."[17] The Canadian Supreme Court's refusal to adopt this position need not lead to as much rigidity as one might expect. The issues that come before the Court are always in some sense unique so that the judges will usually be able to "distinguish" previous decisions which they do not wish to follow as turning on grounds different from those in the case at hand. The immediate effect of "distinguishing" a case is similar to overruling it. But paradoxically, in the long run, the Anglo-Canadian practice of "distinguishing" cases may lead to more uncertainty than the American practice of overruling previous decisions, for the "distinguished" decision remains part of the "law" and can always be returned to in a later judgment.

The real effect of the application of *stare decisis* is not to freeze the law of the Constitution in a fixed mould but to limit the degree of discretion open to the judiciary. Earlier precedents establish boundaries within which judges must manoeuvre in approaching any new issues. On a given point – for instance, the interpretation of the "peace, order and good government" power – there will be considerable room for choice between competing series of cases. But whatever course is taken, the reasoning of

---

[16] *Stuart* v. *Bank of Montreal*, (1909), 41 S.C.R. 516.
[17] *Burnet* v. *Coronado Oil & Gas Co.*, (1932), 285 U.S. 393, at pp. 406-8.

the Court will normally be developed by reference to the authority of previous cases.

Besides *stare decisis* the courts have developed a number of general rules and concepts which are specifically designed to serve as guidelines to the solution of problems involving the division of powers in the B.N.A. Act. Most of these problems stem from the unavoidable amount of overlapping which is inherent in the division of legislative powers. It is difficult to conceive of any piece of legislation which is not potentially related to a matter in both the Dominion's list of powers in Section 91 and the provinces' in Section 92. This is the grounds for the application of the "aspect" doctrine which the Privy Council first formally enunciated in the case of *Hodge* v. *The Queen*.[18] According to this principle, "subjects which in one aspect and for one purpose fall within Section 92 may in another aspect and for another purpose fall within Section 91." Thus, whenever the constitutionality of legislation is challenged the courts must not only carefully examine the impugned legislation with a view to identifying those aspects of it which relate to federal jurisdiction and those which affect provincial matters, but must also decide which of its aspects – national or provincial – is its most essential or primary feature, its leading aspect, its pith and substance. A number of other rules have been enunciated to embellish or complement the "aspect" doctrine, but when analysed functionally they come down essentially to the unavoidable judicial task of identifying the most significant aspect or dimension of the impugned legislation.

There are many areas of legislative activity in which it is possible for both the Dominion and the provinces to enact valid legislation. To deal with collisions in these areas the Judicial Committee formulated the rule of Dominion paramountcy. If there is a direct conflict between the terms of valid provincial legislation and valid federal legislation, such that the two cannot stand together, then the former must give way to the latter. It is easier, of course, to state such a rule than apply it, and the authorities are not entirely consistent on the question of what constitutes a "conflict." Indeed it is very often the case that the court finds that federal and provincial legislation can co-exist in the same area. Laws regulating the sale of liquor are an example of an area which the Privy Council's early decisions identified and implicitly added to those fields of concurrent legislation explicitly stated in Section 95 of the B.N.A. Act. The

[18] (1883), 9 App. Cas. 117, at p. 130.

designation of such areas in which national and provincial authorities may act concurrently undoubtedly has added a badly needed element of flexibility to Canadian federalism. There has been a noticeable tendency in the Supreme Court's recent decisions to recognize new fields of concurrency.[19] Although this liberal attitude to concurrency has contributed to the development of co-operative federalism, on the whole it has tended to permit the provinces to legislate in areas already occupied by Parliament.

With all these rules and principles it cannot be emphasized too strongly that no matter how numerous they may become, nor how elaborately defined, they are not capable of a completely unambiguous application. They determine the kinds of reasoning which are relevant in constitutional adjudication but not the results of such reasoning. One of the overriding interests of political scientists who study judicial review should be to discover exactly where pure legal analysis ends and value judgments, which cannot themselves be determined by such analysis, begin.

To outside observers, particularly in the United States, perhaps the most unusual feature of judicial review in Canada is the use of advisory opinions. In contrast to the United States, where the courts will rule on constitutional issues only in an actual case or controversy between contending parties, in Canada both the provincial Appeal Courts and the Supreme Court are called upon by both levels of government to give advisory opinions on constitutional questions. The original Supreme Court Act empowered the Governor in Council "to refer to the Supreme Court, for hearing and consideration, any matters whatsoever as he may think fit."[20] The provinces have also made similar provision for references to the provincial Appeal Courts. In practice these "reference cases" have been largely confined to assessing the constitutionality of statutes or proposed bills. Originally the federal government's reference of provincial legislation to the Supreme Court was thought of as a means of obtaining judicial advice as to whether or not provincial laws should be disallowed. However, this rationale can no longer account for most reference cases. On many occasions, for instance in all of the "New Deal" references in the 1930's, the federal government has asked the Supreme Court to determine whether or not the national Parliament has exceeded its jurisdiction. Also, unlike the disallowance procedure with which

---

[19] See W. R. Lederman, "The Concurrent Operation of Federal and Provincial Laws in Canada" (1963), 9 *McGill Law Journal* 185.
[20] S.C. 1875, c.11, 3. 52.

only the national government can take the initiative, reference cases can be used by provincial governments to test the constitutionality of federal legislation.

Jurists both in Canada and on the Privy Council have on occasion expressed their disapproval of the practice of giving advisory opinions. To minds trained in the enacting mode of analysis required by the common law tradition the questions put to the court in a reference case are far too general and hypothetical. Usually they concern proposed bills or statutes which have not yet been put into force. In these cases the court must decide the constitutionality of statutes without knowing the precise effects they are likely to have. Many judges and lawyers would agree with Felix Frankfurter that the precedents which flow from such decisions are apt to be "ghosts that slay." But if we are willing to set aside the canons of a meticulous jurisprudence for some broader considerations of public policy, there is much to be said for the reference case. Often it is vital to know as quickly as possible whether a statute is valid or not; the reference case procedure makes it possible for those concerned with the legislation to obtain an opinion on its constitutional validity without waiting months or years for an individual to raise the constitutional question in an ordinary case. In fields where federal and provincial agencies are trying to co-ordinate their activity and jointly maximize their regulatory power, a judgment given in a reference case can serve as a judicious guide to those who must draft the federal and provincial legislation. The Supreme Court's decision in the *Ontario Farm Products Marketing Act* reference is a case in point.[21] In areas where jurisdiction is much more an object of federal-provincial rivalry, while the referring of an issue to the courts undoubtedly has the effect of throwing sensitive political issues into the laps of the judges, there may still be a real advantage in submitting the resolution of the political conflict to the relatively dispassionate ways of the judicial process.

Governments, both federal and provincial, have clearly not shared the jurists' qualms about the merits of the reference case. One-third of all the constitutional cases decided by the Privy Council originated in questions referred to Canadian courts by federal or provincial governments. Among these are many of the most significant decisions concerning the division of legislative powers. Indeed, twelve of the twenty-five cases included in this volume originated as reference cases. The inclination of

[21] *Reference re Farm Products Marketing Act (Ont.)*, [1957] S.C.R. 198.

governments to refer constitutional questions directly to the courts is especially marked in the modern period. Close to two-thirds of the reference case appeals heard by the Privy Council were brought before it in its last three decades as Canada's final court of appeal. During this period reference cases accounted for nearly half of all its constitutional adjudication. Although, since 1949, under the aegis of the Supreme Court of Canada, the use of reference cases has fallen off a little, the difference is very slight. For better or for worse it seems likely that the reference case will continue to play a central role in Canadian judicial review. It is noticeable that during a recent round of federal-provincial negotiations, Premier Lesage of Quebec threatened to resist Ottawa's proposed extension of family allowances by referring the issue to the courts.

The procedures of judicial review in Canada have one other facet which, like the reference case, has the effect of propelling major constitutional disputes into the courts. This is the practice of inviting the governments whose interests are involved in any constitutional case to intervene and take part in the case. In contrast to the practice in the United States, where only the national government has the right to intervene in the federal courts, and then only when an act of Congress is challenged, in Canada, by legislation and custom, the provinces as well as the Dominion are in most instances notified when their legislative powers are being tested in the courts and are given the right to become active parties in the case. The legislation concerning reference cases goes even further by extending to private groups who might have a stake in the outcome of a constitutional case an opportunity to be notified and heard. Thus, even though a constitutional issue may originate in a case between two private parties, the principal public or private bodies concerned with the issues can at some stage intervene and assume a major role in the advocacy of one side of the case. It is paradoxical that in Canada, while the style of constitutional jurisprudence is much more narrowly legalistic than it is in American constitutional law, the interventions of governments and private interest groups, coupled with the frequent use of the reference case, expose judicial review much more directly to the contention of major political forces in the country.

THE IMPORTANCE OF JUDICIAL REVIEW

One of the themes that runs through much of the present literature on Canadian federalism is the view that judicial interpretation of the B.N.A. Act has come to play a much less central role as a determinant of the division of powers. In reviewing the large adjustments which have taken place in federal-provincial relations since World War II, the more conspicuous factors seem to be extra-constitutional. The most decisive changes – the tax-sharing arrangements, the shared cost programs, the recent growth of provincial power and aggressiveness – do not seem to have been dependent upon constitutional changes effected either by constitutional interpretation or amendment. The primary instruments in these developments have not been the courts but federal-provincial negotiations and interaction both at the political and executive levels. Professor D. V. Smiley has drawn attention to the effectiveness of these extra-judicial agencies in shaping Canadian federalism. "The federal aspects of the Canadian constitution," he writes, "using the latter term in its broadest sense, have come to be less what the courts say they are than what the federal and provincial cabinets and bureaucracies in a continuous series of formal and informal relations determine them to be."[22]

There is undoubtedly much truth in this thesis. Politicians and administrators have certainly been more conspicuous than judges in the post-war evolution of Canadian federalism. This so-called "co-operative federalism" of the post-war period has been much less a litigious struggle between Ottawa and the provinces to defend and expand their own enclaves of power than a matter of political compromise and administrative pragmatism. While granting all this, we must still guard against dismissing too categorically the importance of the constitutional text and its application by the courts. In any of the issues that arise in federal-provincial relations, those who are responsible for working out the policies and strategies of the governments involved, no matter how pragmatic and flexible they may appear to be in dealing with the division of powers, must always operate on the basis of some assessment of the constitutional power which could be found to sustain the positions they wish to assume. In making these calculations, they will be guided by their awareness of previous constitutional

---

[22] D. V. Smiley, "The Rowell-Sirois Report and Provincial Autonomy" (1962), 28 *Canadian Journal of Political Science and Economics* 54, at p. 59.

cases and their anticipation of how alternative legislative and administrative schemes would fare if challenged in the courts. The number of major issues that are settled in court should not be regarded as the sole measure of the significance of judicial review. Just as important, but far more difficult to measure, is the extent to which judicial decisions, past, present, and future, enter into the considerations of the principal agents in the decision-making process.

Even if we do confine our attention to actual cases handled by the Supreme Court, the evidence does not indicate a marked decline in the incidence and significance of judicial review. One finds, for instance, that in the first decade, the 1950's, of the emancipated Supreme Court's constitutional adjudication, there were very nearly the same number of cases as in what was, by most accounts, the most notorious decade of the Privy Council's regime as Canada's final court of appeal. In the 1930's the Privy Council ruled on the constitutionality of legislation in 30 of its reported decisions; in the 1950's the Supreme Court of Canada was called upon to make similar decisions in 29 cases. The main difference between these two periods is that in the later decade provincial rather than Dominion statutes became the principal objects of constitutional challenges. Whereas in 18 of the 30 constitutional cases before the Privy Council in the 1930's it was national legislation whose constitutional validity was questioned (and in over half of these cases the federal government initiated the action), in the 1950's provincial statutes were involved in 21 of the 29 cases in which the Supreme Court of Canada dealt with the division of powers. Nor were all of those 29 cases of the trivial variety. Granted the most decisive questions had been brought before the courts prior to 1949, still the *Johannesson*[23] case and the cases which touch on the "trade and commerce" power entailed important contributions to the classical issues of Canadian constitutional law, while the cases which involved the question of inter-governmental delegation and civil liberties decided for the first time some rather critical questions concerning the division of powers.

To understand how the Canadian federal system operates the political scientist should retain some balance in the importance he attaches to judicial review. In his haste to avoid the naïveté of the traditionalist approach that would endeavour to explain the workings of the federal system by the legal rules which formally govern it, he should not fall into the equally

[23] *Johannesson* v. *West St. Paul*, [1952] 1 S.C.R. 292.

misleading mode of analysis which would dismiss the legal rules and their elucidation by the judiciary as one influential determinant of the system. The flow of power in Canadian federalism as in any complex political situation is a two-way affair; institutions such as the courts are undoubtedly affected by the total political context of which they are a part, but as well they react upon and shape that context. The political scientist's task is to ascertain both the way in which the Supreme Court is acted upon by the major forces in Canadian federalism and the way in which the Court in turn operates as one of those forces. It is hoped that the material contained in this volume will stimulate an increasing number of students to follow these avenues of inquiry.

PETER H. RUSSELL
University of Toronto
January, 1965.

LEADING
CONSTITUTIONAL
DECISIONS

PART ONE

PEACE, ORDER, AND GOOD GOVERNMENT

1. Russell v. The Queen, 1882

~ In the case of *Russell* v. *The Queen* the Judicial Committee
of the Privy Council was confronted for the first time with what
has undoubtedly been the classic issue in the Canadian division
of powers – the contest between the Dominion's "peace, order
and good government" power and the provinces' power in
relation to "property and civil rights" and "all matters of a
merely local or private nature in the province." Here the Privy
Council ruled the Dominion's temperance legislation *intra vires*
on the grounds that since the subject matter of the legislation
did not belong to any of the classes of subjects assigned exclusively to the provinces, it must fall under the central Parliament's
residuary power. This decision is usually regarded as the high-
water mark in the early tendency of judicial review to provide a
broad interpretation of the Dominion's legislative capacities.

The direct challenge to the Dominion's Temperance Act
came from Charles Russell, who had been convicted under the
Act of unlawfully selling liquor in Fredericton, New Brunswick.
But the fate of Russell's appeal, the immediate issue of the case,
was less important than the opportunity the case gave to the
Privy Council to review the earlier decision of the Supreme
Court of Canada in *City of Fredericton* v. *The Queen*[1] ruling
the Canada Temperance Act *intra vires*. The Supreme Court
majority in that case sustained the Act under the "trade and
commerce" clause of Section 91, giving a broad interpretation
of that power. In *Russell* v. *The Queen* the Privy Council agreed
with the Supreme Court of Canada that the Act was valid, but
on the basis of Parliament's residuary power, not the "trade and
commerce" power. While not repudiating the possibility of
sustaining the legislation under Section 91(2), Sir Montague
Smith refused to endorse positively the Supreme Court's reasoning. This refusal was more in keeping with the narrower inter-

[1] (1880), 3 S.C.R. 505.

pretation of Section 91(2) which their Lordships had given the previous year in the *Parsons* case.[2]

The reasoning which the Privy Council followed in this case is also notable as one of the best illustrations of what later came to be known as "the aspect doctrine." Sir Montague Smith, speaking for the Judicial Committee, argued that even though the Canada Temperance Act did affect property and civil rights in the provinces as well as some of the other matters, such as licenses, enumerated in Section 92, these aspects of the legislation were incidental to its main purpose – its pith and substance – which was the promotion of public order and safety throughout the nation. It was this latter aspect that should determine the characterization of the legislation for the purpose of bringing it under one of the powers distributed in Sections 91 and 92. ~

RUSSELL *V.* THE QUEEN

In the Privy Council. (1882), 7 App. Cas. 829; 1 Olmsted 145

The judgment of their Lordships was delivered by

SIR MONTAGUE E. SMITH. This is an appeal from an order of the Supreme Court of the Province of New Brunswick, discharging a rule nisi which had been granted on the application of the Appellant for a certiorari to remove a conviction made by the police magistrate of the city of Frederickton against him for unlawfully selling intoxicating liquors, contrary to the provisions of the Canada Temperance Act, 1878.

No question has been raised as to the sufficiency of the conviction, supposing the above-mentioned statute is a valid legislative Act of the Parliament of Canada. The only objection made to the conviction in the Supreme Court of New Brunswick, and in the appeal to Her Majesty in Council, is that, having regard to the provisions of the British North America Act, 1867, relating to the distribution of legislative powers, it was not competent for the Parliament of Canada to pass the Act in question.

The Supreme Court of New Brunswick made the order now appealed from in deference to a judgment of the Supreme Court of Canada in the case of the *City of Frederickton* v. *The Queen.* In that case the question of the validity of the Canada Temperance Act, 1878, though in another shape, directly arose,

[2] *Citizens' Insurance Co.* v. *Parsons* (1881), 7 App. Cas. 96. See below p. 73.

and the Supreme Court of New Brunswick, consisting of six Judges, then decided, Mr. Justice Palmer dissenting, that the Act was beyond the competency of the Dominion Parliament. On the appeal of the City of Frederickton, this judgment was reversed by the Supreme Court of Canada, which held, Mr. Justice Henry dissenting, that the Act was valid. (The case is reported in 3rd Supreme Court of Canada Reports, p. 505.) The present appeal to Her Majesty is brought, in effect, to review the last-mentioned decision.

The preamble of the Act in question states that "it is very desirable to promote temperance in the dominion, and that there should be uniform legislation in all the provinces respecting the traffic in intoxicating liquors." The Act is divided into three parts. The first relates to "proceedings for bringing the second part of this Act into force"; the second to "prohibition of traffic in intoxicating liquors"; and the third to "penalties and prosecutions for offences against the second part."

The mode of bringing the second part of the Act into force, stating it succinctly, is as follows: On a petition to the Governor in Council, signed by not less than one fourth in number of the electors of any county or city in the Dominion qualified to vote at the election of a member of the House of Commons, praying that the second part of the Act should be in force and take effect in such county or city, and that the votes of all the electors be taken for or against the adoption of the petition, the Governor-General, after certain prescribed notices and evidence, may issue a proclamation, embodying such petition, with a view to a poll of the electors being taken for or against its adoption. When any petition has been adopted by the electors of the county or city named in it, the Governor-General in Council may, after the expiration of sixty days from the day on which the petition was adopted, by Order in Council published in the *Gazette*, declare that the second part of the Act shall be in force and take effect in such county or city, and the same is then to become of force and take effect accordingly. Such order in Council is not to be revoked for three years, and only on like petition and procedure.

The most important of the prohibitory enactments contained in the second part of the Act is s. 99, which enacts that, "from the day on which this part of this Act comes into force and takes effect in any county or city, and for so long thereafter as the same continues in force therein, no person, unless it be for exclusively sacramental or medicinal purposes, or for bona fide use in some art, trade, or manufacture, under the regulation contained in the fourth sub-section of this section, or as hereinafter authorized by one of the four next sub-sections of this section, shall, within such county or city, by himself, his clerk, servant, or agent, expose or keep for sale, or directly or indirectly, on any pretence or upon any device, sell or barter, or in consideration of the purchase of any other property give, to any other person, any spirituous or other intoxicating liquor, or any mixed liquor, capable of being used as a beverage and part of which is spirituous or otherwise intoxicating."

Sub-sect. 2 provides that "neither any license issued to any distiller or brewer" (and after enumerating other licenses), "nor yet any other description of license whatever, shall in any wise avail to render legal any act done in violation of this section."

Sub-sect. 3 provides for the sale of wine for sacramental purposes, and sub-sect. 4 for the sale of intoxicating liquors for medicinal and manufacturing purposes, these sales being made subject to prescribed conditions.

Other sub-sections provide that producers of cider, and distillers and brewers, may sell liquors of their own manufacture in certain quantities, which may be termed wholesale quantities, or for export, subject to prescribed conditions, and there are provisions of a like nature with respect to vine-growing companies and manufacturers of native wines.

The third part of the Act enacts (sect. 100) that whoever exposes for sale or sells intoxicating liquors in violation of the second part of the Act should be liable, on summary conviction, to a penalty of not less than fifty dollars for the first offence, and not less than one hundred dollars for the second offence, and to be imprisoned for a term not exceeding two months for the third and every subsequent offence; all intoxicating liquors in respect to which any such offence has been committed to be forfeited.

The effect of the Act when brought into force in any county or town within the Dominion is, describing it generally, to prohibit the sale of intoxicating liquors, except in wholesale quantities, or for certain specified purposes, to regulate the traffic in the excepted cases, and to make sales of liquors in violation of the prohibition and regulations contained in the Act criminal offences, punishable by fine, and for the third or subsequent offence by imprisonment.

It was in the first place contended, though not very strongly relied on, by the Appellant's counsel, that assuming the Parliament of Canada had authority to pass a law for prohibiting and regulating the sale of intoxicating liquors, it could not delegate its powers, and that it had done so by delegating the power to bring into force the prohibitory and penal provisions of the Act to a majority of the electors of counties and cities. The short answer to this objection is that the Act does not delegate any legislative powers whatever. It contains within itself the whole legislation on the matters with which it deals. The provision that certain parts of the Act shall come into operation only on the petition of a majority of electors does not confer on these persons power to legislate. Parliament itself enacts the condition and everything which is to follow upon the condition being fulfilled. Conditional legislation of this kind is in many cases convenient, and is certainly not unusual, and the power so to legislate cannot be denied to the Parliament of Canada, when the subject of legislation is within its competency. . . .

The general question of the competency of the Dominion Parliament to pass the Act depends on the construction of the 91st and 92nd sections of the British North America Act, 1867, which are found in Part VI of the statute under the heading, "Distribution of Legislative Powers."

The 91st section enacts, "It shall be lawful for the Queen by and with the advice and consent of the Senate and House of Commons to make laws for the peace, order, and good government of Canada, in relation to all matters not coming within the classes of subjects by this Act assigned exclusively to the legislatures of the provinces; and for greater certainty, but not so as to restrict the generality of the foregoing terms of this section, it is hereby declared that (notwithstanding anything in this Act) the exclusive legislative authority of the Parliament of Canada extends to all matters coming within the classes of subject next hereinafter enumerated;" then after the enumeration of twenty-nine classes of subjects, the section contains the following words: "And any matter coming within any of the classes of subjects enumerated in this section shall not be deemed to come within the class of matters of a local or private nature comprised in the enumeration of the classes of subjects by this Act assigned exclusively to the Legislature of the province."

The general scheme of the British North America Act with regard to the distribution of legislative powers, and the general scope and effect of sects. 91 and 92, and their relation to each other, were fully considered and commented on by this Board in the case of the *Citizens Insurance Company* v. *Parsons* (7 App. Cas. 96). According to the principle of construction there pointed out, the first question to be determined is, whether the Act now in question falls within any of the classes of subjects enumerated in sect. 92, and assigned exclusively to the Legislatures of the Provinces. If it does, then the further question would arise, *viz.*, whether the subject of the Act does not also fall within one of the enumerated classes of subjects in sect. 91, and so does not still belong to the Dominion Parliament. But if the Act does not fall within any of the classes of subjects in sect. 92, no further question will remain, for it cannot be contended, and indeed was not contended at their Lordships' bar, that, if the Act does not come within one of the classes of subjects assigned to the Provincial Legislatures, the Parliament of Canada had not, by its general power "to make laws for the peace, order, and good government of Canada," full legislative authority to pass it.

Three classes of subjects enumerated in sect. 92 were referred to, under each of which, it was contended by the appellant's counsel, the present legislation fell. These were:

9. Shop, saloon, tavern, auctioneer, and other licenses in order to the raising of a revenue for provincial, local, or municipal purposes.

13. Property and civil rights in the province.

16. Generally all matters of a merely local or private nature in the province.

With regard to the first of these classes, No. 9, it is to be observed that the power of granting licenses is not assigned to the Provincial Legislatures for the purpose of regulating trade, but "in order to the raising of a revenue for provincial, local, or municipal purposes."

The Act in question is not a fiscal law; it is not a law for raising revenue; on the contrary, the effect of it may be to destroy or diminish revenue; indeed it was a main objection to the Act that in the city of Frederickton it did in point of fact diminish the sources of municipal revenue. It is evident, therefore, that the matter of the Act is not within the class of subject No. 9, and consequently that it could not have been passed by the Provincial Legislature by virtue of any authority conferred upon it by that sub-section.

~ Sir Montague E. Smith then pointed out that while national legislation such as the Canada Temperance Act might affect the sale or use of an article covered by a license granted under sub-section 9 of Section 92, this in itself was not grounds for bringing the legislation under that sub-section. ~

Next, their Lordships cannot think that the Temperance Act in question properly belongs to the class of subjects, "Property and Civil Rights." It has in its legal aspect an obvious and close similarity to laws which place restrictions on the sale or custody of poisonous drugs, or of dangerously explosive substances. These things, as well as intoxicating liquors, can, of course, be held as property, but a law placing restrictions on their sale, custody, or removal, on the ground that the free sale or use of them is dangerous to public safety, and making it a criminal offence punishable by fine or imprisonment to violate these restrictions, cannot properly be deemed a law in relation to property in the sense in which those words are used in the 92nd section. What Parliament is dealing with in legislation of this kind is not a matter in relation to property and its rights, but one relating to public order and safety. That is the primary matter dealt with, and though incidentally the free use of things in which men may have property is interfered with, that incidental interference does not alter the character of the law. Upon the same considerations, the Act in question cannot be regarded as legislation in relation to civil rights. In however large a sense these words are used, it could not have been intended to prevent the Parliament of Canada from declaring and enacting certain uses of property, and certain acts in relation to property, to be criminal and wrongful. Laws which make it a criminal offence for a man wilfully to set fire to his own house on the ground that such an act endangers the public safety, or to overwork his horse on the ground of cruelty to the animal, though affecting in some sense property and the right of a man to do as he pleases with his own, cannot properly be regarded as legislation in relation to property or to civil rights. Nor could a law which prohibited or restricted the sale or exposure of cattle having a contagious disease be so regarded. Laws of this nature designed for the promotion of public order, safety, or morals, and which subject those who contravene them to criminal procedure and punishment, belong to the subject of public wrongs rather than to that of civil rights. They are of a nature which fall within the general authority of Parliament to make laws for the order and good government of Canada, and have direct relation to criminal law, which is one of the enumerated classes of subjects assigned exclusively to the Parliament of Canada. It was said in the course of the judgment of this Board in the case of the *Citizens Insurance Company of Canada* v. *Parsons* that the two sections (91 and 92) must be read together, and the language of one interpreted, and, where necessary, modified by that of the other. Few, if any, laws could be made by Parliament for the peace, order, and good government of Canada which did not in some incidental way affect property and civil rights; and it could not have been intended, when assuring to the provinces exclusive legislative authority on the subjects of property and civil rights, to exclude the Parliament from the exercise of this general power whenever any such incidental interference would result from it. The true nature and character of the legislation in the particular instance under discussion must always be determined, in order to ascertain the class of subject to which it really belongs. In the present case it appears to their Lordships, for the reasons already given, that the matter of the Act in question does not properly belong to the class of subjects "Property and Civil Rights" within the meaning of sub-sect. 13. . . .

It was lastly contended that this Act fell within sub-sect. 16 of sect. 92 – "Generally all matters of a merely local or personal nature in the province."

It was not, of course, contended for the appellant that the Legislature of New Brunswick could have passed the Act in question, which embraces in its enactments all the provinces; nor was it denied, with respect to this last contention, that the Parliament of Canada might have passed an Act of the nature of that under discussion to take effect at the same time throughout the whole Dominion. Their Lordships understand the contention to be that, at least in the absence of a general law of the Parliament of Canada, the provinces might have passed a local law of a like kind, each for its own province, and that, as the prohibitory and penal parts of the Act in question were to come into force in those counties and cities only in which it was adopted in the manner prescribed, or, as it was said, "by local option," the legislation was in effect, and on its face, upon a matter of a merely local nature. The judgment of Allen C. J., delivered in the Supreme Court of the Province of New Brunswick in the case of *Barker* v. *City of Frederickton* (3 Pugs & Burb. Sup. Ct. New Br. Rep. 139), which was adverse to the validity of the Act in question, appears to have been founded upon this view of its enactments. The learned Chief Justice says: "Had this Act prohibited the sale of liquor, instead of merely restricting and regulating it, I should have had no doubt about the power of the Parliament to pass such an Act; but I think an Act, which in effect authorizes the inhabitants of each town or parish to regulate the sale of liquor, and to direct for whom, for what purposes, and under what conditions spirituous liquors may be sold therein, deals with matters of a merely local nature, which, by terms of the 16th sub-section of sect. 92 of the British North America Act, are within the exclusive control of the local Legislature."

Their Lordships cannot concur in this view. The declared object of Parliament in passing the Act is that there should be uniform legislation in all the provinces respecting the traffic in intoxicating liquors, with a view to promote temperance in the Dominion. Parliament does not treat the promotion of temperance as desirable in one province more than in another, but as desirable everywhere throughout the Dominion. The Act as soon as it was passed became a law for the whole Dominion, and the enactments of the first part, relating to the machinery for bringing the second part into force, took effect and might be put in motion at once and everywhere within it. It is true that the prohibitory and penal parts of the Act are only to come into force in any county or city upon the adoption of a petition to that effect by a majority of electors, but this conditional application of these parts of the Act does not convert the Act itself into legislation in relation to a merely local matter. The objects and scope of the legislation are still general, viz., to promote temperance by means of a uniform law throughout the Dominion.

The manner of bringing the prohibitions and penalties of the Act into force, which Parliament has thought fit to adopt, does not alter its general and uniform character. Parliament deals with the subject as one of general concern to the Dominion, upon which uniformity of legislation is desirable, and the Parliament alone can so deal with it. There is no ground or pretence for saying that the evil or vice struck at by the Act in question is local or exists only in one province, and that Parliament, under colour of general legislation, is dealing with a provincial matter only. It is therefore unnecessary to discuss the considerations which a state of circumstances of this kind might present. The present legislation is clearly meant to apply a remedy to an evil which is assumed to exist throughout the Dominion, and the local option, as it is called, no more localizes the subject and scope of the Act than a provision in an Act for the prevention of contagious diseases in cattle that a public officer should proclaim in what districts it should come in effect, would make the statute itself a mere local law for each of these districts. In statutes of this kind the legislation is general, and the provision for the special application of it to particular places does not alter its character.

Their Lordships having come to the conclusion that the Act in question does not fall within any of the classes of subjects assigned exclusively to the Provincial Legislatures, it becomes unnecessary to discuss the further question whether its provisions also fall within any of the classes of subjects enumerated in sect. 91. In abstaining from this discussion, they must not be understood as intimating any dissent from the opinion of the Chief Justice of the Supreme Court of Canada and the other Judges, who held that the Act, as a general regulation of the traffic in intoxicating liquors throughout the Dominion, fell within the class of subject, "the regulation of trade and commerce," enumerated in that section, and was, on that ground, a valid exercise of the legislative power of the Parliament of Canada. . . .

2. Attorney-General for Ontario v.
Attorney-General for Canada
(Local Prohibition Case), *1896*

~ In the *Local Prohibition* case of 1896 the "peace, order, and good government" clause underwent its second major examination by the Privy Council. On this occasion, in marked contrast to *Russell* v. *The Queen*, the federal government's general power emerged considerably reduced in significance. In one of the early parts of the judgment – in a paragraph that does not seem essential to the conclusion reached in the case – not only was Parliament's general power severed from the list of enumerated powers which supposedly clarify it but, in addition, the general power was given a position of subordination, first to the enumerated sub-sections of Section 91 and, secondly, to those of Section 92. Yet it should be noted that Lord Watson left what was still potentially a fairly large field for the application of Parliament's general power when he acknowledged that matters which are normally private and local might become questions of national concern, in which case they would come under the national Parliament's power to make laws for the peace, order, and good government of Canada. In succeeding cases this means of invoking the Dominion's general power was largely ignored by the Privy Council.

In this case the Privy Council also repudiated the decision of the Supreme Court of Canada in *City of Fredericton* v. *The Queen*,[1] which had brought the Canada Temperance Act under the "trade and commerce" power. In so doing the Privy Council culminated its implicit overruling of the early tendency of the Supreme Court of Canada to give the "trade and commerce" power a broad interpretation. This, coupled with the attenuation of the Dominion's residual power signified that in so far as the central issues in the division of powers were concerned the Privy Council was set on a course which, on balance, was much more favourable to the provinces than to the national legislature. This turned out to be a course which the Privy Council, with few departures, was to pursue for almost forty years.

[1] (1880), 3 S.C.R. 505. See below p. 66.

The question of the validity of the Ontario local option legislation was first raised in private litigation in the case of *Huson* v. *South Norwich*.[2] But before the Supreme Court could bring down its judgment in this case the federal government referred this question, along with six other more hypothetical questions, to the Supreme Court. In the reference case the Supreme Court ruled that the Ontario legislation was *ultra vires*, a decision which, oddly enough, due to a change in the Court's personnel, reversed its own decision in *Huson* v. *South Norwich*. In appealing this decision to the Privy Council Ontario was joined by Quebec and Manitoba, while the Distillers and Brewers' Association of Ontario intervened on the Dominion's side. Thus the issue of the relative constitutional powers of Parliament and the provincial legislatures to provide for prohibition by local option was propelled from a contest between private litigants to a case involving a direct confrontation of the two levels of government and one of the major interest groups in the affected industry. ~

ATTORNEY-GENERAL FOR ONTARIO *v.*
ATTORNEY-GENERAL FOR CANADA
In the Privy Council. [1896] A.C. 348; 1 Olmsted 343

~ The appeal was made by special leave from a judgment of the Supreme Court of Canada, 24 S.C.R. 170, on a reference to it of seven questions. ~

(1) Has a provincial legislature jurisdiction to prohibit the sale within the province of spirituous, fermented, or other intoxicating liquors?

(2) Or has the legislature such jurisdiction regarding such portions of the province as to which the Canada Temperance Act is not in operation?

(3) Has a provincial legislature jurisdiction to prohibit the manufacture of such liquors within the province?

(4) Has a provincial legislature jurisdiction to prohibit the importation of such liquors into the province?

(5) If a provincial legislature has not jurisdiction to prohibit sales of such liquors, irrespective of quantity, has such legislature jurisdiction to prohibit the sale by retail, according to the definition of a sale by retail either in statutes in force in the

[2] (1895), 24 S.C.R. 145.

province at the time of confederation, or any other definition thereof?

(6) If a provincial legislature has a limited jurisdiction only as regards the prohibition of sales, has the legislature jurisdiction to prohibit sales subject to the limits provided by the several sub-sections of the 99th section of the Canada Temperance Act, or any of them (Revised Statutes of Canada, 49 Vict. c. 106, s. 99)?

(7) Has the Ontario Legislature jurisdiction to enact s. 18 of Ontario Act, 53 Vict. c. 56, intituled "An Act to improve the Liquor Licence Acts," as said section is explained by Ontario Act, 54 Vict. c. 46, intituled "An Act respecting local option in the matter of liquor selling"?

Sect. 18, referred to in the last of the said questions, is as follows:

"18. Whereas the following provision of this section was at the date of confederation in force as a part of the Consolidated Municipal Act (29th and 30th Victoria, chapter 51, section 249, sub-section 9), and was afterwards re-enacted as sub-section 7 of section 6 of 32nd Victoria, chapter 32, being the Tavern and Shop Licence Act of 1868, but was afterwards omitted in subsequent consolidations of the Municipal and the Liquor Licence Acts, similar provisions as to local prohibition being contained in the Temperance Act of 1864, 27th and 28th Victoria, chapter 18; and the said last-mentioned Act having been repealed in municipalities where not in force by the Canada Temperance Act, it is expedient that municipalities should have the powers by them formerly possessed; it is hereby enacted as follows:

"The council of every township, city, town, and incorporated village may pass by-laws for prohibiting the sale by retail of spirituous, fermented, or other manufactured liquors in any tavern, inn, or other house or place of public entertainment, and for prohibiting altogether the sale thereof in shops and places other than houses of public entertainment. Provided that the by-law before the final passing thereof has been duly approved of by the electors of the municipality in the manner provided by the sections in that behalf of the Municipal Act. Provided further that nothing in this section contained shall be construed into an exercise of jurisdiction by the Legislature of the province of Ontario beyond the revival of provisions of law which were in force at the date of the passing of the British North America Act, and which the subsequent legislation of this province purported to repeal."

Act 54 Vict. c. 46, referred to above, declares that s. 18 was not intended to affect the provisions of s. 252 of the Consolidated Municipal Act, being Canada Act, 29 & 30 Vict. c. 51.

A majority of the Supreme Court, after hearing counsel for the Dominion, the provinces of Ontario, Quebec, and Manitoba, and also, under s. 37, sub-s. 4, of the Supreme and Exchequer Courts Act for the Distillers and Brewers' Association of Ontario, answered all the questions in the negative. Strong C.J., and Fournier J., while agreeing in a negative answer to questions 3 and 4, answered the remainder in the affirmative.

The judgment of their Lordships was delivered by

LORD WATSON. Their Lordships think it expedient to deal, in the first instance, with the seventh question, because it raises a practical issue, to which the able arguments of counsel on both sides of the Bar were chiefly directed, and also because it involves considerations which have a material bearing upon the answers to be given to the other six questions submitted in this appeal. In order to appreciate the merits of the controversy, it is necessary to refer to certain laws for the restriction or suppression of the liquor traffic which were passed by the Legislature of the old province of Canada before the Union, or have since been enacted by the Parliament of the Dominion, and by the Legislature of Ontario respectively.

~ Lord Watson then reviewed the history of liquor legislation in Ontario. He related how the Ontario Legislature came to pass the Act referred to in the seventh question. This Act aimed at restoring to Ontario municipalities the power of making by-laws prohibiting the sale of liquor. The right had been bestowed upon them in 1864 but had later been allowed to lapse by the Ontario Legislature and was not in force when the Canada Temperance Act of 1886, which provided for prohibition at the option of localities, purported to repeal it. ~

The seventh question raises the issue, whether, in the circumstances which have just been detailed, the provincial legislature had authority to enact s. 18. In order to determine that issue, it becomes necessary to consider, in the first place, whether the Parliament of Canada had jurisdiction to enact the Canada Temperance Act; and, if so, to consider in the second place, whether, after that Act became the law of each province of the Dominion, there yet remained power with the Legislature of Ontario to enact the provisions of s. 18.

The authority of the Dominion Parliament to make laws for the suppression of liquor traffic in the province is maintained, in the first place, upon the ground that such legislation deals with matters affecting "the peace, order, and good government of Canada," within the meaning of the introductory and general enactments of s. 91 of the British North America Act; and, in the second place, upon the ground that it concerns "the regulation of trade and commerce," being No. 2 of the enumerated classes of subjects which are placed under the exclusive jurisdiction of the Federal Parliament by that section. These sources of jurisdiction are in themselves distinct, and are to be found in different enactments.

It was apparently contemplated by the framers of the Imperial Act of 1867 that the due exercise of the enumerated powers conferred upon the Parliament of Canada by s. 91 might, occasionally and incidentally, involve legislation upon matters which are prima facie committed exclusively to the provincial legislatures by s. 92. In order to provide against that contingency, the concluding part of s. 91 enacts that "any matter coming within any of the classes of subjects enumerated in this section shall not be deemed to come within the class of matters of a local or private nature comprised in the enumeration of the classes of subjects by this Act assigned exclusively to the legislatures of the provinces." It was observed by this Board in *Citizens' Insurance Co. of Canada* v. *Parsons* (7 App. Cas. 108) that the paragraph just quoted "applies in its grammatical construction only to No. 16 of s. 92." The observation was not material to the question arising in that case, and it does not appear to their Lordships to be strictly accurate. It appears to them that the language of the exception in s. 91 was meant to include and correctly describes all the matters enumerated in the sixteen heads of s. 92, as being, from a provincial point of view, of a local or private nature. It also appears to their Lordships that the exception was not meant to derogate from the legislative authority given to provincial legislatures by those sixteen sub-sections, save to the extent of enabling the Parliament of Canada to deal with matters local or private in those cases where such legislation is necessarily incidental to the exercise of the powers conferred upon it by the enumerative heads of clause 91. . . .

The general authority given to the Canadian Parliament by the introductory enactments of s. 91 is "to make laws for the peace, order, and good government of Canada, in relation to all matters not coming within the classes of subjects by this Act assigned exclusively to the legislatures of the provinces"; and it is declared, but not so as to restrict the generality of these words, that the exclusive authority of the Canadian Parliament extends to all matters coming within the classes of subjects which are enumerated in the clause. There may, therefore, be matters not included in the enumeration, upon which the Parliament of Canada has power to legislate, because they concern the peace, order, and good government of the Dominion. But to those matters which are not specified among the enumerated subjects of legislation, the exception from s. 92, which is enacted by the concluding words of s. 91, has no application; and, in legislating with regard to such matters, the Dominion Parliament has no authority to encroach upon any class of subjects which is exclusively assigned to provincial legislatures by s. 92. These enactments appear to their Lordships to indicate that the exercise of legislative power by the Parliament of Canada, in regard to all matters not enumerated in s. 91, ought to be strictly confined to such matters as are unquestionably of Canadian interest and importance, and ought not to trench upon provincial legislation with respect to any of the classes of subjects enumerated in s. 92. To attach any other construction to the general power which, in supplement of its enumerated powers, is conferred upon the Parliament of Canada by s. 91, would, in their Lordships' opinion, not only be contrary to the intendment of the Act, but would practically destroy the autonomy of the provinces. If it were once conceded that the Parliament of Canada has authority to make laws applicable to the whole Dominion, in relation to matters which in each province are substantially of local or private interest, upon the assumption that these matters also concern the peace, order, and good government of the Dominion, there is hardly a subject enumerated in s. 92 upon which it might not legislate, to the exclusion of the provincial legislatures.

In construing the introductory enactments of s. 91, with respect to matters other than those enumerated, which concern the peace, order, and good government of Canada, it must be kept in view that s. 94, which empowers the Parliament of Canada to make provision for the uniformity of the laws relative to property and civil rights in Ontario, Nova Scotia, and New Brunswick does not extend to the province of Quebec; and also that the Dominion legislation thereby authorized is expressly declared to be of no effect unless and until it has been adopted and enacted by the provincial legislature. These enactments would be idle and abortive, if it were held that the Parliament of Canada derives jurisdiction from the introductory provisions of s. 91, to deal with any matter which is in substance local or provincial, and does not truly affect the interest of the Dominion as a whole. Their Lordships do not doubt that some matters, in their origin local and provincial, might attain such dimensions as to affect the body politic of the Dominion, and to justify the Canadian Parliament in passing laws for their regulation or abolition in the interest of the Dominion. But great caution must be observed in distinguishing between that which is local and provincial, and therefore within the jurisdiction of the provincial legislatures, and that which has ceased to be merely local or provincial, and has become matter of national concern, in such sense as to bring it within the jurisdiction of the Parliament of Canada. An Act restricting the right to carry weapons of offence, or their sale to young persons, within the province would be within the authority of the provincial legislature. But traffic in arms, or the possession of them under such circumstances as to raise a suspicion that they were to be used for seditious purposes, or against a foreign State, are matters which, their Lordships conceive, might be competently dealt with by the Parliament of the Dominion.

The judgment of this Board in *Russell* v. *Reg.* (7 App. Cas. 829) has relieved their Lordships from the difficult duty of considering whether the Canada Temperance Act of 1886 relates to the peace, order, and good government of Canada, in such sense as to bring its provisions within the competency of the Canadian Parliament. In that case the controversy related to the validity of the Canada Temperance Act of 1878; and neither the Dominion nor the Provinces were represented in the argument. It arose between a private prosecutor and a person who had been convicted, at his instance, of violating the provisions of the Canadian Act within a district of New Brunswick, in which the prohibitory clauses of the Act had been adopted. But the provisions of the Act of 1878 were in all material respects the same with those which are now embodied in the Canada Temperance Act of 1886; and the reasons which were assigned for sustaining the validity of the earlier, are, in their Lordships' opinion, equally applicable to the later Act. It therefore appears to them that the decision in *Russell* v. *Reg.* must be accepted as an authority to the extent to which it goes, namely, that the restrictive provisions of the Act of 1886, when they have been duly brought into operation in any provincial area within the Dominion, must receive effect as valid enactments relating to the peace, order, and good government of Canada.

That point being settled by decision, it becomes necessary to consider whether the Parliament of Canada had authority to pass the Temperance Act of 1886 as being an Act for the "regulation of trade and commerce" within the meaning of No. 2 of s. 91. If it were so, the Parliament of Canada would, under the exception from s. 92 which has already been noticed, be at liberty to exercise its legislative authority, although in so doing it should interfere with the jurisdiction of the provinces. The scope and effect of No. 2 of s. 91 were discussed by this Board at some length in *Citizens' Insurance Co.* v. *Parsons* (7 App. Cas. 96), where it was decided that, in the absence of legislation upon the subject by the Canadian Parliament, the Legislature of Ontario had authority to impose conditions, as being matters of civil right, upon the business of fire insurance, which was admitted to be a trade, so long as those conditions only affected provincial trade. Their Lordships do not find it necessary to reopen that discussion in the present case. The object of the Canada Temperance Act of 1886 is, not to regulate retail transactions between those who trade in liquor and their customers, but to abolish all such transactions within every provincial area in which its enactments have been adopted by a majority of the local electors. A power to regulate, naturally, if not necessarily, assumes, unless it is enlarged by the context, the conservation of the thing which is to be made the subject of regulation. In that view, their Lordships are unable to regard the prohibitive enactments of the Canadian statute of 1886 as regulations of trade and commerce. . . .

The authority of the Legislature of Ontario to enact s. 18 of 53 Vict. c. 56, was asserted by the appellant on various grounds. The first of these, which was very strongly insisted on, was to the effect that the power given to each province by No. 8 of s. 92 to create municipal institutions in the province necessarily implies the right to endow these institutions with all the administrative functions which had been ordinarily possessed and exercised by them before the time of the Union. Their Lordships can find nothing to support that contention in the language of s. 92, No. 8, which, according to its natural meaning, simply gives provincial legislatures the right to create a legal body for the management of municipal affairs. Until confederation, the Legislature of each province as then constituted could, if it chose, and did in some cases, entrust to a municipality the execution of powers which now belong exclusively to the Parliament of Canada. Since its date a provincial Legislature cannot delegate any power which it does not possess; and the extent and nature of the functions which it can commit to a municipal body of its own creation must depend upon the legislative authority which it derives from the provisions of s. 92 other than No. 8.

Their Lordships are likewise of opinion that s. 92, No. 9, does not give provincial legislatures any right to make laws for the abolition of the liquor traffic. It assigns to them "shop, saloon, tavern, auctioneer and other licences, in order to the raising of a revenue for provincial, local or municipal purposes." It was held by this Board in *Hodge* v. *Reg.* (9 App. Cas. 117) to include the right to impose reasonable conditions upon the licencees which are in the nature of regulation; but it cannot, with any show of reason, be construed as authorizing the abolition of the sources from which revenue is to be raised.

The only enactments of s. 92 which appear to their Lordships to have any relation to the authority of provincial legislatures to make laws for the suppression of the liquor traffic are to be found in Nos. 13 and 16, which assign to their exclusive juris- diction, (1) "property and civil rights in the province," and (2) "generally all matters of a merely local or private nature in the province." A law which prohibits retail transactions and restricts the consumption of liquor within the ambit of the province, and does not affect transactions in liquor between persons in the province and persons in other provinces or in foreign countries, concerns property in the province which would be the subject-matter of the transactions if they were not prohibited, and also the civil rights of persons in the province. It is not impossible that the vice of intemperance may prevail in particular localities within a province to such an extent as to constitute its cure by restricting or prohibiting the sale of liquor a matter of a merely local or private nature, and therefore falling prima facie within No. 16. In that state of matters, it is conceded that the Parliament of Canada could not imperatively enact a prohibitory law adapted and confined to the require- ments of localities within the province where prohibition was urgently needed. . . .

The question must next be considered whether the provincial enactments of s. 18 to any, and if so to what, extent come into collision with the provisions of the Canadian Act of 1886. In so far as they do, provincial must yield to Dominion legislation, and must remain in abeyance unless and until the Act of 1886 is repealed by the parliament which passed it.

~ Lord Watson then examined the differences between the prohibitions authorized by Section 18 of the Ontario Act and the prohibitions of the Canada Temperance Act. ~

It thus appears that, in their local application within the province of Ontario, there would be considerable difference between the two laws; but it is obvious that their provisions could not be in force within the same district or province at one and the same time. In the opinion of their Lordships the question of conflict between their provisions which arises in this case does not depend upon their identity or non-identity, but upon a feature which is common to both. Neither statute is imperative, their prohibitions being of no force or effect until they have been voluntarily adopted and applied by the vote of a majority of the electors in a district or municipality. In *Russell* v. *Reg.* it was observed by this Board, with reference to the Canada Temperance Act of 1878, "The Act as soon as it was passed became a law for the whole Dominion, and the enactments of the first part, relating to the machinery for bringing the second part into force, took effect and might be put in motion at once and everywhere within it." No fault can be found with the accuracy of that statement. Mutatis mutandis, it is equally true as a description of the provisions of s. 18. But in neither case can the statement mean more than this; that, on the passing of the Act, each district or municipality within the Dominion or the province, as the case might be, became vested with a right to adopt and enforce certain prohibitions if it thought fit to do so. But the prohibitions of these Acts, which constitute their object and their essence, cannot with the least degree of accuracy be said to be in force anywhere until they have been locally adopted.

If the prohibitions of the Canada Temperance Act had been made imperative throughout the Dominion, their Lordships might have been constrained by previous authority to hold that the jurisdiction of the Legislature of Ontario to pass s. 18 or any similar law had been superseded. In that case no provincial prohibitions such as are sanctioned by s. 18 could have been enforced by a municipality without coming into conflict with the paramount law of Canada. For the same reason, provincial prohibitions in force within a particular district will necessarily become inoperative whenever the prohibitory clauses of the Act of 1886 have been adopted by that district. But their Lordships can discover no adequate grounds for holding that there exists repugnancy between the two laws in districts of the province of Ontario where the prohibitions of the Canadian Act are not and may never be in force. In a district which has by the votes of its electors rejected the second part of the Canadian Act, the option is abolished for three years from the date of the poll; and it hardly admits of doubt that there could be no repugnancy whilst the option given by the Canadian Act was suspended. The Parliament of Canada has not, either expressly or by implication, enacted that so long as any district delays or refuses to accept the prohibitions which it has authorized the provincial parliament is to be debarred from exercising the legislative authority given it by s. 92 for the suppression of the drink traffic as a local evil. Any such legislation would be unexampled; and it is a grave question whether it would be lawful. Even if the provisions of s. 18 had been imperative, they would not have taken away or impaired the right of any district in Ontario to adopt, and thereby bring into force, the prohibitions of the Canadian Act.

Their Lordships, for these reasons, give a general answer to the seventh question in the affirmative. They are of opinion that the Ontario Legislature had jurisdiction to enact s. 18, subject to this necessary qualification, that its provisions are or will become inoperative in any district of the province which has already adopted, or may subsequently adopt, the second part of the Canada Temperance Act of 1886.

Their Lordships will now answer briefly, in their order, the other questions submitted by the Governor-General of Canada. So far as they can ascertain from the record, these differ from the question which has already been answered in this respect, that they relate to matters which may possibly become litigious in the future, but have not as yet given rise to any real and present controversy. Their Lordships must further observe that these questions, being in their nature academic rather than judicial, are better fitted for the consideration of the officers of the Crown than of a court of law. The replies to be given to them will necessarily depend upon the circumstances in which they may arise for decision; and these circumstances are in this case left to speculation. It must, therefore, be understood that the answers which follow are not meant to have, and cannot have, the weight of a judicial determination, except in so far as their Lordships may have occasion to refer to the opinions which they have already expressed in discussing the seventh question.

Answers to questions 1 and 2 – Their Lordships think it sufficient to refer to the opinions expressed by them in disposing of the seventh question.

Answer to question 3 – In the absence of conflicting legislation by the Parliament of Canada, their Lordships are of opinion that the provincial legislatures would have jurisdiction to that effect if it were shewn that the manufacture was carried on under such circumstances and conditions as to make its prohibition a merely local matter in the province.

Answer to question 4 – Their Lordships answer this question in the negative. It appears to them that the exercise by the provincial legislature of such jurisdiction in the wide and general terms in which it is expressed would probably trench upon the exclusive authority of the Dominion Parliament.

Answers to questions 5 and 6 – Their Lordships consider it unnecessary to give a categorical reply to either of these questions. Their opinion upon the points which the questions involve has been sufficiently explained in their answer to the seventh question.

3. In re Board of Commerce Act and Combines and Fair Prices Act, 1919, *1922*

~ The Privy Council's decision in this case produced the "emergency doctrine" which further restricted the grounds for invoking the Dominion's "peace, order and good government" power. Viscount Haldane contended that only under special circumstances such as war or famine could a matter normally within Section 92 become of such national importance as to be brought under the Dominion's general power. In this instance he reported that their Lordships could find no evidence to indicate that such a critical situation had been reached. It should be remembered that the legislation challenged here, while prompted by the profiteering in scarce commodities which had developed after the war, was not confined to the postwar period.

The six members of the Supreme Court of Canada had been evenly divided in this case. It is interesting to compare the opinion of Justice Anglin with that of the Judicial Committee. Justice Anglin found the federal legislation and the order authorized by it valid. Unlike the Privy Council, Anglin viewed profiteering as "an evil so prevalent and so insidious that in the opinion of many persons it threatens to-day the moral and social well-being of the Dominion."[1] Thus he found that the "true aspect and real purpose" of the legislation was the "public order, safety or morals, . . . of the body politic of the Dominion . . . a matter of national concern."[2] On these grounds he invoked Parliament's general power to sustain the legislation. He also thought that it could be supported by the "trade and commerce" power and, in part, by the "criminal law" power (Section 91 [27]). Justice Duff, on the other hand, rejected what he regarded as the dangerous notion that the Dominion, simply in order to deal with vicissitudes of national trade, could, under its general power, legislate in relation to matters otherwise subject to provincial jurisdiction. Such reasoning would "justify Parliament in any conceivable circumstance forcing upon a province a system of nationalization of industry."[3] These disagreements

[1] (1920), 60 S.C.R. 456, at p. 467.
[2] *Ibid.*, p. 466.
[3] *Ibid.*, p. 513.

between the two judges on the Supreme Court and between Justice Anglin and the Privy Council provide a good illustration of how extra-legal considerations can enter into the judiciary's determination of constitutional issues. ~

IN RE THE BOARD OF COMMERCE ACT, 1919, AND THE COMBINES AND FAIR PRICES ACT, 1919
In the Privy Council. [1922] *1 A.C. 191; II Olmsted 245*

~ This Appeal was by special leave from the Supreme Court of Canada. The appeal related to the validity of two acts passed by the Parliament of Canada in 1919 – namely, the Board of Commerce Act and the Combines and Fair Prices Act. ~

The judgment of their Lordships was delivered by

VISCOUNT HALDANE. This is an appeal from the Supreme Court of Canada, before which were brought, under statute, questions relating to the constitutional validity of the Acts above mentioned. As the six judges who sat in the Supreme Court were equally divided in opinion, no judgment was rendered. The Chief Justice and Anglin and Mignault JJ. considered that the questions raised should be answered in the affirmative, while Idington, Duff and Brodeur JJ. thought that the first question should be answered in the negative and that therefore the second question did not arise. These questions were raised for the opinion of the Supreme Court by a case stated under s. 32 of the Board of Commerce Act, 1919, and were: (1) whether the Board had lawful authority to make a certain order; and (2) whether the Board had lawful authority to require the Registrar, or other proper authority of the Supreme Court of Ontario, to cause the order, when issued, to be made a rule of that Court.

The order in question was to the effect that certain retail dealers in clothing in the City of Ottawa were prohibited from charging as profits on sales more than a certain percentage on cost, which was prescribed as being fair profit. The validity of this order depended on whether the Parliament of Canada had legislative capacity, under the British North America Act of 1867 to establish the Board and give it authority to make the order.

The statutes in question were enacted by the Parliament of Canada in 1919, and were to be read and construed as one Act. By the first of these statutes, the Board of Commerce Act, a

Board was set up, consisting of three commissioners appointed by the Governor-General, which was to be a Court of Record. The duty of the Board was to be to administer the second of the two statutes in question, the Combines and Fair Prices Act, called the Special Act. It was to have power to state a case for the opinion of the Supreme Court of Canada upon any question which, in its own opinion, was one of law or jurisdiction. It was given the right to inquire into and determine the matters of law and fact entrusted to it, and to order the doing of any act, matter or thing required or authorized under either Act, and to forbid the doing or continuing of any act, matter or thing which, in its opinion, was contrary to either Act. The Board was also given authority to make orders and regulations with regard to these, and generally for carrying the Board of Commerce Act into effect. Its finding on any question of fact within its jurisdiction was to be binding and conclusive. Any of its decisions or orders might be made a rule or order or decree of the Exchequer Court, or of any Superior Court of any Province of Canada.

The second statute, the Combines and Fair Prices Act, 1919, was directed to the investigation and restriction of combines, monopolies, trusts and mergers, and to the withholding and enhancement of the prices of commodities. By Part I, the Board of Commerce was empowered to prohibit the formation or operation of combines as defined, and, after investigation, was to be able to issue orders to that effect. A person so ordered to cease any act or practice in pursuance of the operations of a combine, was, in the event of failure to obey the order, to be guilty of an indictable offence, and the Board might remit to the Attorney-General of a Province the duty of instituting the appropriate proceedings. By Part II, the necessaries of life were to include staple and ordinary articles of food, whether fresh, preserved, or otherwise treated, and clothing and fuel, including the materials from which these were manufactured or made, and such other articles as the Board might prescribe. No person was to accumulate or withhold from sale any necessary of life, beyond an amount reasonably required for the use or consumption of his household, or for the ordinary purposes of his business. Every person who held more, and every person who held a stock-in-trade of any such necessary of life, was to offer the excess amount for sale at reasonable and just prices. This, however, was not to apply to accumulating or withholding by farmers and certain other specified persons. The Board was empowered and directed to inquire into any breach or non-observance of any provision of the Act, and the making of such unfair profits as above referred to, and all such practices with respect to the holding or disposition of necessaries of life as, in the opinion of the Board, were calculated to enhance their cost or price. An unfair profit was to be deemed to have been made when the Board, after proper inquiry, so declared. It might call for returns and enter premises and inspect. It might remit what it considered to be offences against this part of the Act to the Attorney-General of the Province, or might declare the guilt of a person concerned, and issue to him orders or prohibitions, for breach of which he should be liable to punishment as for an indictable offence.

The above summary sufficiently sets out the substance of the two statutes in question for the present purpose.

In the first instance the Board stated, for the opinion of the Supreme Court of Canada, a case in which a number of general constitutional questions were submitted. That Court, however, took the view that the case was defective, inasmuch as it did not contain a statement of concrete facts, out of which such questions arose. Finally, a fresh case was stated containing a statement of the facts in certain matters pending before the Board, and formulating questions that had actually arisen. These related to the action of certain retail clothing dealers in the City of Ottawa. An order was framed by the Board which, after stating the facts found, gave directions as to the limits of profit, and a new case was stated which raised the questions already referred to.

In these circumstances the only substantial question which their Lordships have to determine is whether it was within the legislative capacity of the Parliament of Canada to enact the statutes in question.

The second of these statutes, the Combines and Fair Prices Act, enables the Board established by the first statute to restrain and prohibit the formation and operation of such trade combinations for production and distribution in the Provinces of Canada as the Board may consider to be detrimental to the public interest. The Board may also restrict, in the cases of food, clothing and fuel, accumulation of these necessaries of life beyond the amount reasonably required, in the case of a private person, for his household, not less than in the case of a trader for his business. The surplus is in such instances to be offered for sale at fair prices. Certain persons only, such as farmers and gardeners, are excepted. Into the prohibited cases the Board has power to inquire searchingly, and to attach what may be criminal consequences to any breach it determines to be improper. An addition of a consequential character is thus made to the criminal law of Canada.

The first question to be answered is whether the Dominion Parliament could validly enact such a law. Their Lordships observe that the law is not one enacted to meet special conditions in wartime. It was passed in 1919, after peace had been declared, and it is not confined to any temporary purpose, but is to continue without limit in time, and to apply throughout Canada. No doubt the initial words of s. 91 of the British North America Act confer on the Parliament of Canada power to deal with subjects which concern the Dominion generally, provided that they are not withheld from the powers of that Parliament to legislate, by any of the express heads in s. 92, untrammelled by the enumeration of special heads in s. 91. It may well be that the subjects of undue combination and hoarding are matters in which the Dominion has a great practical interest. In special circumstances, such as those of a great war, such an interest might conceivably become of such paramount and overriding importance as to amount to what lies outside the heads in s. 92, and is not covered by them. The decision in *Russell* v. *The Queen* ((1882) 7 App. Cas. 829) appears to recognize this as constitutionally possible, even in time of peace; but it is quite another matter to say that under normal circumstances general Canadian policy can justify interference, on such a scale as the statutes in controversy involve, with the property and civil rights of the inhabitants of the Provinces. It is to the Legislatures of the Provinces that the regulation and restriction of their civil rights have in general been exclusively confided, and as to these the Provincial Legislatures possess quasi-sovereign authority. It can, therefore, be only under necessity in highly exceptional circumstances, such as cannot be assumed to exist in the present case, that the liberty of the inhabitants of the Provinces may be restricted by the Parliament of Canada, and that the Dominion can intervene in the interests of Canada as a whole in questions such as the present one. For, normally, the subject-matter to be dealt with in the case would be one falling within s. 92. Nor do the words in s. 91, the "Regulation of trade and commerce," if taken by themselves, assist the present Dominion contention. It may well be, if the Parliament of Canada had, by reason of an altogether exceptional situation, capacity to interfere, that these words would apply so as to enable that Parliament to oust the exclusive character of the Provincial powers under s. 92.

In the case of Dominion companies their Lordships in deciding the case of *John Deere Plow Co.* v. *Wharton* ([1915]

A.C. 330, 339, 340), expressed the opinion that the language of s. 91, head 2, could have the effect of aiding Dominion powers conferred by the general language of s. 91. But that was because the regulation of the trading of Dominion companies was sought to be invoked only on furtherance of a general power which the Dominion Parliament possessed independently of it. Where there was no such power in that Parliament, as in the case of the Dominion Insurance Act, it was held otherwise, and that the authority of the Dominion Parliament to legislate for the regulation of trade and commerce did not, by itself, enable interference with particular trades in which Canadians would, apart from any right of interference conferred by these words above, be free to engage in the Provinces ([1916] 1 A.C. 588). This result was the outcome of a series of well-known decisions of earlier dates, which are now so familiar that they need not be cited.

For analogous reasons the words of head 27 of s. 91 do not assist the argument for the Dominion. It is one thing to construe the words "the criminal law, except the constitution of courts of criminal jurisdiction, but including the procedure in criminal matters," as enabling the Dominion Parliament to exercise exclusive legislative power where the subject matter is one which by its very nature belongs to the domain of criminal jurisprudence. A general law, to take an example, making incest a crime, belongs to this class. It is quite another thing, first to attempt to interfere with a class of subject committed exclusively to the Provincial Legislature, and then to justify this by enacting ancillary provisions, designated as new phases of Dominion criminal law which require a title to so interfere as basis of their application. For analogous reasons their Lordships think that s. 101 of the British North America Act, which enables the Parliament of Canada, notwithstanding anything in the Act, to provide for the establishment of any additional Courts for the better administration of the laws of Canada, cannot be read as enabling that Parliament to trench on Provincial rights, such as the powers over property and civil rights in the Provinces exclusively conferred on their Legislatures. Full significance can be attached to the words in question without reading them as implying such capacity on the part of the Dominion Parliament. It is essential in such cases that the new judicial establishment should be a means to some end competent to the latter.

As their Lordships have already indicated, the jurisdiction attempted to be conferred on the new Board of Commerce appears to them to be ultra vires for the reasons now discussed. It implies a claim of title, in the cases of non-traders as well as of traders, to make orders prohibiting the accumulation of certain articles required for every-day life, and the withholding of such articles from sale at prices to be defined by the Board, whenever they exceed the amount of the material which appears to the Board to be required for domestic purposes or for the ordinary purposes of business. The Board is also given jurisdiction to regulate profits and dealings which may give rise to profit. The power sought to be given to the Board applies to articles produced for his own use by the householder himself, as well as to articles accumulated, not for the market but for the purposes of their own processes of manufacture by manufacturers. The Board is empowered to inquire into individual cases and to deal with them individually, and not merely as the result of applying principles to be laid down as of general application. This would cover such instances as those of coal mines and of local Provincial undertakings for meeting Provincial requirements of social life.

Legislation setting up a Board of Commerce with such powers appears to their Lordships to be beyond the powers conferred by s. 91. They find confirmation of this view in s. 41 of the Board of Commerce Act, which enables the Dominion Executive to review and alter the decisions of the Board. It has already been observed that circumstances are conceivable, such as those of war or famine, when the peace, order and good Government of the Dominion might be imperilled under conditions so exceptional that they require legislation of a character in reality beyond anything provided for by the enumerated heads in either s. 92 or s. 91 itself. Such a case, if it were to arise would have to be considered closely before the conclusion could properly be reached that it was one which could not be treated as falling under any of the heads enumerated. Still, it is a conceivable case, and although great caution is required in referring to it, even in general terms, it ought not, in the view their Lordships take of the British North America Act, read as a whole, to be excluded from what is possible. For throughout the provisions of that Act there is apparent the recognition that subjects which would normally belong exclusively to a specifically assigned class of subject may, under different circumstances and in another aspect, assume a further significance. Such an aspect may conceivably become of paramount importance, and of dimensions that give rise to other aspects. This is a principle which, although recognized in earlier decisions, such as that of

Russell v. *The Queen*, both here and in the Courts of Canada, has always been applied with reluctance, and its recognition as relevant can be justified only after scrutiny sufficient to render it clear that the circumstances are abnormal. In the case before them, however important it may seem to the Parliament of Canada that some such policy as that adopted in the two Acts in question should be made general throughout Canada, their Lordships do not find any evidence that the standard of necessity referred to has been reached, or that the attainment of the end sought is practicable, in view of the distribution of legislative powers enacted by the Constitution Act, without the co-operation of the Provincial Legislatures. It may well be that it is within the power of the Dominion Parliament to call, for example, for statistical and other information which may be valuable for guidance in questions affecting Canada as a whole. Such information may be required before any power to regulate trade and commerce can be properly exercised, even where such power is construed in a fashion much narrower than that in which it was sought to interpret it in the argument at the Bar for the Attorney-General for Canada. But even this consideration affords no justification for interpreting the words of s. 91, sub-s. 2, in a fashion which would, as was said in the argument on the other side, make them confer capacity to regulate particular trades and businesses.

For the reasons now given their Lordships are of opinion that the first of the questions brought before them must be answered in the negative. As a consequence the second question does not arise.

4. Fort Frances Pulp and Power Co. v. Manitoba Free Press, *1923*

~ The Privy Council in this case gave a positive application of the "emergency doctrine" which it had first enunciated in *The Board of Commerce Act* case. The outbreak of a great war was identified as one of those extraordinary contingencies in the life of the nation which could justify the national government's intervention in matters normally subject to provincial jurisdiction. It should be noted that the statutes and orders challenged in this case had been specifically designed to deal with the wartime and immediate postwar emergency. The Judicial Committee would ordinarily have characterized the laws controlling the price and supply of newsprint as relating to property and civil rights in the province, but it was willing to recognize that under wartime conditions such laws took on a national aspect so that they could be brought under Section 91. Viscount Haldane, speaking for the Judicial Committee, went further and stated that once an emergency was deemed to exist the judiciary must give the national Parliament the benefit of the doubt as to the continued existence of the emergency.

The *Fort Frances* case was followed by the Privy Council after World War II to sustain the national government's scheme for the deportation of Japanese Canadians.[1] The statutes under which the deportation orders were issued were the War Measures Act, 1914, and the National Emergency Transitional Powers Act, 1945. On this occasion the Privy Council declared its reluctance to question Parliament's judgment concerning both the existence and the continuation of a wartime emergency. In 1950 the Supreme Court of Canada followed a similar line of reasoning in ruling *intra vires* the Dominion Government's wartime rent control regulations.[2]

In so far as "the peace, order and good government" clause is concerned, the most important implication of this series of judgments is the view that the exercise of the central govern-

---

[1] *Co-operative Committee on Japanese Canadians* v. *A.-G. Canada*, [1947] A.C. 87.

[2] *Reference re Validity of Wartime Leasehold Regulations*, [1950] S.C.R. 124.

ment's general power under emergency conditions entails a drastic departure from the normal practice of Canadian federalism. In the *Japanese Canadians* case Lord Wright pictured the invocation of the Dominion's emergency power as temporarily setting aside "the rule of law as to the distribution of powers between the . . . Dominion and the . . . Provinces."[3] Of course the other side of this implication is the corollary that during a great war and its immediate aftermath the normal working of the Canadian federal system is, at least potentially, in abeyance. ~

FORT FRANCES PULP AND POWER CO. *v.*
MANITOBA FREE PRESS
In the Privy Council. [*1923*] *A.C. 695; II Olmsted 306*

The judgment of their Lordships was delivered by

VISCOUNT HALDANE. This appeal raises questions of some novelty and delicacy.

The appellants are manufacturers of newsprint paper in Ontario, and the respondents are publishers of newspapers, carrying on business at various places in Canada. The action out of which the appeal arises was brought by the respondents against the appellants to recover sums the former had paid for paper delivered to them at controlled prices. These sums, which the respondents alleged to represent margins in excess of the prices regulated by law, they claimed to be repayable to them as the result of orders of the Paper Control Tribunal of Canada, the final order having been made on July 8, 1920. The sums represented the amounts due after an adjustment of accounts in accordance with the above-mentioned final order and previous orders which it modified. For the balance so arrived at the action was brought in the Supreme Court of Ontario. It was tried before Riddell J., who gave judgment for the plaintiffs, the respondents.

~ Viscount Haldane stated that the Judicial Committee would not follow the Appellate Division of the Supreme Court of Ontario which had ruled in favour of the respondents, the Manitoba Free Press, not on constitutional grounds but on the grounds that the appellants were bound by contract to accept the price set by the Paper Control Tribunal. The Privy Council

[3] [1947] A.C. 101.

considered that to decide the case it was necessary to determine the validity of the Dominion legislation and orders setting up the controlling tribunals.

Viscount Haldane then proceeded to examine the statutes and orders in question. The federal government's control over the supply and price of newsprint had first been instituted in 1917 by Orders in Council under the War Measures Act, 1914. A Paper Commissioner and Controller was established with the power to fix quantities and set prices and, in 1918, a Paper Control Tribunal was set up to hear appeals from the orders of the Paper Commissioner. Another Act in 1919 confirmed both the Commissioner's and the Tribunal's power to settle any matters which were pending before the proclamation of peace. The Privy Council was of the opinion that the Order challenged in this case had been made prior to any formal proclamation of peace. ∼

It is clear that in normal circumstances the Dominion Parliament could not have so legislated as to set up the machinery of control over the paper manufacturers which is now in question. The recent decision of the Judicial Committee in the *Board of Commerce* case ([1922] 1 A.C. 191), as well as earlier decisions, show that as the Dominion Parliament cannot ordinarily legislate so as to interfere with property and civil rights in the Provinces, it could not have done what the two statutes under consideration purport to do had the situation been normal. But it does not follow that in a very different case, such as that of sudden danger to social order arising from the outbreak of a great war, the Parliament of the Dominion cannot act under other powers which may well be implied in the constitution. The reasons given in the *Board of Commerce* case recognize exceptional cases where such a power may be implied.

In the event of war, when the national life may require for its preservation the employment of very exceptional means, the provision of peace, order and good government for the country as a whole may involve effort on behalf of the whole nation, in which the interests of individuals may have to be subordinated to that of the community in a fashion which requires s. 91 to be interpreted as providing for such an emergency. The general control of property and civil rights for normal purposes remains with the Provincial Legislatures. But questions may arise by reason of the special circumstances of the national emergency which concern nothing short of the peace, order and good government of Canada as a whole.

The overriding powers enumerated in s. 91, as well as the general words at the commencement of the section, may then become applicable to new and special aspects which they cover of subjects assigned otherwise exclusively to the Provinces. It may be, for example, impossible to deal adequately with the new questions which arise without the imposition of special regulations on trade and commerce of a kind that only the situation created by the emergency places within the competency of the Dominion Parliament. It is proprietary and civil rights in new relations, which they do not present in normal times, that have to be dealt with; and these relations, which affect Canada as an entirety, fall within s. 91, because in their fullness they extend beyond what s. 92 can really cover. The kind of power adequate for dealing with them is only to be found in that part of the constitution which establishes power in the State as a whole. For it is not one that can be reliably provided for by depending on collective action of the Legislatures of the individual Provinces agreeing for the purpose. That the basic instrument on which the character of the entire constitution depends should be construed as providing for such centralised power in an emergency situation follows from the manifestation in the language of the Act of the principle that the instrument has among its purposes to provide for the State regarded as a whole, and for the expression and influence of its public opinion as such. This principle of a power so implied has received effect also in countries with a written and apparently rigid constitution such as the United States, where the strictly federal character of the national basic agreement has retained the residuary powers not expressly conferred on the Federal Government for the component States. The operation of the scheme of interpretation is all the more to be looked for in a constitution such as that established by the British North America Act, where the residuary powers are given to the Dominion Central Government; and the preamble of the statute declares the intention to be that the Dominion should have a constitution similar in principle to that of the United Kingdom.

Their Lordships, therefore, entertain no doubt that however the wording of ss. 91 and 92 may have laid down a framework under which, as a general principle, the Dominion Parliament is to be excluded from trenching on property and civil rights in the Provinces of Canada, yet in a sufficiently great emergency such as that arising out of war, there is implied the power to deal adequately with that emergency for the safety of the

Dominion as a whole. The enumeration in s. 92 is not in any way repealed in the event of such an occurrence, but a new aspect of the business of Government is recognized as emerging, an aspect which is not covered or precluded by the general words in which powers are assigned to the Legislatures of the Provinces as individual units. Where an exact line of demarcation will lie in such cases it may not be easy to lay down a priori, nor is it necessary. For in the solution of the problem regard must be had to the broadened field covered, in case of exceptional necessity, by the language of s. 91, in which the interests of the Dominion generally are protected. As to these interests the Dominion Government, which in its Parliament represents the people as a whole, must be deemed to be left with considerable freedom to judge.

The other point which arises is whether such exceptional necessity as must be taken to have existed when the war broke out, and almost of necessity for some period subsequent to its outbreak, continued through the whole of the time within which the questions in the present case arose.

When war has broken out it may be requisite to make special provision to ensure the maintenance of law and order in a country, even when it is in no immediate danger of invasion. Public opinion may become excitable, and one of the causes of this may conceivably be want of uninterrupted information in newspapers. Steps may have to be taken to ensure supplies of these and to avoid shortage, and the effect of the economic and other disturbance occasioned originally by the war may thus continue for some time after it is terminated. The question of the extent to which provision for circumstances such as these may have to be maintained is one on which a Court of law is loath to enter. No authority other than the central Government is in a position to deal with a problem which is essentially one of statesmanship. It may be that it has become clear that the crisis which arose is wholly at an end and that there is no justification for the continued exercise of an exceptional interference which becomes ultra vires when it is no longer called for. In such a case the law as laid down for distribution of powers in the ruling instrument would have to be invoked. But very clear evidence that the crisis has wholly passed away would be required to justify the judiciary, even when the question raised was one of ultra vires which it had to decide, in overruling the decision of the Government that exceptional measures were still requisite.

In saying what is almost obvious, their Lordships observe them-selves to be in accord with the view 'taken under analogous circumstances by the Supreme Court of the United States, and expressed in such decisions as that in October, 1919, in *Hamilton* v. *Kentucky Distilleries Co.* (251 U.S. 146).

When then, in the present instance, can it be said that the necessity altogether ceased for maintaining the exceptional measure of control over the newspaper print industry intro-duced while the war was at its height? At what date did the disturbed state of Canada which the war had produced so entirely pass away that the legislative measures relied on in the present case became ultra vires? It is enough to say that there is no clear and unmistakable evidence that the Government was in error in thinking that the necessity was still in existence at the dates on which the action in question was taken by the Paper Control Tribunal. No doubt late in 1919 statements were made to the effect that the war itself was at an end. For example, in the Order in Council made at Ottawa on December 20, 1919, it is stated that it must "be realised that although no proclamation has been issued declaring that the war no longer exists, actual war conditions have in fact long ago ceased to exist, and con-sequently existence of war can no longer be urged as a reason in fact for maintaining these extraordinary regulations as necessary or advisable for the security of Canada."

The Order in Council then goes on to say that in consequence of the armistice of November, 1918, the Expeditionary Force had since been withdrawn and demobilised, and the country generally is devoting its energies to re-establishment in the ordi-nary avocations of peace. In these circumstances, it states, the Minister of Justice considers that the time has arrived when the emergency Government legislation should cease to operate. This was in December, 1919. The Order then goes on to declare repealed all Orders and Regulations of the Governor in Council which depend for their sanction upon s. 6 of the War Measures Act, 1914, and repeals them as from January 1, 1920. But from this repeal it expressly excepts, among other Orders and Regula-tions specified, those relating to paper control, which are to remain in force until the end of another session of Parliament.

It will be observed that this Order in Council deals only with the results following from the cessation of actual war condi-tions. It excepts from repeal certain measures concerned with consequential conditions arising out of war, which may obvi-ously continue to produce effects remaining in operation after war itself is over.

Their Lordships find themselves unable to say that the Dominion Government had no good reason for thus temporarily continuing the paper control after actual war had ceased, but while the effects of war conditions might still be operative. They are, therefore, unable to accept the propositions submitted to them in the powerful argument for the appellants.

5. Toronto Electric Commissioners *v.* Snider, *1925*

~ In this case a major piece of national legislation, the Industrial Disputes Investigation Act, 1907, was cut down by the Privy Council's restrictive interpretation of the Dominion's "peace, order and good government" power. The subject matter of this statute – the establishment of national conciliation services to avoid work stoppages during labour disputes in some of the country's most vital industries such as mines, transportation and communication agencies and public service utilities – did not meet Viscount Haldane's "emergency" test. It should be noted that in this particular case the provisions of the Act were being applied not to an undertaking which was interprovincial or national in scope but to a municipal transportation agency.

As a result of this decision federal legislation providing for the settlement of labour disputes was confined to a much smaller field: industrial activities which are directly subject to federal jurisdiction, such as interprovincial railways or federal Crown agencies. National labour relations legislation limited to these areas was upheld in a reference to the Supreme Court of Canada in 1955.[1]

It would appear from the *Snider* case that the Judicial Committee, under Viscount Haldane's leadership, had come to look upon Parliament's general power almost exclusively as an emergency power. The least plausible, but perhaps most entertaining extension of this approach came in Viscount Haldane's attempt to reconcile the construction of the general power in earlier cases – in particular, in *Russell* v. *The Queen* – with the emergency doctrine. He was only able to do this by arguing that when the Privy Council decided *Russell* v. *The Queen* in 1882 it must have looked upon intemperance as a national menace serious enough to justify bringing the Canada Temperance Act under the "peace, order and good government" clause. ~

---

[1] *Reference re Validity of Industrial Relations and Disputes Investigation Act* [1955] S.C.R. 529.

TORONTO ELECTRIC COMMISSIONERS *v.* SNIDER
In the Privy Council [1925] A.C. 396; II Olmsted 394.

The judgment of their Lordships was delivered by

VISCOUNT HALDANE. It is always with reluctance that their Lordships come to a conclusion adverse to the constitutional validity of any Canadian statute that has been before the public for years as having been validly enacted; but the duty encumbent on the Judicial Committee, now as always, is simply to interpret the British North America Act and to decide whether the statute in question has been within the competence of the Dominion Parliament under the terms of s. 91 of that Act. In this case the Judicial Committee have come to the conclusion that it was not. To that conclusion they find themselves compelled, alike by the structure of s. 91 and by the interpretation of its terms that has now been established by a series of authorities. They have had the advantage not only of hearing full arguments on the question, but of having before them judgments in the Courts of Ontario, from which this appeal to the Sovereign in Council came directly. Some of these judgments are against the view which they themselves take, others are in favour of it, but all of them are of a high degree of thoroughness and ability.

The particular exercise of legislative power with which their Lordships are concerned is contained in a well-known Act, passed by the Dominion Parliament in 1907, and known as the Industrial Disputes Investigation Act. As it now stands it has been amended by subsequent Acts, but nothing turns, for the purposes of the question now raised, on any of the amendments that have been introduced.

The primary object of the Act was to enable industrial disputes between any employer in Canada and any one or more of his employees, as to "matters or things affecting or relating to work done or to be done by him or them, or as to the privileges, rights and duties of employers or employees (not involving any such violation thereof as constitutes an indictable offence)," relating to wages or remuneration, or hours of employment; sex, age or qualifications of employees, and the mode, terms and conditions of employment; the employment of children or any person, or classes of persons; claims as to whether preference of employment should be given to members of labour or other organizations; materials supplied or damage done to work; customs or usages, either general or in particular districts; and the interpretation of agreements. Either of the parties to any such dispute was empowered by the Act to apply to the Minister of Labour for the Dominion for the appointment of a Board of Conciliation and Investigation, to which Board the dispute might be referred. The Act enabled the Governor in Council to appoint a Registrar of such Boards, with the duty of dealing with all applications for reference, bringing them to the notice of the Minister, and conducting the correspondence necessary for the constitution of the Boards. The Minister was empowered to establish a Board when he thought fit, and no question was to be raised in any Court interfering with his decision. Each Board was to consist of three members, to be appointed by the Minister, one on the recommendation of the employer, one on that of the employees, and the third, who was to be chairman, on the recommendation of the members so chosen. If any of them failed in this duty the Minister was to make the appointment. The department of the Minister of Labour was to provide the staffs required. The application for a Board was to be accompanied by a statutory declaration showing that, failing adjustment, a lock-out or strike would probably occur.

The Board so constituted was to make inquiry and to endeavour to affect a settlement. If the parties came to a settlement the Board was to embody it in a memorandum of recommendation which, if the parties had agreed to it in writing, was to have the effect of an award on a reference to arbitration or one made under the order of a Court of record. In such a case the recommendation could be constituted a rule of Court and enforced accordingly. If no such settlement was arrived at, then the Board was to make a full report and a recommendation for settlement to the Minister, who was to make it public.

The Boards set up were given powers to summon and to enforce the attendance of witnesses, to administer oaths and to call for business books and other documents, and also to order into custody or subject to fine, in case of disobedience or contempt. The Board was also empowered to enter any premises where anything was taking place which was the subject of the reference and to inspect. This power was also enforceable by penalty. The parties were to be represented before the Board, but no counsel or solicitors were to appear excepting by consent and subject to the sanction of the Board itself. The proceedings were normally to take place in public.

By s. 56 of the Act, in the event of a reference to a Board, it was made unlawful for the employer to lock-out or for the employees to strike on account of any dispute prior to or pending the reference, and any breach of this provision was made punishable by fine. By s. 57, employers and employed were both bound to give at least thirty days' notice of an intended change affecting conditions of employment with respect to wages or hours. In the event of a dispute arising over the intended change, until the dispute had been finally dealt with by a Board and a report had been made, neither employers nor employed were to alter the conditions, or lock-out or strike, or suspend employment or work, and the relationship of employer and employee was to continue uninterrupted. If, in the opinion of the Board, either party were to use this or any other provision of the Act for the purpose of unjustly maintaining a given condition of affairs through delay, and the Board were so to report to the Minister, such party was to be guilty of an offence and liable to penalties.

By s. 63 (a), where a strike or lock-out had occurred or was threatened, the Minister was empowered, although neither of the parties to the dispute had applied for one, to set up a Board. He might also, under the next section, without any application, institute an inquiry.

Whatever else may be the effect of this enactment, it is clear that it is one which could have been passed, so far as any Province was concerned, by the Provincial Legislature under the powers conferred by s. 92 of the British North America Act. For its provisions were concerned directly with the civil rights of both employers and employed in the Province. It set up a Board of Inquiry which could summon them before it, administer to them oaths, call for their papers and enter their premises. It did not more than what a Provincial Legislature could have done under head 15 of s. 92, when it imposed punishment by way of penalty in order to enforce the new restrictions on civil rights. It interfered further with civil rights when, by s. 56, it suspended liberty to lock-out or strike during a reference to a Board. It does not appear that there is anything in the Dominion Act which could not have been enacted by the Legislature of Ontario, excepting one provision. The field for the operation of the Act was made the whole of Canada.

~ Viscount Haldane then pointed out the similarities between the provisions of the Ontario Trade Disputes Act, 1914, and the Dominion's Industrial Disputes Investigation Act, 1907. ~

The primary respondents in this appeal are the members of a Board of Conciliation appointed by the Dominion Minister of

Labour under the Act first referred to. There was a dispute in 1923 between the appellants and a number of the men whom they employed, which dispute was referred to the first respondents, who proceeded to exercise the powers given by the Dominion Act. The appellants then commenced an action in the Supreme Court of Ontario for an injunction to restrain these proceedings, on the allegation that the Dominion Act was ultra vires. The Attorneys-General of Canada and of Ontario were notified and made parties as intervenants.

There was a motion for an interim injunction, which was heard by Orde J., who, after argument, granted an injunction till the trial. The action was tried by Mowat J., who intimated his dissent from the view of the British North America Act taken by Orde J., who was co-ordinate in authority with him, according to which view the Dominion Act was ultra vires. He, therefore, as he had power by the Provincial Judicature Act to do, directed the action to be heard by a Divisional Court, and it was ultimately heard by the Appellate Division of the Supreme Court of Ontario (Mulock C.J., Magee, Hodgins, Ferguson and Smith JJ.A.). The result was that by the majority (Hodgins J.A. dissenting) the action of the appellants was dismissed.

The broad grounds of the judgment of the majority, which will be referred to later on, was that the Dominion Act was not a law relating to matters as to which s. 92 conferred exclusive jurisdiction, but was a law within the competence of the Dominion Parliament, inasmuch as it was directed to the regulation of trade and commerce throughout Canada, and to the protection of the national peace, order and good government, by reason of (a) confining, within limits, a dispute which might spread over all the Provinces; (b) informing the general public in Canada of the nature of the dispute; and (c) bringing public opinion to bear on it. The power of the Dominion Parliament to legislate in relation to criminal law, under head 27 of s. 91, was also considered to apply.

Before referring to these grounds of judgment their Lordships, without repeating at length what has been laid down by them in earlier cases, desire to refer briefly to the construction which, in their opinion, has been authoritatively put on ss. 91 and 92 by the more recent decisions of the Judicial Committee. The Dominion Parliament has, under the initial words of s. 91, a general power to make laws for Canada. But these laws are not to relate to the classes of subjects assigned to the Provinces by s. 92, unless their enactment falls under heads specifically assigned to the Dominion Parliament by the enumeration in s.

91. When there is a question as to which legislative authority has the power to pass an Act, the first question must therefore be whether the subject falls within s. 92. Even if it does, the further question must be answered, whether it falls also under an enumerated head in s. 91. If so, the Dominion has the paramount power of legislating in relation to it. If the subject falls within neither of the sets of enumerated heads, then the Dominion may have power to legislate under the general words at the beginning of s. 91.

Applying this principle, does the subject of the legislation in controversy fall fully within s. 92? For the reasons already given their Lordships think that it clearly does. If so, is the exclusive power prima facie conferred on the Province trenched on by any of the overriding powers set out specifically in s. 91? It was, among other things, contended in the argument that the Dominion Act now challenged was authorized under head 27, "the Criminal Law, except the Constitution of Courts of Criminal Jurisdiction, but including the Procedure in Criminal Matters." It was further suggested in the argument that the power so conferred is aided by the power conferred on the Parliament of Canada to establish additional Courts for the better administration of the laws of Canada.

But their Lordships are unable to accede to these contentions.

~ Viscount Haldane then advanced arguments and authorities rejecting the attempt to bring matters, which would normally come under provincial jurisdiction, under the criminal law power in Section 91 merely by the insertion of penal sanctions in the legislation. ~

Nor does the invocation of the specific power in s. 91 to regulate trade and commerce assist the Dominion contention. In *Citizens Insurance Co.* v. *Parsons* (7 App. Cas. 96, 112) it was laid down that the collocation of this head (No. 2 of s. 91), with classes of subjects enumerated of national and general concern, indicates that what was in the mind of the Imperial Legislature when this power was conferred in 1867 was regulation relating to general trade and commerce. Any other construction would, it was pointed out, have rendered unnecessary the specific mention of certain other heads dealing with banking, bills of exchange and promissory notes, as to which it had been significantly deemed necessary to insert a specific mention. The contracts of a particular trade or business could not, therefore, be dealt with by Dominion legislation so as to conflict with the powers assigned to the Provinces over property and civil rights relating to the regulation of trade and commerce. The Dominion power has a really definite effect when applied in aid of what the Dominion Government are specifically enabled to do independently of the general regulation of trade and commerce, for instance, in the creation of Dominion companies with power to trade throughout the whole of Canada. This was shown in the decision in *John Deere Plow Co.* v. *Wharton* ([1915] A.C. 330, 340). The same thing is true of the exercise of an emergency power required, as on the occasion of war, in the interest of Canada as a whole, a power which may operate outside the specific enumerations in both ss. 91 and 92. And it was observed in *Attorney-General for Canada* v. *Attorney-General for Alberta* ([1916] 1 A.C. 588, 596), in reference to attempted Dominion legislation about insurance, that it must now be taken that the authority to legislate for the regulation of trade and commerce does not extend to the regulation, for instance, by a licensing system, of a particular trade in which Canadians would otherwise be free to engage in the Provinces ([1915] A.C. 330, 340). It is, in their Lordships' opinion, now clear that, excepting so far as the power can be invoked in aid of capacity conferred independently under other words in s. 91, the power to regulate trade and commerce cannot be relied on as enabling the Dominion Parliament to regulate civil rights in the Provinces.

A more difficult question arises with reference to the initial words of s. 91, which enable the Parliament of Canada to make laws for the peace, order and good government of Canada in matters falling outside the Provincial powers specifically conferred by s. 92. . . .

. . . It appears to their Lordships that it is not now open to them to treat *Russell* v. *The Queen* (7 App. Cas. 829) as having established the general principle that the mere fact that Dominion legislation is for the general advantage of Canada, or is such that it will meet a mere want which is felt throughout the Dominion, renders it competent if it cannot be brought within the heads enumerated specifically in s. 91. Unless this is so, if the subject matter falls within any of the enumerated heads in s. 92, such legislation belongs exclusively to Provincial competency. No doubt there may be cases arising out of some extraordinary peril to the national life of Canada, as a whole, such as the cases arising out of a war, where legislation is required of an order that passes beyond the heads of exclusive Provincial competency. Such cases may be dealt with under the words at the commencement of s. 91, conferring general powers in relation to peace, order and good government, simply because such cases are not otherwise provided for. But instances of this, as was pointed out in the judgment in *Fort Frances Pulp and Power Co.* v. *Manitoba Free Press* ([1923] A.C. 695) are highly exceptional. Their Lordships think that the decision in *Russell* v. *The Queen* can only be supported today, not on the footing of having laid down an interpretation, such as has sometimes been invoked of the general words at the beginning of s. 91, but on the assumption of the Board, apparently made at the time of deciding the case of *Russell* v. *The Queen*, that the evil of intemperance at that time amounted in Canada to one so great and so general that at least for the period it was a menace to the national life of Canada so serious and pressing that the National Parliament was called on to intervene to protect the nation from disaster. An epidemic of pestilence might conceivably have been regarded as analogous. It is plain from the decision in the *Board of Commerce* case ([1922] 1 A.C. 191) that the evil of profiteering could not have been so invoked, for Provincial powers, if exercised, were adequate to it. Their Lordships find it difficult to explain the decision in *Russell* v. *The Queen* as more than a decision of this order upon facts, considered to have been established at its date rather than upon general law. . . .

. . . Their Lordships have examined the evidence produced at the trial. . . . They are of opinion that it does not prove any emergency putting the national life of Canada in unanticipated peril such as the Board which decided *Russell* v. *The Queen* may be considered to have had before their minds.

6. Attorney-General for Canada v. Attorney-General for Ontario (Employment and Social Insurance Act Reference), 1937

~ The Employment and Social Insurance Act, 1935, which the Privy Council ruled *ultra vires* in this case was the first measure of the Conservative government's social reform program (the so-called "New-Deal" legislation) which was introduced by Prime Minister R. B. Bennett at the beginning of the 1935 session of Parliament. The Liberal Opposition under Mr. Mackenzie King's leadership, while approving the principle of the social legislation, contended that it was beyond Parliament's jurisdiction. Accordingly, following the defeat of the Bennett government in the general election of October, 1935, Mr. King's administration referred the question of the validity of eight of the reform measures of the 1935 session of the Supreme Court of Canada and then, on appeal to the Judicial Committee of the Privy Council.[1] While the adversaries in all of these reference cases represented the two levels of government, in some of the cases provincial representatives supported the validity of the federal legislation. In this case, for instance, the Province of Ontario supported the federal government's side of the case, while New Brunswick was alone in maintaining the other side.

The Privy Council's decisions in these cases were a grave disappointment to those in Canada who had hoped that the powers assigned by the Constitution to the central government would be sufficiently broad to enable it to deal effectively with the nation-wide consequence of a severe economic depression. The invalidation of five of the eight federal statutes submitted to the courts in this series of reference cases dashed the hopes raised by the Privy Council's recent decisions in the *Aeronautics* and *Radio* references,[2] which had pointed to a much broader

---

[1] Two other decisions from this series are included in this volume: *Natural Products Marketing Act Reference* (pp. 96-100), *Labour Conventions Reference* (pp. 134-44).

[2] *In re Regulation and Control of Aeronautics*, [1932] A.C. 54; *In re Regulation and Control of Radio Communication*, [1932] A.C. 304. See below pp. 117-27, and pp. 128-33.

construction of the Dominion's legislative capacities. Among those who wished to strengthen the powers of the central government the immediate response was to turn to formal amendment of the B.N.A. Act to overcome what was regarded as the inappropriate division of powers being shaped by judicial review. The only real fruit of this renewal of interest in constitutional amendment was the amendment secured in 1940, which, with the unanimous consent of the Provinces, assigned unemployment insurance to the exclusive jurisdiction of the federal Parliament.

Mr. Louis St. Laurent, who acted as legal counsel for the Dominion in this case, admitted that a scheme of unemployment insurance designed to have permanent effect could not be justified on emergency grounds. Instead, the case for bringing the legislation under the "peace, order and good government" power rested on both the residual aspect of that power and its application to matters of national concern. Counsel for the Dominion argued that the legislation attacked a problem which had not existed when the B.N.A. Act was drawn up and hence was not specifically provided for in any of the enumerated heads of Sections 91 and 92. Further they urged that the problem of unemployment was one which threatened the well-being of the whole Dominion. Lord Atkin, speaking for the Judicial Committee, did not accept this reasoning. His reference to the lack of any special emergency sufficient to justify invoking the federal government's general power suggests an absorption of the residual and national importance phases of that power in the emergency power approach. ~

ATTORNEY-GENERAL FOR CANADA
v. ATTORNEY-GENERAL FOR ONTARIO
In the Privy Council. [1937] A.C. 355; III Olmsted 207

The judgment of their Lordships was delivered by

LORD ATKIN. This is an appeal from the judgment of the Supreme Court, delivered on June 17, 1936, in the matter of a reference by the Governor-General in Council, dated November 5, 1935, asking whether the Employment and Social Insurance Act, 1935, was ultra vires of the Parliament of Canada. The majority of the Supreme Court, Rinfret, Cannon, Crocket, and Kerwin JJ., answered the question in the affirmative, the Chief Justice and Davis J. dissenting. The Act in its preamble recited art. 23 of the Treaty of Peace, by which in the Covenant of the League of Nations the members of the League agreed that they would endeavour to maintain fair and humane conditions of labour (omitting, however, in the recital that this agreement was subject to and in accordance with the provisions of international conventions existing or hereafter to be agreed), and art. 427 of the said treaty, by which it was declared that the well-being, physical, moral and intellectual, of industrial wage earners was of supreme international importance. It then recited that it was desirable to discharge the obligations to Canadian labour assumed under the provisions of the said treaty: and that it was essential for the peace, order and good government of Canada to provide for a national employment service and insurance against unemployment, etc. It consists of five Parts, Employment and Social Insurance Commission (ss. 4-9), Employment Service (ss. 10-14), Unemployment Insurance (ss. 15-38), National Health (ss. 39-41) and General (ss. 42-48). In substance the Act provides for a system of compulsory unemployment insurance. Part I sets up a commission charged with administering the Act and obtaining information and making proposals to the Governor in Council for making provision for the assistance of persons during unemployment who would not be entitled to unemployment insurance benefit under Part III. Part II provides for the organization by the commission of employment offices similar to the labour exchanges in the United Kingdom. Part III provides for unemployment insurance, while Part IV merely provides that the commission shall co-operate with other authorities in the Dominion or Provinces, and shall collect information concerning any plan for providing medical care or compensation in case of ill-health. Part V provides for regulations and reports. There are three schedules. The first defines employment within the meaning of Part III, and excepted employments, which include employment in agriculture and forestry, in fishing, and in lumbering and logging. The second enacts the weekly rates of contribution, and rules as to payment and recovery of contributions paid by employers on behalf of employed persons. The third enacts the rates of unemployment benefit, and supplementary provisions concerning the payment of unemployment benefit.

The substance of the Act is contained in the sections constituting Part III. They set up a now familiar system of unemployment insurance under which persons engaged in unemployment as defined in the Act are insured against unemployment. The funds required for making the necessary payments are to be provided partly from money provided by Parliament, partly from contributions by employed persons, and partly from contributions by the employers of those persons. The two sets of contributions are to be paid by revenue stamps. Every employed person and every employer is to be liable to pay contributions in accordance with the provisions of the second schedule, the employer being liable to pay both contributions in the first instance, recovering the employed person's share by deduction from his wages, or, if necessary, in certain cases by action.

There can be no doubt that, prima facie, provisions as to insurance of this kind, especially where they affect the contract of employment, fall within the class of property and civil rights in the Province, and would be within the exclusive competence of the Provincial Legislature. It was sought, however, to justify the validity of Dominion legislation on grounds which their Lordships on consideration feel compelled to reject. Counsel did not seek to uphold the legislation on the ground of the treaty-making power. There was no treaty or labour convention which imposed any obligation upon Canada to pass this legislation, and the decision on this question in the reference on the three labour Acts does not apply. A strong appeal, however, was made on the ground of the special importance of unemployment insurance in Canada at the time of, and for some time previous to, the passing of the Act. On this point it becomes unnecessary to do more than to refer to the judgment of this Board in the reference on the three labour Acts, and to the judgment of the Chief Justice in the Natural Products Marketing Act which, on this matter, the Board have approved and adopted. It is sufficient to say that the present Act does not purport to deal with any special emergency. It founds itself in the preamble on general world-wide conditions referred to in the Treaty of Peace: it is an Act whose operation is intended to be permanent: and there is agreement between all the members of the Supreme Court that it could not be supported upon the suggested existence of any special emergency. Their Lordships find themselves unable to differ from this view.

It only remains to deal with the argument which found favour with the Chief Justice and Davis J., that the legislation can be supported under the enumerated heads, 1 and 3 of s. 91 of the British North America Act, 1867: (1) The public debt and property, namely (3) The raising of money by any mode or system of taxation. Shortly stated, the argument is that the obligation imposed upon employers and persons employed is a mode of taxation: that the money so raised becomes public property, and that the Dominion have then complete legislative authority to direct that the money so raised, together with assistance from money raised by general taxation, shall be applied in forming an insurance fund and generally in accordance with the provisions of the Act.

That the Dominion may impose taxation for the purpose of creating a fund for special purposes, and may apply that fund for making contributions in the public interest to individuals, corporations or public authorities, could not as a general proposition be denied. Whether in such an Act as the present compulsion applied to an employed person to make a contribution to an insurance fund out of which he will receive benefit for a period proportionate to the number of his contributions is in fact taxation it is not necessary finally to decide. It might seem difficult to discern how it differs from a form of statutory obligation to pay insurance premiums to the State or to an insurance company. But assuming that the Dominion has collected by means of taxation a fund, it by no means follows that any legislation which disposes of it is necessarily within Dominion competence.

It may still be legislation affecting the classes of subjects enumerated in s. 92, and, if so, would be ultra vires. In other words, Dominion legislation, even though it deals with Dominion property, may yet be so framed as to invade civil rights within the Province, or encroach upon the classes of subjects which are reserved to Provincial competence. It is not necessary that it should be a colourable device, or a pretence. If on the true view of the legislation it is found that in reality in pith and substance the legislation invades civil rights within the Province, or in respect of other classes of subjects otherwise encroaches upon the provincial field, the legislation will be invalid. To hold otherwise would afford the Dominion an easy passage into the Provincial domain. In the present case, their Lordships agreed with the majority of the Supreme Court in holding that in pith and substance this Act is an insurance Act affecting the civil rights of employers and employed in each Province, and as such is invalid. The other parts of the Act are so inextricably mixed up with the insurance provisions of Part III that it is impossible to sever them. It seems obvious, also, that in its truncated form, apart from Part III, the Act would never have come into existence. It follows that the whole Act must be pronounced ultra vires, and in accordance with the view of the majority of the Supreme Court their Lordships will humbly advise His Majesty that this appeal be dismissed.

7. Attorney-General for Ontario v.
Canada Temperance Federation, *1946*

~ This case originated in 1939 when the Government of
Ontario referred the question of the validity of the Canada
Temperance Act, 1927, to the Supreme Court of Ontario. As
this Act had substantially the same provisions as the Act which
had been upheld in 1882 by the Judicial Committee in *Russell*
v. *The Queen*, the real object of the reference was to challenge
that decision and consolidate the much narrower construction
of the "peace, order and good government" clause which the
Privy Council had been developing since 1882. This challenge
to the central Parliament's legislative capacities brought about
a major confrontation of the two levels of government. The
Attorneys-General of Alberta and New Brunswick intervened
to support Ontario and received further support from both
Nova Scotia and Saskatchewan.

The Board's judgment, delivered by Viscount Simon, constitutes a sharp break from the Privy Council's restrictive interpretation of Parliament's general power. Viscount Simon not only
refuted the explanation of *Russell* v. *The Queen* which Viscount
Haldane had provided in the *Snider* case[1] but also effectively
undermined the emergency doctrine as the exclusive way of
interpreting the opening words of Section 91. According to his
reasoning the validity of Dominion legislation does not depend
on the existence of an emergency but on the subject matter of
the legislation: "if it is such that it goes beyond local or provincial concern or interests and must from its inherent nature be
the concern of the Dominion as a whole . . . then it will fall
within the competence of the Dominion Parliament as a matter
affecting the peace, order and good government of Canada,
though it may in another aspect touch on matters specially
reserved to the Provincial Legislatures."[2] Despite Viscount
Simon's disavowal of any intention of embarking on a fresh
interpretation of the relationship between Sections 91 and 92,
his words in effect provided jurists in later cases with a method

[1] *Toronto Electric Commn.* v. *Snider,* [1925] A.C. 412. See above p.
44.

[2] *A.-G. Ont.* v. *Canada Temperance Federation* [1946] A.C. 205. See
below p. 54.

of constructing the "peace, order and good government" clause which is a decisive alternative to the emergency power conception.

In the Privy Council's few remaining years as Canada's final court of appeal there were only two more cases which tested their Lordship's approach to the opening words of Section 91. In neither of these did the Privy Council show any inclination to follow the path opened up by Viscount Simon's judgment in the *Canada Temperance Federation* case. On the contrary, its decision in both of these cases suggested a return to the emergency doctrine. The 1946 decision upholding the federal government's deportation of Japanese Canadians under the general power was based entirely on the grounds of war-time and post-war emergency.[3] In 1951 the Judicial Committee rejected the attempt to use Viscount Simon's reasoning as a means of bringing federal legislation prohibiting the sale of margarine in Canada under Parliament's general power. In dismissing this ground for validating the legislation the judgment referred to the absence of any conditions grave enough to justify invoking the Dominion's general power and implied that the exercise of that power entails an overriding of the normal distribution of powers in Sections 91 and 92.[4] Thus it remained for the Supreme Court of Canada to follow Viscount Simon's lead and apply the national aspect test to the interpretation of Parliament's power to legislate for the peace, order and good government of Canada. ~

ATTORNEY-GENERAL FOR ONTARIO
v. CANADA TEMPERANCE FEDERATION
In the Privy Council. [1946] *A.C. 193; III Olmsted 424.*

The judgment of their Lordships was delivered by

VISCOUNT SIMON. On June 1, 1939, the Lieutenant-Governor of Ontario in Council referred to the Supreme Court of Ontario under the provisions of the Constitutional Questions Act, R.S.O., c. 130, the following question: "Are Parts I, II and III of the Canada Temperance Act, R.S.C. 1927, c. 196, constitutionally valid in whole or in part, and if in part, in what respect?"

---

[3] *Co-operative Comm. on Japanese Canadians* v. *A.-G. Canada.* [1947] A.C. 87.

[4] *Canadian Federation of Agriculture* v. *A.-G. Quebec.* [1951] A.C. 198.

On September 26, 1939, the Supreme Court by a majority (Riddell, Fisher, McTague and Gillanders JJ.A.) answered the question as follows: "This court is of opinion (Henderson J. dissenting) that Parts I, II and III of the Canada Temperance Act, R.S.C. 1927, c. 196, are within the legislative competence of the Parliament of Canada." Against this judgment the Attorney-General for Ontario and the Moderation League of Ontario have appealed to the Judicial Committee, and their appeal has been supported by the Attorneys-General for Alberta and New Brunswick, who were admitted as interveners and were represented on the hearing. The appeal was opposed by counsel appearing for the Attorney-General for Canada and for several Temperance Federations.

The object of the appeal is to challenge the decision of this Board in the case of *Russell* v. *The Queen* (7 App. Cas. 829), or at any rate to deny its applicability to the Act now in question. The majority of the Supreme Court held that that decision governed the present case and obliged it to answer the question referred to it in the affirmative. The statute which was declared to be within the legislative competence of the Dominion Parliament in *Russell's* case was the Canada Temperance Act, 1878. That Act has been amended from time to time by the Dominion Parliament, and has been revised and re-enacted in a consolidated form on more than one occasion under the provisions of the Acts relating to the revision of Statutes of Canada. The last revision took place in 1927 under the provisions of the Dominion Act, 1924 (14 & 15 Geo. 5, c. 65) and now appears on the Statute Roll as the Canada Temperance Act, R.S.C. of 1927, c. 196. The material provisions of the Act of 1927 are admittedly identical with those of the Act of 1878.

~.Viscount Simon then stated the main provision of the Canada Temperance Act, 1878. Following this he stated the grounds of the Judicial Committee's decision in *Russell* v. *The Queen* and traced the citation of that case by the Privy Council in subsequent decisions. ~

But in 1925 *Russell's* case was commented on in a judgment of the Judicial Committee delivered by Lord Haldane in *Toronto Electric Commissioners* v. *Snider* ([1925] A.C. 396), and it is on this comment that the present appellants largely rely in support of their contention that it was wrongly decided. After contrasting that case with other decisions of the Board already mentioned above, Lord Haldane said: "It appears to their Lordships that it is not now open to them to treat *Russell*

v. *The Queen* as having established the general principle that the mere fact that Dominion legislation is for the general advantage of Canada, or is such that it will meet a mere want which is felt throughout the Dominion, renders it competent if it cannot be brought within the heads enumerated specifically in s. 91. . . . No doubt there may be cases arising out of some extraordinary peril to the national life of Canada, as a whole, such as the cases arising out of a war, where legislation is required of an order that passes beyond the heads of exclusive Provincial competency" ([1925] A.C. 412). And later he said "Their Lordships think that the decision in *Russell* v. *The Queen* can only be supported today, not on the footing of having laid down an interpretation, such as has sometimes been invoked, of the general words at the beginning of s. 91, but on the assumption of the Board, apparently made at the time of deciding the case of *Russell* v. *The Queen*, that the evil of intemperance at that time amounted in Canada to one so great and so general that at least for the period it was a menace to the national life of Canada so serious and pressing that the National Parliament was called on to intervene to protect the nation from disaster. An epidemic of pestilence might conceivably have been regarded as analogous" ([1937] A.C. 863).

The first observation which their Lordships would make on this explanation of *Russell's* case is that the British North America Act nowhere gives power to the Dominion Parliament to legislate in matters which are properly to be regarded as exclusively within the competence of the provincial legislatures merely because of the existence of an emergency. Secondly, they can find nothing in the judgment of the Board in 1882 which suggests that it proceeded on the ground of emergency; there was certainly no evidence before that Board that one existed. The Act of 1878 was a permanent, not a temporary, Act, and no objection was raised to it on that account. In their Lordships' opinion, the true test must be found in the real subject matter of the legislation: if it is such that it goes beyond local or provincial concern or interests and must from its inherent nature be the concern of the Dominion as a whole (as, for example, in the *Aeronautics* case ([1932] A.C. 54) and the *Radio* case ([1932] A.C. 304), then it will fall within the competence of the Dominion Parliament as a matter affecting the peace, order and good government of Canada, though it may in another aspect touch on matters specially reserved to the provincial legislatures. War and pestilence, no doubt, are instances; so, too, may be the drink or drug traffic, or the carrying of arms. In *Russell* v. *The Queen*, Sir Montague Smith gave as an instance of valid Dominion legislation a law which prohibited or restricted the sale or exposure of cattle having a contagious disease. Nor is the validity of the legislation, when due to its inherent nature, affected because there may still be room for enactments by a provincial legislature dealing with an aspect of the same subject in so far as it specially affects that province.

It is to be noticed that the Board in *Snider's* case nowhere said that *Russell* v. *The Queen* was wrongly decided. What it did was to put forward an explanation of what it considered was the ground of the decision, but in their Lordships' opinion the explanation is too narrowly expressed. True it is that an emergency may be the occasion which calls for the legislation, but it is the nature of the legislation itself, and not the existence of emergency, that must determine whether it is valid or not.

The appellants' first contention is that *Russell's* case was wrongly decided and ought to be overruled. Their Lordships do not doubt that in tendering humble advice to His Majesty they are not absolutely bound by previous decisions of the Board, as is the House of Lords by its own judgments. In ecclesiastical appeals, for instance, on more than one occasion, the Board has tendered advice contrary to that given in a previous case, which further historical research has shown to have been wrong. But on constitutional questions it must be seldom indeed that the Board would depart from a previous decision which it may be assumed will have been acted on both by governments and subjects. In the present case the decision now sought to be overruled has stood for over sixty years; the Act has been put into operation for varying periods in many places in the Dominion; under its provisions businesses must have been closed, fines and imprisonments for breaches of the Act have been imposed and suffered. Time and again the occasion has arisen when the Board could have overruled the decision had it thought it wrong. Accordingly, in the opinion of their Lordships, the decision must be regarded as firmly embedded in the constitutional law of Canada, and it is impossible now to depart from it. Their Lordships have no intention, in deciding the present appeal, of embarking on a fresh disquisition as to relations between ss. 91 and 92 of the British North America Act, which have been expounded in so many reported cases; so far as the Canada Temperance Act, 1878, is concerned the question must be considered as settled once and for all.

The second contention of the appellants was that in 1927,

when the statute now in force was enacted, there were no circumstances which enabled the Parliament of the Dominion to legislate anew. As has already been said, the Act of 1927 is, in all respects material for this appeal, identical in its terms with the Act of 1878, and also with the Act of 1886, which itself was a revised edition of 1878 and was the Act in force in 1896 when the case of *Att.-Gen. for Ontario* v. *Att.-Gen. for the Dominion* ([1896] A.C. 348) was heard. It was not contended that if the Act of 1878 was valid when it was enacted it would have become invalid later on by a change of circumstances, but it was submitted that as that Act and the Act of 1886 have been repealed, the Act of 1927 was new legislation and consequently circumstances must exist in 1927 to support the new Act. Then it was said (and this, apparently, was the opinion of Henderson J.A., who dissented from the other members of the Supreme Court of Ontario) that no circumstances could exist in 1927 to support the Act, in view of the legislation that had been passed in the provinces, including Ontario, for the regulation of the liquor traffic. Their Lordships do not find it necessary to consider the true effect either of s. 5 or s. 8 of the Act of 1924 for the revision of the Statutes of Canada, for they cannot agree that if the Act of 1878 was constitutionally within the powers of the Dominion Parliament it could be successfully contended that the Act of 1927 which replaced it was ultra vires. The same ground is not covered by provincial legislation setting up a licensing system and making the sale of liquor a government monopoly. Moreover, if the subject-matter of the legislation is such that it comes within the province of the Dominion Parliament that legislature must, as it seems to their Lordships, have power to re-enact provisions with the object of preventing a recurrence of a state of affairs which was deemed to necessitate the earlier statute. To legislate for prevention appears to be on the same basis as legislation for cure. A pestilence has been given as an example of a subject so affecting, or which might so affect, the whole Dominion that it would justify legislation by the Parliament of Canada as a matter concerning the order and good government of the Dominion. It would seem to follow that if the Parliament could legislate when there was an actual epidemic it could do so to prevent one occurring and also to prevent it happening again. Once it has been decided that the Act of 1878 was constitutionally valid, it follows that an Act which replaces it and consolidates therewith the various amending Acts that have from time to time been enacted must be equally valid. . . .

8. Johannesson v. West St. Paul, 1952

~ This case originated in private litigation between Johannesson, the operator of a commercial aviation enterprise in western Canada and the Manitoba town of West St. Paul which had passed a by-law preventing Johannesson from establishing an aerodrome in a location he had chosen in that municipality. Johannesson challenged the validity of the provincial Municipal Act which had delegated to the municipality the power to make the by-law in question. Both the trial judge and a majority of the Manitoba Court of Appeal had ruled the Manitoba legislation *intra vires*. On the appeal to the Supreme Court of Canada the Attorney-General of Manitoba and the Attorney-General of Canada intervened to support their respective sides of the case. The Supreme Court was unanimous in reversing the decision of the lower courts and finding that the Dominion's power in relation to aeronautics left no room for a province to regulate the location of aerodromes.

This was the first case since the abolition of appeals to the Privy Council in 1949 that provided a test of the Supreme Court's approach to the opening words of Section 91. Six of the seven judges who took part in the decision supported the validity of the federal Aeronautics Act and Air Regulations as an exercise of the "peace, order and good government" power. In doing so, it is significant that they cited the conception of that power presented by Viscount Simon in the *Canada Temperance Federation* case. Justice Locke's opinion (part of which is reproduced below) indicates the highly functional considerations which may be involved in deciding whether a matter is one which concerns the country as a whole.

While the decision in this case points to a more expansive treatment of Parliament's general power, its implications for the treaty-implementing power are less clear.[1] The Court was divided on the question of whether Section 132 which gives Parliament the power of implementing any obligations arising from treaties entered into by Canada as part of the British Empire, could be used, as it had been in the Aeronautics

---

[1] See Part Three below for the leading cases dealing with this issue in the division of powers.

Reference,[2] to support the validity of the federal Aeronautics Act. The International Convention in support of which the Aeronautics Act had originally been enacted was ratified on behalf of the British Empire. But this Convention had been abrogated by the Civil Aviation Convention which Canada had signed in her own right at Chicago in 1944. In the light of these facts three of the judges were of the opinion that Section 132 could no longer be used to sustain the Dominion's Aeronautics legislation, while three others took the view that even though the Chicago Convention was not, strictly speaking, a British Empire treaty still "it comes to the same thing."[3] The seventh, Justice Locke, does not appear to have committed himself on this point.

Nearly a decade and half went by before the Supreme Court gave any further indication of its approach to the "peace, order and good government" clause. But in two cases in the 1960's, with only three of the judges who participated in the *Johannesson* decision still serving, the Supreme Court again turned to the "peace, order and good government" clause to uphold federal power.

The first case, *Munro* v. *The National Capital Commission*,[4] in 1966, involved a challenge to certain powers of zoning and expropriation in the Ottawa area conferred by the National Capital Act on the National Capital Commission. Justice Cartwright, who wrote the Court's opinion, was unable to find explicit jurisdiction over the development of the nation's capital in either the provincial or federal lists of powers and reasoned that the matter could, therefore, be brought within the residual function of "peace, order and good government." But he did not stop there. He went on to invoke the national aspect dimension of that clause. "I find it difficult," he said, "to suggest a subject matter of legislation which more clearly goes beyond local or provincial interests and is the common concern of Canada as a whole than the development, conservation and improvement of the National Capital Region. . . ." The fact that such legislation would incidentally affect the civil rights of residents of both Ontario and Quebec could not, he argued, be an objection to its validity.

[2] *In re Regulation and Control of Aeronautics in Canada*, [1932] A.C. 54. See below pp. 117-18.

[3] This was the phrase used by Viscount Dunedin in *In re Regulation and Control of Radio Communication in Canada*, [1932] A.C. 305, at p. 312. See below p. 131.

[4] *Munro* v. *The National Capital Commission*, [1966] S.C.R. 663.

A year later in the *Offshore Mineral Rights Reference*[5] the Court again used the national importance test (as well as the residual function of peace, order and good government and Section 91(1A)) in citing the federal Parliament's general power as the basis of Ottawa's claim to ownership of and juris-diction over the mineral and other natural resources in the land under the sea off British Columbia's coast. The Court provided little evidence to support its assertion that "the mineral resources of the lands underlying the territorial sea are of concern to Canada as a whole and go beyond local or provincial concern or interests" – an assertion which seems less self-evident than Justice Cartwright's earlier assertion of the inherent national character of national capital legislation. The central thrust of the Court's reasoning focused on the international arrange-ments which Canada as a sovereign nation must enter into in relation to the territorial sea and the continental shelf. Here it is significant that the Court did not take a dualistic view of sovereignty in Canada. It assumed that the sovereign rights transferred from the British Empire to "Canada" as an indé-pendent member of the international community attached exclusively to the federal level of government.[6]

There can be no mistaking the centralist thrust of these two judgments. It is worth noting that in both cases the Court was unanimous and, in contrast with *Johannesson*, produced a single opinion. ∼

JOHANNESSON *v.* WEST ST. PAUL
In the Supreme Court of Canada. [1952] 1 S.C.R. 292

KERWIN J.: This is an appeal by Mr. and Mrs. Johannesson against a judgment of the Court of Appeal for Manitoba af-firming an order of Campbell J. dismissing their application for an order declaring that s. 921 of The Municipal Act, R.S.M. 1940, c. 141, was *ultra vires* as not being within the legislative competence of the Legislature, and that by-law 292 of the rural municipality of West St. Paul, passed May 27, 1948, in pursuance of such section, was, therefore, null and void.

Section 921 of The Municipal Act appears in Division II "Public Safety and Amenity" under the sub-head "Aerodromes" and reads as follows:

[5] *Reference Re: Offshore Mineral Rights* [1967] S.C.R. 792.
[6] For the bearing of this case on the treaty-implementing power, see below, page 152.

*921. Any municipal corporation may pass by-laws for licens-
ing, regulating, and, within certain defined areas, preventing the
erection, maintenance and continuance of aerodromes or places
where aeroplanes are kept for hire or gain.*

~ Justice Kerwin then reviewed the history of this legislation.
He also set out the provisions of the West St. Paul by-law 292,
which banned aerodromes from the area in which Johannesson
wished to locate his airport. This by-law was authorized by
Section 921 of Manitoba's Municipal Act. ~

The circumstances which give rise to the present dispute are
important as showing the far-reaching effect of the provisions
of the section. The appellant Johannesson had been engaged
in commercial aviation since 1928 and held an air transport
licence, issued by the Air Transport Board of Canada, to operate
an air service at Winnipeg and Flin Flon. The charter service
which he operated under this licence covers territory in central
and northern Manitoba and northern Saskatchewan, and had
substantially increased in volume over the years. This service
was operated with light and medium weight planes, which in the
main were equipped in summer with floats and in winter with
skis in order to permit landing on the numerous lakes and rivers
in this territory, and these planes had to be repaired and serviced
in Winnipeg, which was the only place within the territory where
the necessary supplies and any facilities were available for that
purpose. The use by small planes of a large airfield, such as
Stevenson Airport near Winnipeg which was maintained for the
use of large transcontinental airplanes, was impractical and
would eventually be prohibited. No facilities existed on the Red
River in Winnipeg for the repairing and servicing of planes
equipped with floats, and repairs could only be made to such
planes by dismantling them at some private dock and transporting them, by truck, through Winnipeg to Stevenson Airport.
After a long search by Johannesson in the suburbs of Winnipeg
for a site that would combine an area of level land of sufficient
area and dimensions and location to comply with the regulations
of the Civil Aviation Branch of the Canadian Department of
Transport relating to a licensed air strip with access to a straight
stretch of the Red River of sufficient length to be suitable for the
landing of airplanes equipped with floats, he found such a location (but one only) in the rural municipality of West St. Paul
and acquired an option to purchase it but, before the transaction
was completed By-law 292 was passed. Title to the land was
subsequently taken in the name of both appellants and these

proceedings ensued. The Attorney-General of Canada and the Attorney-General of Manitoba were notified but only the latter was represented before the judge of first instance and the Court of Appeal. Leave to appeal to this Court was granted by the latter.

On behalf of the appellants and the Attorney-General of Canada, reliance is placed upon the decision of the Judicial Committee in the *Aeronautics* case ([1932] A.C. 54). Irrespective of later judicial comments upon this case, in my view it is a decision based entirely upon the fact that the Dominion Aeronautics Act there in question had been enacted pursuant to an International Convention of 1919 to which the British Empire was a party and, therefore, within s. 132 of the British North America Act, 1867:

132. The Parliament and Government of Canada shall have all Powers necessary or proper for performing the obligations of Canada or of any Province thereof, as part of the British Empire, towards foreign countries arising under treaties between the Empire and such foreign countries.

However, in the subsequent decision in the *Labour Conventions* case (*A.-G. for Canada* v. *A.-G. for Ontario* ([1937] A.C. 326)), Lord Atkin, who had been a member of the Board in the *Aeronautics* case, said with reference to the judgment therein:

The Aeronautics *case ([1932] A.C. 54 at 351) concerned legislation to perform obligations imposed by a treaty between the Empire and foreign countries. Sect. 132, therefore, clearly applied, and but for a remark at the end of the judgment, which in view of the stated ground of the decision was clearly obiter, the case could not be said to be an authority on the matter now under discussion.*

The remarks of Viscount Simon in *A.-G. for Ontario* v. *Canada Temperance Federation* ([1946] A.C. 193), must be read when considering the words of Lord Sankey in the *Aeronautics* case in another connection. At the moment all I am concerned with emphasizing is that the *Aeronautics* case decided one thing, and one thing only, and that is that the matter there discussed fell within the ambit of s. 132 of the British North America Act.

At this stage it is necessary to refer to a matter that was not explained to the Courts below. According to a certificate from the Under-Secretary of State for Foreign Affairs, the Convention of 1919 was denounced by Canada, which denunciation became effective in 1947. This was done because on February 13, 1947, Canada had deposited its Instrument of Ratification of the Convention on International Civil Aviation signed at Chicago December 8, 1944, and which Convention came into force on April 4, 1947. With the exception of cértain amendments that are not relevant to the present discussion, the Aeronautics Act remains on the statute books of Canada in the same terms as those considered by the Judicial Committee in the *Aeronautics* case. Section 132 of the B.N.A. Act, therefore ceased to have any efficacy to permit Parliament to legislate upon the subject of aeronautics.

Nevertheless the fact remains that the Convention of 1919 was a treaty between the Empire and foreign countries and that pursuant thereto the Aeronautics Act was enacted. It continues as c. 3 of the Revised Statutes of Canada, 1927, as amended. Under s. 4 of that Act, as it stood when these proceedings were commenced, the Minister, with the approval of the Governor in Council, had power to regulate and control aerial navigation over Canada and the territorial waters of Canada, and in particular but not to restrict the generality of the foregoing, he might make regulations with respect to * * * (c) the licensing, inspection and regulation of all aerodromes and air stations. Pursuant thereto regulations have been promulgated dealing with many of the matters mentioned in the section, including provisions for the licensing of air ports. If, therefore, the subject of aeronautics goes beyond local or provincial concern.because it has attained such dimensions as to affect the body politic of Canada, it falls under the "peace, order and good government" clause of s. 91 of the B.N.A. Act since aeronautics is not a subject-matter confined to the provinces by s. 92. It does not fall within head 8, "Municipal Institutions," as that head "simply gives the provincial legislature the right to create a legal body for the management of municipal affairs. . . . The extent and nature of the functions" the provincial legislature "can commit to a municipal body of its own creation must depend upon the legislative authority which it derives from the provisions of s. 92 other than No. 8": *Attorney General for Ontario* v. *Attorney General for Canada* ([1896] A.C. 348 at 364). Nor, on the authority of the same decision is it within head 9: "shop, saloon, tavern, auctioneer, and other licences in order to the raising of a revenue for provincial, local, or municipal purposes." Once it is held that the subject-matter transcends "Property and Civil Rights in the Province" (head 13) or

"Generally all matters of a merely local or private nature in the Province" (head 16), these two heads of s. 92 have no relevancy.

Now, even at the date of the *Aeronautics* case, the Judicial Committee was influenced (i.e. in the determination of the main point) by the fact that in their opinion the subject of air navigation was a matter of national interest and importance and had attained such dimensions. That that is so at the present time is shown by the terms of the Chicago Convention of 1944 and the provisions of the Dominion Aeronautics Act and the regulations thereunder referred to above. The affidavit of the appellant Johannesson, from which the statement of facts was culled, also shows the importance that the subject of air navigation has attained in Canada. To all of which may be added those matters of everyday knowledge of which the Court must be taken to be aware.

It is with reference to this phase of the matter that Viscount Simon's remarks in *A.G. for Canada* v. *Canada Temperance Federation* ([1946] A.C. 193 at 205), must be read. What was there under consideration was the Canada Temperance Act, originally enacted in 1878, and Viscount Simon stated: "In their Lordships' opinion, the true test must be found in the real subject-matter of the legislation: if it is such that it goes beyond local or provincial concern or interests and must from its inherent nature be the concern of the Dominion as a whole (as, for example, in the *Aeronautics* case and the *Radio* case ([1932] A.C. 304), then it will fall within the competence of the Dominion Parliament as a matter affecting the peace, order and good government of Canada, though it may in another aspect touch on matters specially reserved to the provincial legislatures." This statement is significant because, while not stating that the *Aeronautics* case was a decision on the point, it is a confirmation of the fact that the Board in the *Aeronautics* case considered that the subject of aeronautics transcended provincial legislative boundaries.

The appeal should be allowed, the orders below set aside, and judgment should be entered declaring s. 921 of the Act *ultra vires* and By-law 292 of the rural municipality of West St. Paul null and void.

LOCKE J.: . . . In my opinion, the position taken by the province and by the municipality in this matter cannot be maintained. Whether the control and direction of aeronautics in all its branches be one which lies within the exclusive jurisdiction of Parliament, and this I think to be the correct view, or whether it be a domain in which Provincial and Dominion legislation may overlap, I think the result must be the same. It has been said on behalf of the respondents that the by-law is merely a zoning regulation passed in exercise of the powers vested in the municipality elsewhere in the Municipal Act. . . . The by-law, in so far as it prohibits the erection, maintenance or continuation of aerodromes, must depend for its validity upon s. 921: subsec. 3 is apparently based upon subsec. (h) of s. 896. . . . The powers sought to be conferred upon the Municipal Council appear to me to be in direct conflict with those vested in the Minister of National Defence by the Aeronautics Act. Section 3(a) of that statute imposes upon the Minister the duty of supervising all matters connected with aeronautics and prescribing aerial routes and by s. 4 he is authorized, with the approval of the Governor in Council, to make regulations with respect to, *inter alia*, the areas within which aircraft coming from any place outside of Canada are to land and as to aerial routes, their use and control. The power to prescribe the aerial routes must include the right to designate where the terminus of any such route is to be maintained, and the power to designate the area within which foreign aircraft may land, of necessity includes the power to designate such area, whether of land or water, within any municipality in any province of Canada deemed suitable for such purpose.

If the validity of the Aeronautics Act and the Air Regulations be conceded, it appears to me that this matter must be determined contrary to the contentions of the respondent. It is, however, desirable, in my opinion, that some of the reasons for the conclusion that the field of aeronautics is one exclusively within federal jurisdiction should be stated. There has been since the First World War an immense development in the use of aircraft flying between the various provinces of Canada and between Canada and other countries. There is a very large passenger traffic between the provinces and to and from foreign countries, and a very considerable volume of freight traffic not only between the settled portions of the country but between those areas and the northern part of Canada, and planes are extensively used in the carriage of mails. That this traffic will increase greatly in volume and extent is undoubted. While the largest activity in the carrying of passengers and mails east and west is in the hands of a government-controlled company, private companies carry on large operations, particularly between the settled parts of the country and the North and mails are carried by some of these lines. The maintenance and extension of this traffic, particularly to the North, is essential to the opening up of the country and the development of the resources of the nation. It requires merely a statement of these well-recognized facts to demonstrate that the field of aeronautics is one which concerns the country as a whole. It is an activity, which to adopt the language of Lord Simon in the *Attorney General for Ontario* v. *Canada Temperance Federation*, must from its inherent nature be a concern of the Dominion as a whole. The field of legislation is not, in my opinion, capable of division in any practical way. If, by way of illustration, it should be decided that it was in the interests of the inhabitants of some northerly part of the country to have airmail service with centres of population to the south and that for that purpose some private line, prepared to undertake such carriage, should be licensed to do so and to establish the southern terminus for their route at some suitable place in the Municipality of West St. Paul where, apparently, there is an available and suitable field and area of water where planes equipped in a manner enabling them to use the facilities of such an airport might land, it would be intolerable that such a national purpose might be defeated by a rural municipality, the Council of which decided that the noise attendant on the operation of airplanes was objectionable. Indeed, if the argument of the respondents be carried to its logical conclusion the rural municipalities of Manitoba through which the Red River passes between Emerson and Selkirk, and the City of Winnipeg and the Town of Selkirk might prevent the operation of any planes equipped for landing upon water by denying them the right to use the river for that purpose. . . .

While the statement of Lord Sankey in the *Aeronautics Reference* that aerial navigation is a class of subjects which has attained such dimensions as to affect the body politic of the Dominion as a whole, and that of Lord Simon in the Canada Temperance matter in referring to that case and the *Radio* case, were perhaps unnecessary to the decision of those matters, they support what I consider to be the true view of this matter that the whole subject of aeronautics lies within the field assigned to Parliament as a matter affecting the peace, order and good government of Canada. S. 921 of The Municipal Act (R.S.M. 1940 c. 141) clearly trespasses upon that field and must be declared *ultra vires* the province. As to the by-law I am unable, with respect, to agree with the contention that it is a mere zoning regulation or that, even if it were, it could be sustained. On the contrary, I consider it to be a clear attempt to prevent the carrying on of the operation of commercial aerodromes within the municipality. As the right to do this must depend upon s. 921, the by-law must also be declared *ultra vires*. . . .

~ Chief Justice Rinfret and Justices Kellock and Estey also wrote opinions in which they concluded that the provincial legislation in question was *ultra vires*. Justice Cartwright concurred with Justice Kellock and Justice Taschereau concurred with Justice Estey. ~

PART TWO

TRADE AND COMMERCE

9. Severn v. The Queen, 1878

~ This case provided the first opportunity for the Supreme Court of Canada to interpret the B.N.A. Act. The case arose out of charges brought against Severn, a liquor manufacturer who was licensed under federal customs legislation, for violating an Ontario Act requiring brewers to purchase provincial licences before selling liquor by wholesale. Severn's refusal to pay the licence fee was based on his contention that the Ontario legislation establishing the licensing system was *ultra vires*. The Ontario Court of Appeal dismissed Severn's argument but this decision was reversed by the Supreme Court of Canada, which by a four-to-two majority found the provincial Act invalid both on the ground that it provided for an indirect tax which could not be supported as a licence under head No. 9 of Section 92 and also on the ground that it interfered with trade and commerce, a subject assigned exclusively to the national Parliament.

As a legal precedent this case is of little importance: the reasoning of the Supreme Court's majority on the "trade and commerce" power was overruled by later decisions of the Privy Council. The real significance of the case is the indication it provides of the basic attitudes of senior Canadian jurists to the division of powers in Canadian federalism at a time when the main issues and events of Confederation must still have been fresh in their minds and when their interpretation of the B.N.A. Act was not yet fettered by Privy Council decisions. The remarkable feature of their general approach to the division of powers is their concern for upholding the national power. This is particularly marked in the opening paragraphs of the Chief Justice's judgment which echo the sentiments of those Fathers of Confederation who, like Sir John A. Macdonald, were anxious to eliminate from the Canadian federal system the centrifugal tendencies which in their view were inherent in the American system.

It is apparent that at this stage the Canadian Supreme Court in applying the federal terms of the Canadian Constitution was inclined to look to American jurisprudence for guidance. As far as the federal commerce power was concerned American experience could only support a broad interpretation of the Canadian Parliament's power in relation to trade and commerce. The opinion of Justice Fournier points to the obvious conclusion that if in the United States the central legislature's commerce power which is a limited one, restricted to interstate commerce, has been construed in broad enough terms to cut down local laws interfering with the flow of trade through the States, in Canada the national legislature's power over trade and commerce which is subject to no express limitations should be given an even more generous construction. Even the two dissenting judges (Justices Ritchie and Strong) while willing to support the Ontario Act under Section 92 (9), did not otherwise differ with the majority's view of the Dominion's "trade and commerce" power.

Two years later in *City of Fredericton* v. *The Queen*[1] the Supreme Court once again gave an extremely wide interpretation of Parliament's power in relation to trade and commerce when it upheld, by a five-to-one majority, the Canada Temperance Act under Section 91 (2). But this early treatment of the "trade and commerce" clause by the Supreme Court was to undergo a sharp reversal by the Judicial Committee of the Privy Council.[2] In a series of cases the Privy Council evolved a number of implied limitations which had the effect of reducing the federal commerce power in Canada to a pale shadow of its counterpart in the United States' Constitution. ~

SEVERN *v.* THE QUEEN
In the Supreme Court of Canada. (1878), 2 S.C.R. 70

RICHARDS, C.J.C.: In deciding important questions arising under the Act passed by the Imperial Parliament for federally uniting the Provinces of Canada, Nova Scotia and New Brunswick, and forming the Dominion of Canada, we must consider the circumstances under which that Statute was passed, the condition of the different Provinces themselves, their relation to one another, to the Mother Country, and the state of things existing in the great country adjoining Canada, as well as the

[1] (1880), 3 S.C.R. 505.
[2] See above pp. 1-2 and pp. 11-12.

systems of government which prevailed in these Provinces and countries. The framers of the Statute knew the difficulties which had arisen in the great Federal Republic, and no doubt wished to avoid them in the new government which it was intended to create under that Statute. They knew that the question of State rights as opposed to the authority of the General Government under their constitution was frequently raised, aggravating, if not causing, the difficulties arising out of their system of government, and they evidently wished to avoid these evils, under the new state of things about to be created here by the Confederation of the Provinces.

In distributing the Legislative powers, the British North America Act declares the Parliament of Canada shall, or, as the 91st section reads,

It shall be lawful for the Queen, by and with the advice and consent of the Senate and House of Commons, to make laws, for the peace, order and good government of Canada, in relation to all matters not coming within the classes of subjects assigned exclusively to the Legislatures of the Provinces.

And then, for greater certainty, that section defines certain subjects to which the exclusive legislative authority of the Parliament extends. Amongst other things are mentioned:

2. The regulation of trade and commerce.
3. The raising of money by any mode or system of taxation.

Certain other subjects of a general and quasi-national character are then referred to and mentioned, as coming within the powers of the Dominion Parliament.

The causing a brewer to take out a licence and pay a certain sum of money therefor, as required by the Ontario Statutes, is a means of raising money, and it, of course, is a tax? And there can be no doubt it is an indirect tax; and it is equally beyond a doubt that it is a means which may be resorted to by the Dominion Parliament for the raising of money. When, then, it is mentioned in the Statute under consideration that the Dominion Parliament may raise money under any mode or system of taxation, and when, in the same Act, the taxing power of the Provincial Legislature is confined to *direct taxation* within the Province, in order to the raising of a revenue for provincial purposes, it seems to me beyond all doubt (except so far as the same may be qualified by No. 9 of section 92) that it was introduced not to allow the Provincial Legislature the right to impose indirect taxes for provincial or local purposes. . . .

The anomaly of allowing the Local Legislatures to compel a manufacturer to take out a licence from the Local Government to sell an article which has already paid a heavy excise duty to the Dominion Government, and after he has paid for and obtained a licence from the Dominion Government to do the very same thing, is obvious to every one. It is not doubted that the Dominion Legislature had a right to lay on this excise tax and to grant this licence, and the act of the Local Legislature forbids and punishes the brewer for doing that which the Dominion Statute permits and allows. Here surely is *what seems* a direct conflict and interference with the act of the Dominion Legislature, and such a conflict as the framers of the British North America Act never contemplated or intended. . . .

. . . I consider the power now claimed to interfere with the paramount authority of the Dominion Parliament in matters of trade and commerce and indirect taxation, so pregnant with evil, and so contrary to what appears to me to be the manifest intention of the framers of the British North America Act, that I cannot come to the conclusion that it is conferred by the language cited as giving that power. . . .

[*Translated*]

FOURNIER, J.: The only question to be decided in this case arises on the constitutionality of a law of the Province of Ontario, imposing upon brewers and distillers the obligation of taking out a licence of $50, in order that they may sell their products within the said Province.

The question we have therefore to consider is, whether the law in question is, or is not, in direct conflict with the British North America Act, and, more particularly, first, with No. 2 of section 91, relating to the "regulation of trade and commerce," and, secondly, with section 122, which gives to the Parliament of Canada the control over the custom and excise laws, and, therefore, beyond the limits of the jurisdiction of the Ontario Legislature. . . .

The 91st section gives to the Federal Parliament the general power of taxation, a sovereignty over all subjects, except those specifically mentioned in section 92, as being subjects exclusively belonging to the Local Legislatures. We find, among the exclusive powers given to the Federal Parliament, the power of *regulating trade and commerce*.

This power, being full and complete, cannot be restricted, unless by some specific provision to be found in the British North America Act.

For this reason, the relative position of the Provinces towards the Federal Parliament is far different from that of the States towards the United States Congress. Here the power to regulate trade and commerce, without any distinction as to interior and exterior commerce, belongs *exclusively* to the Dominion Parliament, whilst, in the United States, Congress has power only to deal with exterior or foreign commerce, commerce between the different States and that with the Indian tribes. The States, not having delegated to Congress the power of regulating interior commerce, still have power to legislate on it as they please. We should not, therefore, look to the numerous decisions rendered on the laws relating to the interior commerce as precedents applicable to the present case, but rather to the decisions given on laws passed by the State Legislatures which happened to come in conflict with the power of Congress to deal with exterior commerce.

There is a decision, rendered as early as 1827, which has always been looked upon as being the true construction of that article of the Constitution of the United States which gives Congress power to regulate exterior commerce, and which is very applicable to the present case. It is that rendered in the case of *Brown* v. *State of Maryland* (12 Wheaton 419). In order to raise revenue to meet the expenses of the State, the Legislature of Maryland passed a law, by which, amongst other things, importers of foreign merchandise enumerated in the law, or such other persons as should sell by wholesale such merchandise, were directed to take out a licence, for which they were to pay $50, before selling any of the imported goods, subjecting them, in case of neglect or refusal, to forfeit the amount due for the licence and to a penalty of $100.

Brown, who was an importer residing in the city of Baltimore, refused to pay this tax, and an information was, in consequence, laid against him before the State Court, which declared the law to be valid and condemned him to pay the penalty prescribed.

This judgment was appealed by means of a writ of error to the Supreme Court, which Court, for the reasons so ably propounded by the learned Chief Justice Marshall, declared the law void as coming in conflict with the power of Congress to regulate exterior commerce.

The question here naturally arises, what was the extent of that power? This question was considered at great length in the case of *Gibbons* v. *Ogden* (9 Wheaton 231), by Chief Justice Marshall, who answered it as follows:

It is the power to regulate; that is, to prescribe the rule by which commerce is to be governed. This power, like all others vested in Congress, is complete in itself, may be exercised to its utmost extent, and acknowledges no limitations other than are prescribed by the Constitution.

Since this is the law in the United States, there is an additional reason why it should be so declared here, where our Constitution does not acknowledge, as in the United States, a division of power as to commerce. . . .

. . . I will add in support of my mode of reasoning, a passage of Chief Justice Marshall's opinion in the case of *Brown* v. *The State of Maryland* (12 Wheaton 448), and I also contend that in this case we should apply this ordinary rule of construction, that when a law is doubtful or ambiguous, it should be interpreted in such a way as to fulfil the intentions of the legislator, and attain the object for which it was passed. Marshall, C. J., says:

We admit this power to be sacred [the State power to tax its own citizens, on their property within its own territory]; *but cannot admit that it may be used so as to obstruct the free course of a power given to Congress. We cannot admit that it may be used so as to obstruct or defeat the power to regulate commerce. It has been observed, that the powers remaining with the States may be so exercised as to come in conflict with those vested in Congress. When this happens that which is not supreme must yield to that which is supreme. This great and universal truth is inseparable from the nature of things, and the constitution has applied it to the often interfering powers of the General and State Governments as a vital principle of perpetual operation. It results necessarily from this principle, that the taxing power of the State must have some limits. It cannot reach and restrain the action of the National Government within its proper sphere. It cannot reach the administration of justice in the Courts of the Union, or the collection of the taxes of the United States or restrain the operation of any law which Congress may constitutionally pass. It cannot interfere with any regulation of commerce. If the States may tax all persons and property found on their territory, what shall restrain them from taxing in their transit through the State from one port to another for the purpose of re-exportation? The laws of trade authorize this operation, and general convenience requires it. Or what should restrain a State from taxing any article passing from the State itself to another State, for commercial purposes? These are all within the sovereign power of taxation, but would obviously derange the measures of Congress to regulate commerce, and effect materially the purpose for which that power was given. We deem it unnecessary to press the argument further, or to give additional illustrations of it, because the subject was taken up, and considered with great attention in* McCulloch v. The State of Maryland *(4 Wheaton 316), the decision in which case is, we think, entirely applicable to this.*

The reasoning of the Supreme Court in that case, under a system of Government which left to the States the regulation of the interior commerce, is not only applicable to the present question, but should have more weight from the fact that under our system the Federal Government has the *exclusive* power over commerce. . . .

HENRY, J.: . . . The legislative power given to the Dominion Parliament is unlimited

To make laws for the peace, order and good government of Canada, in relation to all matters not coming within the classes of subjects by this Act assigned exclusively *to the Legislatures of the Provinces,*

and we need not necessarily consider the provisions of sub-sections 2 and 3 of section 91.

Everything in the shape of legislation for the peace, order and good government of Canada is embraced, except as before mentioned. But sub-section 29 goes further and provides for exceptions and reservations in regard to matters otherwise included in the power of legislation given to the Local Legislatures, and also provides that:

Any matter coming within any of the classes of subjects enumerated in this section shall not be deemed to come within the class of matters of a local or private nature comprised in the enumeration of the classes of subjects by this Act assigned exclusively to the Legislatures of the Provinces.

"The regulation of trade and commerce" and "the raising of money by any mode or system of taxation" is, however, specially mentioned, and both include the right to make and have carried out all the provisions in the Dominion Act. This position has not been, and cannot be, successfully assailed. The subjects in all their details of which trade and commerce are composed, and the regulation of them, and the raising of revenue by indirect taxation, must, therefore, be matters referred to and included in the latter clause of sub-section 29, before mentioned, and if so,

Shall not be deemed to come within the class of matters of a local or private nature comprised in the enumeration of the classes of subjects by this Act assigned exclusively to the Legislature of the Provinces.

Every constituent, therefore, of trade and commerce, and the subject of indirect taxation, is thus, as I submit, withdrawn from the consideration of the Local Legislatures, even if it should otherwise be *apparently* included. The Imperial Act fences in those twenty-eight subjects wholesale and in detail, and the Local Legislatures were intended to be, and are, kept out of the inclosure, and when authorized to deal with the subject of "direct taxation within the Province," as in sub-section 2 of section 92, and "shop, saloon, tavern, auctioneer, and other licences," they are commanded, by the concluding clause of sub-section 29, sec. 91, not to interfere by measures for what they may call "direct taxation," or in regard at least to "other licences," or in reference to "municipal institutions," with the prerogatives of the Dominion Parliament as to the "regulation of trade and commerce," including "Customs and Excise laws" and "the raising of money by any mode or system of taxation." I have already shown, that the exercise of the power contended for by the Legislature of Ontario is incompatible with the full exercise of that of the Dominion Parliament, and might be used to its total destruction. The object of the Imperial Act was clearly to give plenary powers of legislation to the Dominion Parliament with the exceptions before stated, and just as clearly to restrict local legislation so as to prevent any conflict with that of the former in regard to the subjects with which it was given power to deal. . . .

~ Justice Taschereau also wrote an opinion in which he concluded that the Ontario legislation was *ultra vires.* Justices Ritchie and Strong wrote dissenting opinions. ~

10. Citizens Insurance Co. v. Parsons;
Queen Insurance Co. v. Parsons, 1881

~ The constitutional issue in this case concerned the validity of the Ontario Fire Insurance Policy Act which prescribed uniform conditions for all fire insurance contracts unless variations from the statutory conditions were properly indicated. Parsons, the respondent in the case, had taken actions against two fire insurance companies to obtain compensation for damages caused by fire in a warehouse insured by the companies. The companies' defence was that Parsons should not receive compensation because he had failed to observe conditions which had been written into the companies' policies or which were prescribed by the Ontario statute. Parson's reply was that he was not bound by the conditions written into the contracts because they were not written on the contracts as variations from the statutory conditions in the manner prescribed by the Ontario Fire Insurance Policy Act. The companies' counsel attempted to counter this contention by arguing that the Ontario statute was *ultra vires*. The judgments of the Ontario Court of Appeal and the Supreme Court of Canada both were in favour of Parsons.

The Privy Council, in reaching the conclusion that the Ontario Act challenged by the companies was within provincial jurisdiction as a law relating to property and civil rights in the province rather than one that could be brought under the Dominion's trade and commerce power, applied the first and most significant limitations to the scope of the "trade and commerce" power. The specific limitation immediately germane to the issue in this case was that the national Parliament could not under Section 91 (2) regulate the contracts of a particular business or trade, such as the business of fire insurance, in a province. But Sir Montague Smith, speaking for the Judicial Committee, prefaced this specific restriction by a much more general one when he stated that the "trade and commerce" power embraced only international trade, interprovincial trade and, perhaps general trade affecting the whole of Canada.

While this general restriction of the scope of the federal commerce power was not essential to the conclusion reached in the *Parsons* case, it was returned to in many subsequent decisions. The consolidation in later cases of the doctrine that the "trade and commerce" power does not extend to intra-provincial, as distinguished from interprovincial, trade had the effect of excluding from the scope of that power all business or commercial transactions completed within a province. By thus excluding intra-provincial trade from federal jurisdiction, judicial review introduced into the Canadian Constitution a restriction on the federal commerce power similar to that which the United States' Constitution by express provision applies to the commerce power of its federal legislature. Although, ironically, the express restrictions in the American Constitution have proved to be far less of a barrier to the development of national economic policies than have the judicially created restrictions in Canada. ~

CITIZENS INSURANCE CO. *v.* PARSONS;
QUEEN INSURANCE CO. *v.* PARSONS.
In the Privy Council. (1881), 7 App. Cas. 96; 1 Olmsted 94.

The judgment of their Lordships was delivered by

SIR MONTAGUE SMITH. The questions in these appeals arise in two actions brought by the same plaintiff (the respondent) upon contracts of insurance against fire of buildings situate in the province of Ontario, in the Dominion of Canada.

The most important question in both appeals is one of those, already numerous, which have arisen upon the provisions of the British North America Act, 1867, relating to the distribution of legislative powers between the parliament of Canada and the legislatures of the provinces, and, owing to the very general language in which some of these powers are described, the question is one of considerable difficulty. Their Lordships propose to deal with it before approaching the facts on which the particular questions in the actions depend. . . .

. . . The distribution of legislative powers is provided for by sects. 91 to 95 of the British North America Act, 1867; the most important of these being sect. 91, headed "Powers of the Parliament," and sect. 92, headed "Exclusive Powers of Provincial Legislatures." . . .

. . . The scheme of this legislation, as expressed in the first branch of sect. 91, is to give to the dominion parliament authority to make laws for the good government of Canada in all matters not coming within the classes of subjects assigned exclusively to the provincial legislature. If the 91st section had stopped here, and if the classes of subjects enumerated in sect. 92 had been altogether distinct and different from those in sect. 91, no conflict of legislative authority could have arisen. The provincial legislatures would have had exclusive legislative power over the sixteen classes of subjects assigned to them, and the dominion parliament exclusive power over all other matters relating to the good government of Canada. But it must have been foreseen that this sharp and definite distinction had not been and could not be attained, and that some of the classes of subjects assigned to the provincial legislatures unavoidably ran into and were embraced by some of the enumerated classes of subjects in sect. 91; hence an endeavour appears to have been made to provide for cases of apparent conflict; and it would seem that with this object it was declared in the second branch of the 91st section, "for greater certainty, but not so as to restrict the generality of the foregoing terms of this section" that (notwithstanding anything in the Act) the exclusive legislative authority of the parliament of Canada should extend to all matters coming within the classes of subjects enumerated in that section. With the same object, apparently, the paragraph at the end of sect. 91 was introduced, though it may be observed that this paragraph applies in its grammatical construction only to No. 16 of sect. 92.

Notwithstanding this endeavour to give pre-eminence to the dominion parliament in cases of a conflict of powers, it is obvious that in some cases where this apparent conflict exists, the legislature could not have intended that the powers exclusively assigned to the provincial legislature should be absorbed in those given to the dominion parliament. Take as one instance the subject "marriage and divorce," contained in the enumeration of subjects in sect. 91; it is evident that solemnization of marriage would come within this general description; yet "solemnization of marriage in the province" is enumerated among the classes of subjects in sect. 92, and no one can doubt, notwithstanding the general language of sect. 91, that this subject is still within the exclusive authority of the legislatures of the provinces. So "the raising of money by any mode or system of taxation" is enumerated among the classes of subjects in sect. 91; but, though the description is sufficiently large and general to include "direct taxation within the province, in order to the raising of a revenue for provincial purposes," assigned to the provincial legislatures by sect. 92, it obviously could not have been intended that, in this instance also, the general power should override the particular one. With regard to certain classes of subjects, therefore, generally described in sect. 91, legislative power may reside as to some matters falling within the general description of these subjects in the legislatures of the provinces. In these cases it is the duty of the Courts, however difficult it may be, to ascertain in what degree, and to what extent, authority to deal with matters falling within these classes of subjects exists in each legislature, and to define in the particular case before them the limits of their respective powers. It could not have been the intention that a conflict should exist; and, in order to prevent such a result, the two sections must be read together, and the language of one interpreted, and, where necessary, modified, by that of the other. In this way it may, in most cases, be found possible to arrive at a reasonable and practical construction of the language of the sections, so as to reconcile the respective powers they contain, and give effect to all of them. In performing this difficult duty, it will be a wise course for those on whom it is thrown, to decide each case which arises as best they can, without entering more largely upon an interpretation of the statute than is necessary for the decision of the particular question in hand.

The first question to be decided is, whether the Act impeached in the present appeals falls within any of the classes of subjects enumerated in sect. 92, and assigned exclusively to the legislatures of the provinces; for if it does not, it can be of no validity, and no other question would then arise. It is only when an Act of the provincial legislature prima facie falls within one of these classes of subjects that the further questions arise, *viz.*, whether, notwithstanding this is so, the subject of the Act does not also fall within one of the enumerated classes of subjects in sect. 91, and whether the power of the provincial legislature is or is not thereby overborne.

The main contention on the part of the respondent was that the Ontario Act in question had relation to matters coming within the class of subjects described in No. 13 of sect. 92, *viz.*, "Property and civil rights in the province." The Act deals with policies of insurance entered into or in force in the province of Ontario for insuring property situate therein against fire, and prescribes certain conditions which are to form part of such contracts. These contracts, and the rights arising from them, it was argued, came legitimately within the class of subject, "Property and civil rights." The appellants, on the other hand, contended that civil rights meant only such rights as flowed from the law, and gave as an instance the status of persons. Their Lordships cannot think that the latter construction is the correct one. They find no sufficient reason in the language itself, nor in the other parts of the Act, for giving so narrow an interpretation to the words "civil rights." The words are sufficiently large to embrace, in their fair and ordinary meaning, rights arising from contract, and such rights are not included in express terms in any of the enumerated classes of subjects in sect. 91.

It becomes obvious, as soon as an attempt is made to construe the general terms in which the classes of subjects in sects. 91 and 92 are described, that both sections and the other parts of the Act must be looked at to ascertain whether language of a general nature must not by necessary implication or reasonable intendment be modified and limited. In looking at sect. 91, it will be found not only that there is no class including, generally, contracts and the rights arising from them, but that one class of contracts is mentioned and enumerated, *viz.*, "18, bills of exchange and promissory notes," which it would have been unnecessary to specify if authority over all contracts and the rights arising from them had belonged to the dominion parliament.

The provision found in sect. 94 of the British North America Act, which is one of the sections relating to the distribution of legislative powers, was referred to by the learned counsel on both sides as throwing light upon the sense in which the words "property and civil rights" are used. By that section the parliament of Canada is empowered to make provision for the uniformity of any laws relative to "property and civil rights" in Ontario, Nova Scotia, and New Brunswick, and to the procedure of the Courts in these three provinces, if the provincial legislatures choose to adopt the provision so made. The province of Quebec is omitted from this section for the obvious reason that the law which governs property and civil rights in Quebec is in the main the French law as it existed at the time of the cession of Canada, and not the English law which prevails in the other provinces. The words "property and civil rights" are, obviously, used in the same sense in this section as in No. 13 of sect. 92, and there seems no reason for presuming that contracts and the rights arising from them were not intended to be included in this provision for uniformity. If, however, the narrow construction of the words "civil rights," contended for by the appellants were to prevail, the dominion parliament could, under its general power, legislate in regard to contracts in all and each of the provinces and as a consequence of this the province of Quebec, though now governed by its own Civil Code, founded on the French law, as regards contracts and their incidents, would be subject to have its law on that subject altered by the dominion legislature, and brought into uniformity with the English law prevailing in the other three provinces, notwithstanding that Quebec has been carefully left out of the uniformity section of the Act.

It is observed that the same words, "civil rights," are employed in the Act of 14 Geo. 3, c. 83, which made provision for the Government of the province of Quebec. Sect. 8 of that Act enacted that His Majesty's Canadian subjects within the province of Quebec should enjoy their property, usages, and other civil rights, as they had before done, and that in all matters of controversy relative to property and civil rights resort should be had to the laws of Canada, and be determined agreeably to the said laws. In this statute the words "property" and "civil rights" are plainly used in their largest sense; and there is no reason for holding that in the statute under discussion they are used in a different and narrower one.

The next question for consideration is whether, assuming the Ontario Act to relate to the subject of property and civil rights, its enactments and provisions come within any of the classes of subjects enumerated in sect. 91. The only one which the Appellants suggested as expressly including the subject of the Ontario Act is No. 2, "the regulation of trade and commerce."

A question was raised which led to much discussion in the Courts below and this bar, *viz.*, whether the business of insuring buildings against fire was a trade. This business, when carried on for the sake of profit, may, no doubt, in some sense of the word, be called a trade. But contracts of indemnity made by insurers can scarcely be considered trading contracts, nor were insurers who made them held to be "traders" under the English bankruptcy laws; they have been made subject to those laws by special description. Whether the business of fire insurance properly falls within the description of a "trade" must, in their Lordships' view, depend upon the sense in which that word is used in the particular statute to be construed; but in the present case their Lordships do not find it necessary to rest their decision on the narrow ground that the business of insurance is not a trade.

The words "regulation of trade and commerce," in their unlimited sense are sufficiently wide, if uncontrolled by the context and other parts of the Act, to include every regulation of trade ranging from political arrangements in regard to trade with foreign governments, requiring the sanction of parliament, down to minute rules for regulating particular trades. But a consideration of the Act shows that the words were not used in this unlimited sense. In the first place the collocation of No. 2 with classes of subjects of national and general concern affords an indication that regulations relating to general trade and commerce were in the mind of the legislature, when conferring this power on the dominion parliament. If the words had been intended to have the full scope of which in their literal meaning they are susceptible, the specific mention of several of the other classes of subjects enumerated in sect. 91 would have been unnecessary; as, 15, banking; 17, weights and measures; 18, bills of exchange and promissory notes; 19, interest; and even 21, bankruptcy and insolvency.

"Regulation of trade and commerce" may have been used in some such sense as the words "regulations of trade" in the Act of Union between England and Scotland (6 Anne, c. 11), and as these words have been used in Acts of State relating to trade and commerce. Article V of the Act of Union enacted that all the subjects of the United Kingdom should have "full freedom and intercourse of trade and navigation" to and from all places in the United Kingdom and the colonies; and Article VI enacted that all parts of the United Kingdom from and after the Union should be under the *same* "prohibitions, restrictions, and *regulations of trade*." Parliament has at various times since the Union passed laws affecting and regulating specific trades in one part of the United Kingdom only, without its being supposed that it thereby infringed the Articles of Union. Thus the Acts for regulating the sale of intoxicating liquors notoriously vary in the two kingdoms. So with regard to Acts relating to bankruptcy, and various other matters.

Construing therefore the words "regulation of trade and commerce" by the various aids to their interpretation above suggested, they would include political arrangements in regard to trade requiring the sanction of parliament, regulation of trade in matters of interprovincial concern, and it may be that they would include general regulation of trade affecting the whole Dominion. Their Lordships abstain on the present occasion from any attempt to define the limits of the authority of the dominion parliament in this direction. It is enough for the decision of the present case to say that, in their view, its authority to legislate for the regulation of trade and commerce does not comprehend the power to regulate by legislation the contracts of a particular business or trade, such as the business of fire insurance in a single province, and therefore that its legislative authority does not in the present case conflict or compete with the power over property and civil rights assigned to the legislature of Ontario by No. 13 of sect. 92. . . .

. . . The opinions of the majority of the Judges in Canada, as summed up by Ritchie, C.J., are in favour of the validity of the Ontario Act. In the present actions, the Court of Queen's Bench and the Court of Appeal of Ontario unanimously supported its legality; and the Supreme Court of Canada, by a majority of three Judges to two, have affirmed the judgments of the provincial Courts. The opinions of the learned Judges of the Supreme Court are stated with great fullness and ability, and clearly indicate the opposite views which may be taken of the Act, and the difficulties which surround any construction that may be given to it.

Taschereau, J., in the course of his vigorous judgment, seeks to place the plaintiff in the action against the Citizens Company in a dilemma. He thinks that the assertion of the right of the province to legislate with regard to the contracts of insurance companies amounts to a denial of the right of the dominion parliament to do so, and that this is, in effect, to deny the right of that parliament to incorporate the Citizens Company, so that the plaintiff was suing a non-existent defendant. Their Lordships cannot think that this dilemma is established. The learned Judge assumes that the power of the dominion parliament to incorporate companies to carry on business in the dominion is derived from one of the enumerated classes of subjects, *viz.*, "the regulation of trade and commerce," and then argues that if the authority to incorporate companies is given by this clause, the exclusive power of regulating them must also be given by it, so that the denial of one power involves the denial of the other. But, in the first place, it is not necessary to rest the authority of the dominion parliament to incorporate companies on this specific and enumerated power. The authority would belong to it by its general power over all matters not coming within the classes of subjects assigned exclusively to the legislatures of the provinces, and the only subject on this head assigned to the provincial legislature being "the incorporation of companies with provincial objects," it follows that the incorporation of companies for objects other than provincial falls within the general powers of the parliament of Canada. But it by no means follows (unless indeed the view of the learned judge is right as to the scope of the words "the regulation of trade and commerce") that because the dominion parliament has alone the right to create a corporation to carry on business throughout the dominion that it alone has the right to regulate its contracts in each of the provinces. Suppose the dominion parliament were to incorporate a company, with power, among other things, to purchase and hold lands throughout Canada in mortmain, it could scarcely be contended if such a company were to carry on business in a province where a law against holding land in mortmain prevailed (each province having exclusive legislative power over "property and civil rights in the province") that it could hold land in that province in contravention of the provincial legislation; and, if a company were incorporated for the sole purpose of purchasing and holding land in the Dominion, it might happen that it could do no business in any part of it, by reason of all the provinces having passed Mortmain Acts, though the corporation would still exist and preserve its status as a corporate body.

On the best consideration they have been able to give to the arguments addressed to them and to the judgments of the learned judges in Canada, their Lordships have come to the conclusion that the Act in question is valid. . . .

11. Attorney-General for Canada v.
Attorney-General for Alberta
(1916 Insurance Reference), *1916*

~ The federal government initiated this case by referring to the
Supreme Court of Canada the question of the validity of those
sections of the Dominion's Insurance Act of 1910 which provided for a compulsory licensing system for insurance companies. The Supreme Court by a four-to-two majority found
the impugned sections of the statute *ultra vires*. On the appeal
to the Privy Council six of the provinces (Alberta, British
Columbia, Saskatchewan, Ontario, Quebec, and New Brunswick) were represented in the attack on the federal legislation,
while a major interest group in the insurance industry, The
Insurance Federation, intervened to defend the validity of the
statute. The Privy Council confirmed the Supreme Court's
decision finding that Sections 4 and 70 of the Insurance Act
were *ultra vires*.

In the *Parsons* case the Privy Council's judgment had pointed
to three kinds of trade which might be brought under the federal
commerce power – international, interprovincial, and general
trade affecting the whole of Canada. This *Insurance Reference*
of 1916 indicates the limitations which the Privy Council was
ready to apply to the third of these possible grounds for invoking
the federal commerce power. According to Viscount Haldane's
judgment Parliament could not under its "trade and commerce"
power establish a general scheme for regulating a business such
as insurance throughout the Dominion. On the other hand
Viscount Haldane, in answering the second question in the
reference, was willing to invoke the Parliament's commerce
power (as well as its power in relation to aliens) to sustain
national legislation regulating foreign insurance companies even
where such companies confine their operations to a single province. This could presumably be justified on the grounds that
such legislation would concern an international commercial
activity.

A year before this, the Privy Council's decision in *Jóhn
Deere Plow Co., Ltd.* v. *Wharton*[1] provided the one example of

[1] *John Deere Plow Co., Ltd.* v. *Wharton*, [1915] A.C. 330, at p. 340.

a general trade matter which could be brought under the federal commerce power. Here the commerce power was used to sustain legislation defining the rights and capacities of companies which had been incorporated by the national Parliament. The federal legislation providing for the incorporation of national companies was supported by Viscount Haldane as coming under Parliament's residual power, but legislation determining the fashion in which such national companies would be permitted to operate he considered a matter of "general interest throughout the Dominion" and consequently a proper exercise of the "trade and commerce" power.

But this positive application of the general trade aspect of the federal commerce power was thoroughly undermined by a later dictum of Viscount Haldane's in the *Board of Commerce* case.[2] Viscount Haldane explained his invocation of the commerce power in the *John Deere Plow* case on the grounds that it had been used there to support a general power which the Dominion parliament possessed independently of it. Thus, aside from its possible application to international and interprovincial trade, the trade and commerce power at this stage had been assigned by judicial review to a position in the division of powers which was inferior to all the other heads of power: it was now regarded as essentially an auxiliary power incapable of serving on its own as a primary source of legislative capacity. ~

ATTORNEY-GENERAL FOR CANADA
v. ATTORNEY-GENERAL FOR ALBERTA
In the Privy Council. [1916] 1 A.C. 589; II Olmsted 1.

The judgment of their Lordships was delivered by

VISCOUNT HALDANE. This is an appeal from a judgment of the Supreme Court of Canada answering certain questions put to the judges by a reference from the Government of the Dominion. The questions so referred were as follows:

1. Are ss. 4 and 70 of the Insurance Act, 1910, or any and what part or parts of the said sections, ultra vires of the Parliament of Canada?

2. Does s. 4 of the Insurance Act, 1910, operate to prohibit an insurance company incorporated by a foreign State from carrying on the business of insurance within Canada, if such

---

[2] *Re The Board of Commerce Act and The Combines and Fair Prices Act, 1919*, [1922] 1 A.C. 191, at p. 198. See above pp. 27-28.

company does not hold a licence from the Minister under the said Act, and if such carrying on of the business is confined to a single province?

Sect. 4 is in these terms: "In Canada, except as otherwise provided by this Act, no company or underwriters or other person shall solicit or accept any risk, or issue or deliver any receipt or policy of insurance, or grant any annuity on a life or lives, or collect or receive any premium, or inspect any risk, or adjust any loss, or carry on any business of insurance, or prosecute or maintain any suit, action, or proceeding, or file any claim in insolvency relating to such business, unless it be done by or on behalf of a company or underwriters holding a licence from the Minister." The Minister is defined in the Act to mean the Minister of Finance of the Dominion.

Sect. 70 is an ancillary section which imposes a penalty on every person who contravenes or attempts to contravene the provisions of the above and other sections. . . .

. . . It will be observed that s. 4 deprives private individuals of their liberty to carry on the business of insurance, even when that business is confined within the limits of a province. It will also be observed that even a provincial company operating within the limits of the province where it has been incorporated cannot, notwithstanding that it may obtain permission from the authorities of another province, operate within that other province without the licence of the Dominion Minister. In other words, the capacity is interfered with which, according to the judgment just delivered by their Lordships in the case of the Bonanza Company (See ante, p. 566. (A.C.)), such a company possesses to take advantage of powers and rights proffered to it by authorities outside the provincial limits. Such an interference with its status appears to their Lordships to interfere with its civil rights within the province of incorporation, as well as with the power of the Legislature of every other province to confer civil rights upon it. Private individuals are likewise deprived of civil rights within their provinces.

It must be taken to be now settled that the general authority to make laws for the peace, order, and good government of Canada, which the initial part of s. 91 of the British North America Act confers, does not, unless the subject-matter of legislation falls within some one of the enumerated heads which follow, enable the Dominion Parliament to trench on the subject-matters entrusted to the provincial Legislatures by the enumeration in s. 92. There is only one case, outside the heads enumerated in s. 91, in which the Dominion Parliament can

legislate effectively as regards a province, and that is where the
subject-matter lies outside all of the subject-matters enumera-
tively entrusted to the province under s. 92. *Russell* v. *The Queen*
(7App. Cas. 829) is an instance of such a case. There the Court
considered that the particular subject-matter in question lay
outside the provincial powers. What has been said in subsequent
cases before this Board makes it clear that it was on this ground
alone, and not on the ground that the Canada Temperance Act
was considered to be authorized as legislation for the regulation
of trade and commerce, that the Judicial Committee thought
that it should be held that there was constitutional authority for
Dominion legislation which imposed conditions of a prohibitory
character on the liquor traffic throughout the Dominion. No
doubt the Canada Temperance Act contemplated in certain
events the use of different licensing boards and regulations in
different districts and to this extent legislated in relation to local
institutions. But the Judicial Committee appear to have thought
that this purpose was subordinate to a still wider and legitimate
purpose of establishing a uniform system of legislation for
prohibiting the liquor traffic throughout Canada excepting
under restrictive conditions. The case must therefore be regarded
as illustrating the principle which is now well established, but
none the less ought to be applied only with great caution, that
subjects which in one aspect and for one purpose fall within the
jurisdiction of the provincial Legislatures may in another aspect
and for another purpose fall within Dominion legislative jurisdiction. There was a good deal in the Ontario Liquor Licence
Act, and the powers of regulation which it entrusted to local
authorities in the province, which seems to cover part of the
field of legislation recognized as belonging to the Dominion in
Russell v. *The Queen*. But in *Hodge* v. *The Queen* (9 App. Cas.
117) the Judicial Committee had no difficulty in coming to the
conclusion that the local licensing system which the Ontario
statute sought to set up was within provincial powers. It was
only the converse of this proposition to hold, as was done
subsequently by this Board, though without giving reasons, that
the Dominion licensing statute, known as the McCarthy Act,
which sought to establish a local licensing system for the liquor
traffic throughout Canada, was beyond the powers conferred on
the Dominion Parliament by s. 91. Their Lordships think that
as the result of these decisions it must now be taken that the
authority to legislate for the regulation of trade and commerce
does not extend to the regulation by a licensing system of a
particular trade in which Canadians would otherwise be free to

engage in the provinces. Sect. 4 of the statute under consideration cannot, in their opinion, be justified under this head. Nor do
they think that it can be justified for any such reasons as appear
to have prevailed in *Russell* v. *The Queen*. No doubt the business
of insurance is a very important one, which has attained to great
dimensions in Canada. But this is equally true of other highly
important and extensive forms of business in Canada which are
today freely transacted under provincial authority. Where the
British North America Act has taken such forms of business out
of provincial jurisdiction, as in the case of banking, it has done
so by express words which would have been unnecessary had the
argument for the Dominion Government addressed to the Board
from the Bar been well founded. Where a company is incorporated to carry on the business of insurance throughout Canada,
and desires to possess rights and powers to that effect operative
apart from further authority, the Dominion Government can
incorporate it with such rights and powers, to the full extent
explained by the decision in the case of *John Deere Plow Co*. v.
Wharton ([1915] A.C. 330). But if a company seeks only
provincial rights and powers, and is content to trust for the
extension of these in other provinces to the Governments of
those provinces, it can at least derive capacity to accept such
rights and powers in other provinces from the province of its
incorporation, as has been explained in the case of the Bonanza
Company.

Their Lordships are therefore of opinion that the majority
in the Supreme Court were right in answering the first of the
two questions referred to them in the affirmative.

The second question is, in substance, whether the Dominion
Parliament has jurisdiction to require a foreign company to
take out a licence from the Dominion Minister, even in a case
where the company desires to carry on its business only within
the limits of a single province. To this question their Lordships'
reply is that in such a case it would be within the power of the
Parliament of Canada, by properly framed legislation, to impose
such a restriction. It appears to them that such a power is given
by the heads in s. 91, which refer to the regulation of trade and
commerce and to aliens. This question also is therefore answered
in the affirmative.

12. Proprietary Articles Trade Association v. Attorney-General for Canada, *1931*

~ In 1929 the federal government referred to the Supreme Court of Canada the question of the validity of the Dominion's anti-combines legislation after doubts as to the constitutionality of the legislation had been raised by counsel and judges in the provincial courts. The Supreme Court unanimously declared the legislation *intra vires*. The Proprietary Articles of Trade Association which had been charged with an infraction of the anti-combines legislation appealed this decision to the Privy Council. It was joined in this appeal by the governments of Ontario and Quebec.

Although counsel for the Dominion had cited the federal commerce power as one of the possible constitutional supports for the legislation, this was not the grounds upon which the Privy Council rested its opinion that the legislation was valid. It was Parliament's power to legislate in relation to criminal law (Section 91 [27]) which Lord Atkin used to sustain the main provisions of the legislation. To support those sections which could not be characterized as criminal law – the remedies which were designed to enforce the anti-combines policy through reductions of customs duty and revocation of patents – he cited the Dominion's taxation power (Section 91 [3]), its power in relation to patents (Section 21 [22]), and its power over customs and excise laws (Section 122).

While the commerce power was not invoked here to sustain this extremely important piece of national economic legislation, Lord Atkin's references to Section 91 (2) indicated a considerable expansion in the Judicial Committee's construction of that power. He took care to guard against the possibility of interpreting his judgment in this case as implying the elimination of the federal commerce power as a possible support for national anti-combines legislation. More positively, and most importantly, he discredited the notion put forward by Viscount Haldane in the *Board of Commerce* case[1] and repeated in the *Snider*[2] case that the power to regulate trade and commerce was

---

[1] See above pp. 27-28 and pp. 82-83.

[2] *Toronto Electric Commissioners* v. *Snider.* [1925] A.C. 409. See above pp. 43-44.

a subordinate one which could only be invoked when used in support of some other federal power. He cautiously avoided, however, any attempt at defining the extent of the commerce power as an independent source of legislative authority.

This case also demonstrates how the failure of the "trade and commerce" power to develop as a significant source of national legislative capacity in the fields of economic management and regulation could be in large measure compensated by other elements in the division of powers. In this case the criminal law power emerged as the principal support for federal anti-combines measures. Parliament's power to incorporate national companies, as indicated in the *John Deere Plow*[3] case, is capable of providing the central government with effective means of affecting the operations of national business agencies and, negatively it poses a major limitation to the provincial governments' power to nationalize industry. Further, the exceptions to Section 92 (10) establish a broad field for federal control over interprovincial transportation and communications systems as well as public works, while the banking, currency, interest and taxation powers in Section 91 arm the federal government, constitutionally, with the major instruments of monetary and fiscal management. Thus it would be wrong to attribute what some regard as the undue degree of decentralization in Canada's federal system solely to the effects of judicial review. It is necessary to look to extra-constitutional factors to explain the failure of federal authorities to exercise fully all the powers at their disposal. ~

PROPRIETARY ARTICLES TRADE ASSOCIATION
v. ATTORNEY-GENERAL FOR CANADA
In the Privy Council. [1931] A.C. 310; II Olmsted 668.

The judgment of their Lordships was delivered by

LORD ATKIN. This is an appeal from the Supreme Court of Canada on a reference by the Governor in Council under s. 55 of the Supreme Court Act. The questions submitted to the Court were:

1. Is the Combines Investigation Act, R.S. Can., 1927, c. 26, ultra vires the Parliament of Canada either in whole or in part, and if so, in what particular or particulars or to what extent?

---

[3] *John Deere Plow Co. Ltd.* v. *Wharton*, [1915] A.C. 330. See above pp. 82-83.

2. Is s. 498 of the Criminal Code ultra vires the Parliament of Canada, and if so, in what particular or particulars or to what extent?

The Supreme Court answered both questions in the negative.

The appellants are the Proprietary Articles Trade Association, who had been found by a Commission appointed under the Combines Investigation Act to have been party to a combine as defined in the Act, and had been admitted to be heard on the reference under s. 55, sub-s. 4, of the Supreme Court Act. The other appellants are the Attorney-General for the Province of Quebec and the Attorney-General for the Province of Ontario. The reference involved important questions of constitutional law within the Dominion, and their Lordships have had the assistance of full and able argument in which all the numerous relevant authorities were brought to their notice. After careful consideration of the arguments and the authorities their Lordships are of opinion that the decision of the Supreme Court is right.

In determining judicially the distribution of legislative powers between the Dominion and the Provinces made by the two famous ss. 91 and 92 of the British North America Act two principles have to be observed. First, the accepted canon of construction as to the general effect of the sections must be maintained. This is that the general powers of legislation for the peace, order and good government of Canada are committed to the Dominion Parliament, though they are subject to the exclusive powers of legislation committed to the Provincial legislatures and enumerated in s. 92. But the Provincial powers are themselves qualified in respect of the classes of subjects enumerated in s. 91, as particular instances of the general powers assigned to the Dominion. Any matters coming within any of those particular classes of subjects is not to be deemed to come within the classes of matters assigned to the Provincial legislatures. This almost reproduces the express words of the sections, and this rule is well settled.

The second principle to be observed judicially was expressed by the Board in 1881, "it will be a wise course . . . to decide each case which arises as best they can, without entering more largely upon an interpretation of the statute than is necessary for the decision of the particular question in hand": *Citizens Insurance Co. of Canada* v. *Parsons* ((1881) 7 App. Cas. 96, 109). It was restated in 1914: "The structure of ss. 91 and 92, and the degree to which the connotation of the expressions used overlaps, render it, in their Lordships' opinion, unwise on this or any other occasion to attempt exhaustive definitions of the meaning and scope of these expressions. Such definitions, in the case of language used under the conditions in which a constitution such as that under consideration was framed, must almost certainly miscarry": *John Deere Plow Co.* v. *Wharton* ([1915] A.C. 330, 338). The object is as far as possible to prevent too rigid declarations of the Courts from interfering with such elasticity as is given in the written constitution.

With these two principles in mind the present task must be approached.

The claim of the Dominion is that the Combines Act and s. 498 of the Criminal Code can be supported as falling within two of the enumerated classes in s. 91 – namely, "(2) The regulation of trade and commerce," and "(27) The criminal law, except the constitution of courts of criminal jurisdiction, but including the procedure in criminal matters." Reliance is also placed on "(3) The raising of money by any mode or system of taxation," "(22) Patents of invention and discovery," and on the general power of legislating for peace, order and good government. The appellants, on the other hand, say that the Act and the section of the Code violate the exclusive right of the Provinces under s. 92 to make laws as to "(13) property and civil rights in the Province," and "(14) the administration of justice in the Province."

~ Lord Atkin then reviewed the legislative history of both the section in the Criminal Code which makes combinations in restraint of trade criminal offences and the legislation providing for the investigation and prosecution of trade combinations. He also set down the main provisions of the Board of Commerce and Fair Prices Acts of 1919 which had been ruled *ultra vires* by the Privy Council in the *Board of Commerce* case. ~

Their Lordships have dealt at some length with the provisions of the Acts of 1919 inasmuch as the appellants relied strongly on the judgment of the Board, in *In re Board of Commerce Act, 1919* ([1922] 1 A.C. 191), which held both Acts to be ultra vires. Unless there are material distinctions between those Acts and the present, it is plainly the duty of this Board to follow the previous decision. It is necessary therefore to contrast the provisions of the Acts of 1919 with the provisions of the Act now in dispute. The judgment above referred to was given in November, 1921, and in June 13, 1923, there was passed the Combines Investigation Act, 1923 (13 & 14 Geo. 5, c. 9), which repealed the two Acts of 1919 and enacted provisions which were substantially those of the present Act. The Act of 1923 was revised in 1927 and appears substantially in the original form in the revised Act – the Combines Investigation Act (R.S. Can., 1927, c. 26). By this Act "combines" are defined as combines "which have operated or are likely to operate to the detriment or against the interest of the public, whether consumers, producers or others," and which "are mergers, trusts or monopolies so-called" or result from the acquisition by any person of any control over the business of any other person or result from any agreement which has the effect of limiting facilities for production, manufacture or transport or of fixing a common price, or enhancing the price of articles or of preventing or lessening competition in or substantially controlling production or manufacture, or "otherwise restraining or injuring trade or commerce." By the Act the Governor in Council may name a Minister of the Crown to be charged with the administration of the Act, and must appoint a registrar of the Combines Investigation Act. The registrar is charged with the duty to inquire whether a combine exists, whenever an application is made for that purpose by six persons supported by evidence, or whenever he has reason to believe that a combine exists, or whenever he is directed by the Minister so to inquire. Provision is made for holding further inquiry by Commissioners appointed from time to time; and the registrar and a commissioner are armed with large powers of examining books and papers, demanding returns, and summoning witnesses. The proceedings are to take place in private unless the Minister directs that they should be public. The registrar is to report the result of any inquiry to the Minister, and every commissioner is to report to the registrar who is to transmit the report to the Minister. Any report of a commissioner is to be made public unless the commissioner reports that public interest requires publication to be withheld, in which case the Minister has a discretion as to publicity.

By s. 32 "Every one is guilty of an indictable offence and liable to a penalty not exceeding ten thousand dollars or to two years' imprisonment, or if a corporation to a penalty not exceeding twenty-five thousand dollars, who is a party or privy to or knowingly assists in the formation or operation of a combine within the meaning of this Act. (2) No prosecution for any offence under this section shall be commenced otherwise than at the instance of the Solicitor-General of Canada or of the Attorney-General of a Province." By subsequent sections, refusal to obey orders as to discovery and other interference with an investigation are made offences for the most part subject to summary conviction and appropriate penalties are imposed.

Under a group of ss. 29 to 31, entitled "Remedies" powers are given as in previous Acts for the Governor in Council to reduce customs duties, and for the Exchequer Court to revoke licences where the duties are used to facilitate a combine or when the holder of a patent uses it so as unduly to limit the manufacture, or enhance the price of any article. Power is given to the Minister to remit to the Attorney-General of a Province any returns made in pursuance of the Act or any report of the registrar, or any commissioner; and if no action is taken thereon by the Attorney-General of the Province, the Solicitor-General (representing the Dominion) may take the appropriate action.

In their Lordships' opinion s. 498 of the Criminal Code and the greater part of the provisions of the Combines Investigation Act fall within the power of the Dominion Parliament to legislate as to matters falling within the class of subjects, "the criminal law including the procedure in criminal matters" (s. 91, head 27). The substance of the Act is by s. 2 to define, and by s. 32 to make criminal, combines which the legislature in the public interest intends to prohibit. The definition is wide, and may cover activities which have not hitherto been considered to be criminal. But only those combines are affected "which have operated or are likely to operate to the detriment or against the interest of the public, whether consumers, producers, or others"; and if Parliament genuinely determines that commercial activities which can be so described are to be suppressed in the public interest, their Lordships see no reason why Parliament should not make them crimes. "Criminal law" means "the criminal law in its widest sense": *Attorney-General for Ontario* v. *Hamilton Street Ry Co.* ([1903] A.C. 524). It certainly is not confined to what was criminal by the law of England or of any Province in 1867. The power must extend to legislation to make new crimes. Criminal law connotes only the quality of such acts or omissions as are prohibited under appropriate penal provisions by authority of the State. The criminal quality of an act cannot be discerned by intuition; nor can it be discovered by reference to any standard but one: Is the act prohibited with penal consequences? Morality and criminality are far from co-extensive; nor is the sphere of criminality necessarily part of a more extensive field covered by morality – unless the moral code necessarily disapproves all acts prohibited by the State, in which case the argument moves in a circle. It appears to their Lordships to be of little value to seek to confine crimes to a category of acts which by their very nature belong to the domain of "criminal jurisprudence"; for the domain of criminal jurisprudence can only be ascertained by examining what acts at any particular period are declared by the State to be crimes, and the only common nature they will be found to possess is that they are prohibited by the State and that those who commit them are punished. Their Lordships agree with the view expressed in the judgment of Newcombe J. ([1929] S.C.R. 409, 422) that the passage in the judgment of the Board in the *Board of Commerce* case ([1922] 1 A.C. 191, 198, 199) to which allusion has been made, was not intended as a definition. In that case their Lordships appear to have been contrasting two matters – one obviously within the line, the other obviously outside it. For this purpose it was clearly legitimate to point to matters which are such serious breaches of any accepted code of morality as to be obviously crimes when they are prohibited under penalties. The contrast is with matters which are merely attempts to interfere with Provincial rights, and are sought to be justified under the head of "criminal law" colourably and merely in aid of what is in substance an encroachment. The Board considered that the Combines and Fair Prices Act of 1919 came within the latter class, and was in substance an encroachment on the exclusive power of the Provinces to legislate on property and civil rights. The judgment of the Board arose in respect of an order under Part II of the Act. Their Lordships pointed out five respects in which the Act was subject to criticism. It empowered the Board of Commerce to prohibit accumulations in the case of non-traders; to compel surplus articles to be sold at prices fixed by the Board; to regulate profits; to exercise their powers over articles produced for his own use by the householder himself; to inquire into individual cases without applying any principles of general application. None of these powers exists in the provisions now under discussion. There is a general definition, and a general condemnation; and if penal consequences follow, they can only follow from the determination by existing courts of an issue of fact defined in express words by the statute. The greater part of the statute is occupied in setting up and directing machinery for making preliminary inquiries whether the alleged offence has been committed. It is noteworthy that no penal consequences follow directly from a report of either commissioner or registrar that a combine exists. It is not even made evidence. The offender, if he is to be punished, must be tried on indictment, and the offence proved in due course of law. Penal consequences, no doubt, follow the breach of orders made for the discovery of evidence; but if the main object be intra vires, the enforcement of orders genuinely authorized and genuinely made to secure that object are not open to attack.

It is, however, not enough for Parliament to rely solely on the powers to legislate as to the criminal law for support of the whole Act. The remedies given under ss. 29 and 30 reducing customs duty and revoking patents have no necessary connection with the criminal law and must be justified on other grounds. Their Lordships have no doubt that they can both be supported as being reasonably ancillary to the powers given respectively under s. 91, head 3, and affirmed by s. 122, "the raising of money by any mode or system of taxation," and under s. 91, head 22, "patents of invention and discovery." It is unfortunately beyond dispute that in a country where a general protective tariff exists persons may be found to take advantage of the protection, and within its walls form combinations that may work to the public disadvantage. It is an elementary point of self-preservation that the legislature which creates the protection should arm the executive with powers of withdrawing or relaxing the protection if abused. The same reasoning applies to grants of monopolies under any system of patents.

The view that their Lordships have expressed makes it unnecessary to discuss the further ground upon which the legislation has been supported by reference to the power to legislate under s. 91, head 2, for "The regulation of trade and commerce." Their Lordships merely propose to disassociate themselves from the construction suggested in argument of a passage in the judgment in the *Board of Commerce* case under which it was contended that the power to regulate trade and commerce could be invoked only in furtherance of a general power which Parliament possessed independently of it. No such restriction is properly to be inferred from that judgment. The words of the statute must receive their proper construction where they stand as giving an independent authority to Parliament over the particular subject-matter. But following the second principle noticed in the beginning of this judgment their Lordships in the present case forbear from defining the extent of that authority. They desire, however, to guard themselves from being supposed to lay down that the present legislation could not be supported on that ground.

If then the legislation in question is authorized under one or other of the heads specifically enumerated in s. 91, it is not to the purpose to say that it affects property and civil rights in the Provinces. Most of the specific subjects in s. 91 do affect property and civil rights but so far as the legislation of Parliament in pith and substance is operating within the enumerated powers there is constitutional authority to interfere with property and civil rights. The same principle would apply to s. 92, head 14, "the administration of justice in the Province," even if the legislation did, as in the present case it does not, in any way interfere with the administration of justice. Nor is there any ground for suggesting that the Dominion may not employ its own executive officers for the purpose of carrying out legislation which is within its constitutional authority, as it does regularly in the case of revenue officials and other matters which need not be enumerated.

13. Attorney-General for British Columbia *v.* Attorney-General for Canada (Natural Products Marketing Act Reference), *1937*

~ The Natural Products Marketing Act, 1934 (as amended in 1935) was one of the eight federal statutes submitted to the courts in the series of "New Deal" reference cases initiated by the King administration in 1935. This statute, provoked by the severe consequences of the worldwide depression in agricultural markets, was designed to provide orderly marketing arrangements for natural products. In framing the legislation the Dominion draughtsmen had been sensitive to the difficulties of divided jurisdiction in the field of marketing legislation and had included provisions which anticipated the need for co-operation between national and provincial marketing agencies. Indeed each of the nine provinces in 1934 had passed statutes designed to dovetail provincial coverage of marketing problems with Dominion legislation so that provincial and Dominion marketing boards could together deal completely with all the trade – domestic and foreign – in a given product. Despite this, Ontario, Quebec, and New Brunswick before the Privy Council all supported the charge that the Dominion Act invaded provincial jurisdiction. British Columbia, however, argued in favour of upholding those parts of the federal Act relating to interprovincial and export trade.

Two earlier decisions of the Supreme Court had revealed the constraints which the application of a rigid constitutional formula could impose upon effective government action in the field of marketing. In *The King* v. *Eastern Terminal Elevator Co.*,[1] a majority of the Court had thrown out the Canada Grain Act, 1912, which had provided a broad national scheme for regulating the marketing, grading, storing, and shipping of Canadian grain. The majority had reasoned that even though most of the grain affected by the Act was involved in export trade still the Act would also incidentally affect grain involved only in intra-provincial trade and hence it must be considered *ultra vires*.

[1] [1925] S.C.R. 434.

A few years later in *Lawson* v. *Interior Tree Fruit & Vegetable Committee of Direction*[2] the Supreme Court reversed its application of this rigid approach to marketing questions when it unanimously found the British Columbia Produce Marketing Act *ultra vires*. This Act provided for the regulation of marketing of all tree fruits and vegetables grown in a designated area in the province. Although the Act dealt with local trade, a substantial portion of the produce subject to its provisions would be shipped outside the province. Because of its interference with interprovincial and export trade four of the five judges considered it infringed on Parliament's jurisdiction under Section 91 (2).

Coming after these decisions the Judicial Committee's (and the Supreme Court's) refusal to support the Dominion's Natural Products Marketing Act in this *Reference* indicated that there were virtually insurmountable obstacles to the successful exercise of the federal commerce power in relation to export and interprovincial trade. Federal legislation designed to organize the export and interprovincial marketing of major crops or products to be valid could not touch any aspect of intra-provincial trade. But this line of cases also pointed to a possible no man's land where neither the Dominion nor the provinces could find constitutional support for effective marketing legislation. The fact that at the point where marketing legislation must take effect products often cannot be distinguished in terms of those destined for extra-provincial as opposed to those destined for intra-provincial markets made it doubtful whether Parliament or the provincial legislatures could regulate the marketing of products in which intra- and extra-provincial elements are inextricably combined. ~

ATTORNEY-GENERAL FOR BRITISH COLUMBIA
v. ATTORNEY-GENERAL FOR CANADA
In the Privy Council. [1937] A.C. 377. III Olmsted 228.

The judgment of their Lordships was delivered by

LORD ATKIN. This is an appeal from the Supreme Court on a reference by the Governor-General in Council, dated November 5, 1935, raising the question whether the Natural Products Marketing Act, 1934, as amended by the Natural Products

[2] *Lawson* v. *Interior Tree Fruit & Vegetable Committee of Direction*, [1931] S.C.R. 357.

Marketing Act Amendment Act, 1935, is ultra vires of the Parliament of Canada. The Supreme Court unanimously answered the question in the affirmative.

The Act consists of two parts. The first provides for the establishment of a Dominion Marketing Board whose powers include powers to regulate the time and place at which, and the agency through which, natural products to which an approved scheme relates shall be marketed, and to determine the manner of distribution and the quantity, quality, grade or class of the product that shall be marketed by any person at any time, and to prohibit the marketing of any of the regulated products of any grade, quality or class.

There are other regulatory powers which need not be further specified. A scheme to regulate the marketing of a natural product is initiated by a representative number of persons engaged in the production or marketing of the natural product. It can be referred by the appropriate Minister to the Board, and if they approve the scheme as submitted or amended by them, and it is further approved by the Minister, the Governor-General in Council may approve the scheme. It is essential that the Governor-General in Council shall be satisfied either that the principal market for the natural product is outside the Province of production, or that some part of the product produced may be exported. The latter provision makes it clear that the regulation may apply to marketing transactions in natural products which have nothing to do with foreign export or inter-Provincial trade. If the Minister is satisfied that trade and commerce in a natural product are injuriously affected by the absence of a scheme prepared as above he may himself propose a scheme for approval of the Governor in Council. The Governor in Council is given power by order or regulation to regulate or restrict importation into Canada of a natural product which enters Canada in competition with a regulated product: and to regulate or restrict the exportation from Canada of any natural product. Part II contains provision for the appointment by the Minister of a Committee who may be entrusted with the duty of investigating all matters connected with the production or marketing of natural or regulated products for the purpose of ascertaining the charges made in distribution of a natural or regulated product. The receipt against the interest of the public of an excessive charge is made an indictable offence, and there are provisions for the trial of such offences.

There can be no doubt that the provisions of the Act cover transactions in any natural product which are completed within the Province, and have no connection with inter-Provincial or export trade. It is therefore plain that the Act purports to affect property and civil rights in the Province, and if not brought within one of the enumerated classes of subjects in s. 91 must be beyond the competence of the Dominion Legislature. It was sought to bring the Act within the class (2) of s. 91 – namely, The Regulation of Trade and Commerce. Emphasis was laid upon those parts of the Act which deal with inter-Provincial and export trade. But the regulation of trade and commerce does not permit the regulation of individual forms of trade or commerce confined to the Province. In his judgment the Chief Justice says ([1936] Can. S.C.R. 412): "The enactments in question, therefore, in so far as they relate to matters which are in substance local and provincial are beyond the jurisdiction of Parliament. Parliament cannot acquire jurisdiction to deal in the sweeping way in which these enactments operate with such local and provincial matters by legislating at the same time respecting external and inter-provincial trade and committing the regulation of external and inter-provincial trade and the regulation of trade which is exclusively local and of traders and producers engaged in trade which is exclusively local to the same authority: *The King* v. *Eastern Terminal Elevator Co.* ([1925] Can. S.C.R. 434)."

Their Lordships agree with this, and find it unnecessary to add anything. There was a further attempt to support the Act upon the general powers to legislate for the peace, order and good government of Canada. Their Lordships have already dealt with this matter in their previous judgments in this series and need not repeat what is there said. The judgment of the Chief Justice in this case is conclusive against the claim for validity on this ground. In the result, therefore, there is no answer to the contention that the Act in substance invades the Provincial field and is invalid. . . .

~ Lord Atkin then dismissed the Dominion's request that the valid provisions of the Act be severed from the invalid provisions and allowed to stand alone. ~

The Board was given to understand that some of the Provinces attach much importance to the existence of marketing schemes such as might be set up under this legislation: and their attention was called to the existence of Provincial legislation setting up Provincial schemes for various Provincial products. It was said that as the Provinces and the Dominion between them possess a totality of complete legislative authority, it must be possible to combine Dominion and Provincial legislation so that each within its own sphere could in co-operation with the other achieve the complete power of regulation which is desired. Their Lordships appreciate the importance of the desired aim. Unless and until a change is made in the respective legislative functions of Dominion and Province it may well be that satisfactory results for both can only be obtained by co-operation. But the legislation will have to be carefully framed, and will not be achieved by either party leaving its own sphere and encroaching upon that of the other. In the present case their Lordships are unable to support the Dominion legislation as it stands. They will therefore humbly advise His Majesty that this appeal should be dismissed.

14. Reference re The Farm Products Marketing Act (Ontario), *1957*

~ In 1957 the federal government submitted to the Supreme Court of Canada eight questions which were designed to measure the extent to which a province could provide a comprehensive system of regulatory boards for organizing the marketing of farm products within the province. Three of the questions concerned the validity of two provisions of Ontario's Farm Products Marketing Act authorizing a system of marketing by means of a central pool and distribution of payments to producers and a proposed amendment which would enable local marketing boards to purchase and market the surplus of a regulated product using a system of licensing fees to recoup any losses suffered. The other five questions involved specific schemes and regulations passed under the Act dealing with the marketing of hogs, peaches and vegetables. A majority of the judges sitting found the impugned provisions of the Act and regulations *intra vires* with the qualification that they not affect extra-provincial trade. Only the proposed amendment to the Act was ruled invalid. But this latter decision was based not on considerations of extra-provincial *versus* intra-provincial trade but on the doctrine developed in earlier cases that an equalization scheme such as the one envisaged by the proposed amendment constituted an indirect tax and hence was beyond provincial jurisdiction.

The implications which this case has for the development of the federal commerce power have little to do with the specific answers which the Court gave to the questions posed by the reference. The most significant element in this decision is the pragmatic way in which a number of the judges tackled the task of drawing the boundary lines between national and provincial jurisdiction in the field of regulating commercial activities. The order of reference had instructed the Court to assume that the statute and regulations extended only to "intra-provincial" transactions. A more cautious Court might have left the matter there. But more than half of the majority (Chief Justice Kerwin and Justices Rand, Locke and Nolan) took this as an invitation to abandon the mechanical, unreflective application of the categories of intra-provincial and extra-provincial trade and explore the realities of the movement of produce in trade with a view to describing in concrete terms the kind of economic activity which is inherently extra-provincial. This functional approach lead this group of judges by rather different routes to the common conclusion that in business operations such as food-processing which involve a number of steps between the original producer and the final consumer even though some parts of the operation (or "transactions") might be completed within the province, the business as a whole might still be primarily extra-provincial in scope and hence subject to federal jurisdiction. Instead of simply taking all "intra-provincial transactions" to be coterminous with provincial authority these opinions in effect imply the application of the "aspect" doctrine to trading activities: looked at from the point of view of economic regulation a transaction might be one stage in an extra-provincial business and hence part of federal trade and commerce, whereas from the point of view of the law of contracts it might be a matter of provincial concern.

All the members of the majority did not join this rather liberal exploration of the domain of extra-provincial trade and commerce. The judgment of Justice Fauteux (part of which is included below) indicates the more traditional and cautious approach to the issue. Also it should be noted that Justice Rand, towards the end of his opinion acknowledged that his own reasoning had not removed the barrier which would prevent either the Dominion or a province, acting alone, from regulating trade in a product before it can be identified as either extra-provincial or intra-provincial. But this does not detract from the general impression created by the judgments of Chief Justice Kerwin and Justices Locke and Rand that the Dominion's "trade and commerce" power could serve as a source of legislative authority for major economic policies in the field of international and interprovincial trade. This impression was given some further confirmation a year later in *Murphy* v. *C.P.R. and A.-G. Canada*[1] when both Justice Locke and Justice Rand, speaking for a unanimous Court cited the federal "trade and commerce" power as the constitutional basis for the Canadian Wheat Board Act which provides for the regulation of the export trade in grains. ~

---

[1] [1958] S.C.R. 626.

REFERENCE RE THE FARM PRODUCTS
MARKETING ACT (ONTARIO)
In the Supreme Court of Canada. [1957] S.C.R. 198.

KERWIN, C.J.C.: This is a reference by His Excellency the Governor-General in Council as to the validity of one clause of one section of The Farm Products Marketing Act of the Province of Ontario, R.S.O. 1950, c. 131, of certain regulations made thereunder, of an order of The Ontario Hog Producers' Marketing Board, of a proposed amendment to the Act, and of a suggested authorization by the Farm Products Marketing Board if that amendment be held to be *intra vires*. On such a reference one cannot envisage all possible circumstances which might arise and it must also be taken that it is established that it is not to be presumed that a Provincial Legislature intended to exceed its legislative jurisdiction under the British North America Act, although the Court may, on what it considers the proper construction of a given enactment, determine that the Legislature has gone beyond its authority.

Subsequent to the date of the order of reference, the Act was amended by c. 20 of the statutes of 1956, which came into force the day it received Royal Assent, s. 1 of which reads as follows:

1. The Farm Products Marketing Act is amended by adding thereto the following section:
1a. The purpose and intent of this Act is to provide for the control and regulation in any or all respects of the marketing within the Province of farm products including the prohibition of such marketing in whole or in part.

Without entering into discussion as to what is a declaratory law, since the term may have different connotations depending upon the matter under review, it is arguable that, for the present purposes, this amendment should be read as part of The Farm Products Marketing Act, but, in any event, the first question submitted to us directs us to assume that that Act as amended down to the date of the reference applies only in the case of 'intra-provincial transactions." This term means "existing or occurring within a province"; see Shorter Oxford English Dictionary, including "intraparochial" as an example under the word "intra." As will appear later, the word "marketing" is defined in the Act, but, in accordance with what has already been stated, I take it as being confined to marketing within the Province.

Question 1 is as follows:

1. Assuming that the said Act applies only in the case of intra-provincial transactions, is clause (l) of subsection 1 of section 3 of The Farm Products Marketing Act, R.S.O. 1950 chapter 131 as amended by Ontario Statutes 1951, chapter 25, 1953, chapter 36, 1954, chapter 29, 1955 chapter 21, ultra vires *the Ontario Legislature?*

Clause (*l*) of subs. (1) of s. 3 referred to, as re-enacted by 1955, c. 21, s. 2, provides:

3. (1) The Board may, . . .

(l) authorize any marketing agency appointed under a scheme to conduct a pool or pools for the distribution of all moneys received from the sale of the regulated product and requiring any such marketing agency, after deducting all necessary and proper disbursements and expenses, to distribute the proceeds of sale in such manner that each person receives a share of the total proceeds in relation to the amount, variety, size, grade and class of the regulated product delivered by him and to make an initial payment, on delivery of the product and subsequent payments until the total net proceeds are distributed.

For a proper understanding of the terms used in this clause and of the provisions of the Act it is necessary to refer to what is proposed by the latter.

The Board is the Farm Products Marketing Board and " 'farm products' includes animals, meats, eggs, poultry, wool, dairy products, grains, seeds, fruit, fruit products, vegetables, vegetable products, maple products, honey, tobacco and such articles of food or drink manufactured or derived in whole or in part from any such product and such other natural products of agriculture as may be designated by the regulations" (s. 1 (*b*)). " 'Regulated product' means a farm product in respect of which a scheme is in force" (s. 1(*g*)). Provision is made for the formulation of a scheme for the marketing or regulating of any farm product upon the petition of at least 10 per cent of all producers engaged in the production of the farm product in Ontario, or in that part thereof to which the proposed scheme is to apply. " 'Marketing' means buying, selling and offering for sale and includes advertising, assembling, financing, packing and shipping for sale or storage and transporting in any manner by any person, and 'market' and 'marketed' have corresponding meanings" (s. 1(e), as re-enacted by 1955, c. 21, s. 1). The scheme may provide for a "marketing agency" designated by the Board in its regulations. Once the scheme is approved by the Board the latter's regulations will apply according to the farm products dealt with thereby.

It seems plain that the Province may regulate a transaction of sale and purchase in Ontario between a resident of the Province and one who resides outside its limits; that is, if an individual in Quebec comes to Ontario and there buys a hog, or vegetables, or peaches, the mere fact that he has the intention to take them from Ontario to Quebec does not deprive the Legislature of its power to regulate the transaction, as is evidenced by such enactments as The Sale of Goods Act, R.S.O. 1950, c. 345. That is a matter of the regulation of contracts and not of trade as trade and in that respect the intention of the purchaser is immaterial. However, if the hog be sold to a packing plant or the vegetables or peaches to a cannery, the products of those establishments in the course of trade may be dealt with by the Legislature or by Parliament depending, on the one hand, upon whether all the products are sold or intended for sale within the Province or, on the other, whether some of them are sold or intended for sale beyond Provincial limits. It is, I think, impossible to fix any minimum proportion of such last-mentioned sales or intended sales as determining the jurisdiction of Parliament. This applies to the sale by the original owner. Once a statute aims at "regulation of trade in matters of inter-provincial concern" (*The Citizens Insurance Company of Canada* v. *Parsons; The Queen Insurance Company* v. *Parsons* ((1881), 7 App. Cas. 96 at 113), it is beyond the competence of a Provincial Legislature. The ambit of head 2 of s. 91 of the British North America Act, "The Regulation of Trade and Commerce" has been considerably enlarged by decisions of the Judicial Committee and expressions used in some of its earlier judgments must be read in the light of its later pronouncements, as is pointed out by Sir Lyman Duff in *Re Alberta Statutes* ([1938] S.C.R. 100 at 121). In fact, his judgment in *Re The Natural Products Marketing Act, 1934* ([1936] S.C.R. 398), which is justly considered as the *locus classicus*, must be read in conjunction with and subject to his remarks in the later case. The concept of trade and commerce, the regulation of which is confided to Parliament, is entirely separate and distinct from the regulation of mere sale and purchase agreements. Once an article enters into the flow of interprovincial or external trade, the subject-matter and all its attendant circumstances cease to be a mere matter of local concern. No change has taken place in the theory underlying the construction of the British North America Act that what is not within the legislative jurisdiction of Parliament must be within that of the Provincial Legislatures. This, of course, still leaves the question as to how far either may proceed, and, as Lord Atkin pointed out in the *Natural Products Marketing Act* case, *supra*, at p. 389, neither party may leave its own sphere and encroach upon that of another. . . .

. . . In view of the wording of question 1, I take clause (*l*) of subs. (1) of s. 3 of The Farm Products Marketing Act as being a successful endeavour on the part of the Ontario Legislature to fulfil its part while still keeping within the ambit of its powers. On the assumption directed to be made and reading the clause so as not to apply to transactions which I have indicated would be of a class beyond the powers of the Legislature, my answer to the first question is "No." . . .

RAND J.: This reference raises questions going to the scope of Provincial authority over trade. They arise out of The Farm Products Marketing Act, R.S.O. 1950, c. 131, as amended, which deals comprehensively with the matter connoted by its name and out of certain schemes formed under it. Its object is to accord primary producers of farm products the advantages of various degrees of controlled marketing, for which it provides provincial and local machinery.

General jurisdiction over its administration is exercised by the Farm Products Marketing Board; regulation is by way of schemes for the marketing of any product; under a scheme, a local board, district committees and county groups are organized; and the marketing may be carried out exclusively by an agency designated by the Board upon the recommendation of the local board.

The questions put, which assume the Act to be limited in application to local trade, call for answers which make it necessary to examine and define the scope of local trade to the extent of the regulation provided. The enquiry must take into account regulatory power over acts and transactions which while objectively appearing to be consummated within the Province may involve or possess an interest of interprovincial or foreign trade, which for convenience I shall refer to as external trade. . . .

. . . Although not specifically mentioned in s. 92 of the British North America Act, there is admittedly a field of trade within provincial power, and the head or heads of s. 92 from which it is to be deduced will be considered later. The power is a subtraction from the scope of the language conferring on the Dominion by head 2 of s. 91 exclusive authority to make laws in relation to the regulation of trade and commerce, and was derived under an interpretation of the Act which was found necessary

in order to preserve from serious curtailment, if not from virtual extinction, the degree of autonomy which, as appears from the scheme of the Act as a whole, the provinces were intended to possess

(*per* Duff J. in *Lawson* v. *Interior Tree, Fruit and Vegetable Committee of Direction* ([1931] S.C.R. 357 at 366). In examining the legislation for the purpose mentioned we should bear in mind Lord Atkin's admonition in *Attorney-General for British Columbia* v. *Attorney-General for Canada et al* ([1937] A.C. 377 at 389), that

the legislation will have to be carefully framed, and will not be achieved by either party leaving its own sphere and encroaching upon that of the other.

The definitive statement of the scope of Dominion and Provincial jurisdiction was made by Duff C.J. in *Re The Natural Products Marketing Act, 1934* ([1936] S.C.R. 398 at 414 *et seq.*). The regulation of particular trades confined to the Province lies exclusively with the Legislature subject, it may be, to Dominion general regulation affecting all trade, and to such incidental intrusion by the Dominion as may be necessary to prevent the defeat of Dominion regulation; interprovincial and foreign trade are correspondingly the exclusive concern of Parliament. That statement is to be read with the judgment of this Court in *The King* v. *Eastern Terminal Elevator Company* ([1925] S.C.R. 434), approved by the Judicial Committee in *Attorney-General for British Columbia* v. *Attorney-General for Canada, supra,* at p. 387, to the effect that Dominion regulation cannot embrace local trade merely because in undifferentiated subject-matter the external interest is dominant. But neither the original statement nor its approval furnishes a clear guide to the demarcation of the two classes when we approach as here the origination, the first stages of trade, including certain aspects of manufacture and production.

That demarcation must observe this rule, that if in a trade activity, including manufacture or production, there is involved a matter of extraprovincial interest or concern its regulation thereafter in the aspect of trade is by that fact put beyond Provincial power. This is exemplified in *Lawson* v. *Interior Tree Fruit and Vegetable Committee of Direction, supra,* where the Province purported to regulate the time and quantity of shipment, the shippers, the price and the transportation of fruit and vegetables in both unsegregated and segregated local and interprovincial trade movements.

A producer is entitled to dispose of his products beyond the Province without reference to a provincial marketing agency or price, shipping or other trade regulation; and an outside purchaser is entitled with equal freedom to purchase and export. Processing is one of a number of trade services that may be given products in the course of reaching the consumer: milling (as of grain or lumber), sorting, packing, slaughtering, dressing, storing, transporting, etc. The producer or purchaser may desire to process the product either within or beyond the Province and if he engages for that with a local undertaking (using that expression in a non-technical sense), such as a packing plant – and it would apply to any sort of servicing – he takes that service as he finds it but free from such Provincial impositions as are strictly trade regulations such as prices or the specification of standards, which could no more be imposed than Provincial trade marks. Regulation of that nature could directly nullify external trade vital to the economy of the country. Trade arrangements reaching the dimensions of world agreements are now a commonplace; interprovincial trade, in which the Dominion is a single market, is of similar importance, and equally vital to the economic functioning of the country as a whole. The Dominion power implies responsibility for promoting and maintaining the vigour and growth of trade beyond Provincial confines, and the discharge of this duty must remain unembarrassed by local trade impediments. If the processing is restricted to external trade, it becomes an instrumentality of that trade and its single control as to prices, movements, standards, etc., by the Dominion follows: *Re The Industrial Relations and Disputes Investigation Act* ([1955] S.C.R. 529). The licensing of processing plants by the Province as a trade regulation is thus limited to their operations in local trade. Likewise the licensing of shippers, whether producers or purchasers, and the fixing of the terms and conditions of shipment, including prices, as trade regulation, where the goods are destined beyond the Province, would be beyond Provincial power.

Local trade has in some cases been classed as a matter of

property and civil rights and related to head 13 of s. 92, and the propriety of that allocation was questioned. The production and exchange of goods as an economic activity does not take place by virtue of positive law or civil right; it is assumed as part of the residual free activity of men upon or around which law is imposed. It has an identity of its own recognized by head 2 of s. 91. I cannot agree that its regulation under that head was intended as a species of matter under head 13 from which by the language of s. 91 it has been withdrawn. It happened that in *The Citizens Insurance Company of Canada* v. *Parsons; The Queen Insurance Company* v. *Parsons* ((1881), 7 App. Cas. 96), assuming insurance to be a trade, the commodity being dealt in was the making of contracts, and their relation to head 13 seemed obvious. But the true conception of trade (in contradistinction to the static nature of rights, civil or property) is that of a dynamic, the creation and flow of goods from production to consumption or utilization, as an individualized activity.

The conclusive answer to the question is furnished by a consideration of s. 94 which provides for the uniformity in Ontario, New Brunswick and Nova Scotia of "all or any of the laws relative to property and civil rights." It is, I think, quite impossible to include within this provision regulation of local trades; that appears to be one feature of the internal economy of each Province in which no such uniformity could ever be expected. What the language is directed to are laws relating to civil status and capacity, contracts, torts and real and personal property in the common law Provinces, jural constructs springing from the same roots, already more or less uniform, and lending themselves to more or less permanence. In some degree uniformity has been achieved by individual Provincial action in such legislation, for instance, as that of contributory negligence.

Head 16 contains what may be called the residuary power of the Province: *Attorney-General for Ontario* v. *Attorney-General for the Dominion et al.* ([1896] A.C. 348 at 365), and it is within that residue that the autonomy of the Province in local matters, so far as it might be affected by trade regulation, is to be preserved. As was recognized in the *Parsons* case, *supra*, this points up the underlying division of the matters of legislation into those which are primarily of national and those of local import. But this is not intended to derogate from regulation as well as taxation of local trade through licence under head 9 of s. 92, nor from its support under head 13.

It is important to keep in mind, as already observed, that the broad language of head 2 of s. 91 has been curtailed not by any express language of the statute but as a necessary implication of the fundamental division of powers effected by it. The interpretation of this head has undergone a transformation. When it was first considered by this Court in *Severn* v. *The Queen* ((1878), 2 S.C.R. 70) and *The City of Fredericton* v. *The Queen* ((1880), 3 S.C.R. 505), the majority views did not envisage the limitation now established; that was introduced by the judgment in the *Parsons* case, *supra*. The nadir of its scope was reached in what seemed its restriction to a function ancillary to other Dominion powers; but that view has been irretrievably scotched.

The powers of this Court in the exercise of its jurisdiction are no less in scope than those formerly exercised in relation to Canada by the Judicial Committee. From time to time the Committee has modified the language used by it in the attribution of legislation to the various heads of ss. 91 and 92, and in its general interpretative formulations, and that incident of judicial power must, now, in the same manner and with the same authority, wherever deemed necessary, be exercised in revising or restating those formulations that have come down to us. This is a function inseparable from constitutional decision. It involves no departure from the basic principles of jurisdictional distribution; it is rather a refinement of interpretation in application to the particularized and evolving features and aspects of matters which the intensive and extensive expansion of the life of the country inevitably presents.

The reaches of trade may extend to aspects of manufacture. In *Attorney-General for Ontario* v. *Attorney-General for the Dominion et al., supra*, the Judicial Committee dealt with the question whether the Province could prohibit the manufacture within the Province of intoxicating liquor, to which the answer was given that, in the absence of conflicting legislation of Parliament, there would be jurisdiction to that effect if it were shown that the manufacture was carried on under such circumstances and conditions as to make its prohibition a merely local matter in the Province. This involves a limitation of the power of the Province to interdict, as a trade matter, the manufacture or production of articles destined for external trade. Admittedly, however, local regulation may affect that trade: wages, workmen's compensation, insurance, taxes and other items that furnish what may be called the local conditions underlying economic activity leading to trade.

The federal character of our constitution places limits on legislative acts in relation to matters which as an entirety span, so to speak, the boundary between the two jurisdictions. In *The King* v. *Eastern Terminal Elevator Company, supra,* for example, there was a common storage of grain destined both to local and external trade. The situation in *City of Montreal* v. *Montreal Street Railway* ([1912] A.C. 333, 1 D.L.R. 681, 13 C.R.C. 541) was equally striking: there Parliament was held incapable of imposing through rates over a local railway on traffic passing between points on that line and points on a connecting Dominion railway; the only regulation open was declared to be parallel action by Legislature and Parliament, each operating only on its own instrumentality. Although by that means the substantial equivalent of a single administration may be attained, there is a constitutional difference between that co-operating action and action by an overriding jurisdiction.

It follows that trade regulation by a Province or the Dominion, acting alone, related to local or external trade respectively, before the segregation of products or manufactures of each class is reached, is impracticable, with the only effective means open, apart from conditional regulation, being that of co-operative action; this, as in some situations already in effect, may take the form of a single board to administer regulations of both on agreed measures. . . .

FAUTEUX J.:
~ The learned Justice answered the first question in the negative but on grounds which did not depend on an analysis of the distinction between intra-provincial and external trade. He then addressed himself to questions 2, 3, and 4 which related to the Ontario hog-marketing scheme. ~

The first question related to this scheme is whether Regulation 104 of C.R.O. 1950, as amended by O.Reg. 100/55 and O.Reg. 104/55, is *ultra vires* the Lieutenant-Governor in council, either in whole or in part, and if so, in what particular or particulars and to what extent.

The main submission is that the scheme is applicable to the sale of hogs generally, for import and export as well, and as such regulates trade within the meaning of head 2 of s. 91 of the British North America Act and therefore is *ultra vires*. In support of this submission, reference was made to ss. 1*a* and 1*b* of sched. 1, reading:

Interpretation

1*a*. *In this scheme*
(a) *"hogs" means hogs produced in Ontario except that part*

thereof comprising the territorial districts and the Provisional County of Haliburton;
(b) "processing" means the slaughtering of hogs; and
(c) "producer" means a producer engaged in production of hogs.

Application of Scheme

1b. This scheme applies to hogs marketed either directly or indirectly for processing but does not apply to
(a) hogs sold by a producer
  (i) to a producer, or
  (ii) to a consumer, or
  (iii) to a retail butcher, and
(b) hogs resold by a processor who bought the hogs under this scheme.

With respect to importation: It is clear from the above provisions that hogs produced elsewhere than in Ontario are not covered by the scheme. It is equally clear from s. 1a(c) read with the provisions of s. 4 of the scheme, which for the whole purpose thereof provides for the grouping of hog producers by districts within the Province, that producers beyond its boundaries are not affected either. In the result, anyone in Ontario is free to import therein and anyone beyond its boundaries to export thereto the regulated product.

With respect to exportation: Were the words "within the Province," expressed or held to be implied after each of the words "marketed" and "processing" appearing in the opening provision of s. 1b, the submission that an Ontario producer is barred from marketing the regulated product elsewhere than in the Province would fail; and in my view it must be so held for the following reasons.

Reference has already been made to the declaratory provision, added to the Act by the Legislature in 1956, and formally stating that: "The purpose and intent of the Act is to provide for the control and regulation, in any or all respects, of the marketing *within the Province* of farm products, including the prohibition of such marketing in whole or in part." This provision imports an all-embracing rule of construction with respect to the Act and also with respect to the legislative provisions authorized to be made thereunder, for expressions used in orders in council, orders, schemes and regulations are to be given "the same meaning as in the Act conferring the power" to make them: The Interpretation Act, R.S.O. 1950, c. 184, s. 6. Thus, the word "marketing" defined in s. 1(e) of the Act means "marketing within the Province" and a similar meaning attends the word "marketed" appearing in the opening provisions of s. 1*b* of Reg. 104. . . . The marketing in Ontario of hogs produced in Ontario for processing, *i.e.*, slaughtering, in Ontario, is the sole transaction or particular business controlled and regulated under the scheme.

Other considerations also attend such interpretation. There is a *presumptio juris* as to the existence of the *bona fide* intention of a legislative body to confine itself to its own sphere and a presumption of similar nature that general words in a statute are not intended to extend its operation beyond the territorial authority of the Legislature. These presumptions are not displaced by the language used in the relevant legislative provisions applicable to this scheme when read as a whole. Indeed such provisions consistently imply the intention of the Legislature to restrict the application of the scheme to intraprovincial transactions. Section 2(1) of Reg. 102/55 prohibiting processors from commencing or continuing in the business of processing except under the authority of a licence surely cannot be said to be applicable to processors beyond the limits of the Province of Ontario.

Having reached the view that the transaction covered by the scheme is intraprovincial, I do not find it necessary or expedient to define in general terms what constitutes an intraprovincial transaction. The suggestion that to be intraprovincial a transaction must be completed within the Province, in the sense that the product, object of the transaction, must be ultimately and exclusively consumed or be sold for delivery therein for such consumption, is one which would, if carried to its logical conclusion, strip from a Province its recognized power to provide for the regulation of marketing within such Province in disregard of the decisions of the Judicial Committee in *Attorney-General for British Columbia* v. *Attorney-General for Canada et al., supra,* and in *Shannon* v. *Lower Mainland Dairy Products Board, supra.*

That joint action of Parliament and of the Legislature may better solve the difficulties arising in particular cases is well known to those entrusted with the government of the nation and the Provinces but provides no answer to the questions here referred for consideration. . . .

~ The head-note to this case in the Supreme Court Reports gives the following summary of the Court's answers to the questions contained in the reference. ~

The questions were answered by the Court as follows:

1. Section 3(1) (*l*), as re-enacted in 1955, empowers the Farm Products Marketing Board to authorize a marketing agency "to conduct a pool or pools for the distribution of all moneys received from the sale of the regulated product and [require] any such marketing agency, after deducting all necessary and proper disbursements and expenses, to distribute the proceeds of sale in such manner that each person receives a share of the total proceeds in relation to the amount, variety, size, grade and class of the regulated product delivered by him."

Per Kerwin C.J. and Rand J.: On the assumption that the Act applies only to intraprovincial transactions as defined in the reasons, this clause is not *ultra vires*.

Per Taschereau, Fauteux and Abbott JJ.: The clause is *intra vires*.

Per Locke and Nolan JJ.: If the pool is limited to products marketed for use within the Province and excludes products marketed or purchased for export either in their natural state or after treatment the clause is *intra vires*.

Per Cartwright J.: The clause is *ultra vires*, since it empowers the Board to authorize a marketing agency to make an equalization of returns to producers, taking from some a part of the price they have received and paying it to others who have obtained a less favourable price.

2. Regulation 104 of C.R.O. 1950, as amended, purports to set up a "scheme" for the marketing of hogs for processing and providing for a local board and a committee in each of seven districts of the Province.

Per Kerwin C.J., Taschereau, Rand, Locke, Fauteux, Abbott and Nolan JJ.: This regulation is *intra vires*.

Per Cartwright J.: The regulation is invalid because it does not constitute a "scheme" within the meaning of the Act.

3. Regulation 102/1955 provides for compulsory licensing of all processors (*i.e.*, persons who slaughter hogs or have hogs slaughtered for them) and shippers, and for the creation or a marketing agency through which all hogs must be marketed.

Per Kerwin C.J.: Assuming that this regulation deals with control of the sale of hogs for consumption within the Province, or to packing plants or other processors whose products will be consumed therein, the regulation is *intra vires*.

Per Taschereau, Fauteux and Abbott JJ.: The regulation is *intra vires*.

Per Rand J.: The licences provided for by this regulation are trade regulating licences and not for revenue purposes only, and since there is nothing in the regulation to restrict the ordinary meaning of its language it is in excess of the powers given to the Board by the statute and is therefore *ultra vires*.

Per Locke and Nolan JJ.: The regulation is *ultra vires* except to the extent that it authorizes the control of the marketing of hogs sold for consumption within the Province or to packing plants or other processors purchasing them for the manufacture of pork products within the Province. The provision for licensing is *intra vires* so long as the power is not used to prevent those desiring to purchase hogs or pork products for export.

Per Cartwright J.: The regulation is invalid for the reason given under question 2.

4. An order of the marketing agency prescribes a "service charge" for each hog marketed under the scheme.

Per Kerwin C.J., Taschereau, Rand, Locke, Fauteux, Abbott and Nolan JJ.: This order is *intra vires*.

Per Cartwright J.: The order is invalid for the reason given under question 2.

5 and 6. Regulation 145/54, dealing with the marketing of peaches, requires every grower to pay licence fees at a stated rate for each ton or fraction thereof of peaches delivered to a processor and requires the processor to deduct these licence fees and forward them to the local board. Regulation 126/52 contains similar provisions in respect of the marketing of vegetables for processing.

Per Kerwin C.J., Taschereau, Rand, Locke, Fauteux, Abbott and Nolan JJ.: These orders are *intra vires*.

Per Cartwright J.: On the material before the Court it is impossible to determine the validity of these orders.

7. A proposed amendment to the Act would empower the Board to authorize a local board "(i) to inquire into and determine the amount of surplus of a regulated product, (ii) to purchase or otherwise acquire the whole or such part of such surplus of a regulated product as the marketing agency may determine, (iii) to market any surplus of a regulated product so purchased or acquired, (iv) to require processors who receive the regulated product from producers to deduct from the moneys payable to the producer any licence fees payable by the producer to the local board and to remit such licence fees to the local board, (v) to use

such licence fees to pay the expenses of the local board and the losses, if any, incurred in the marketing of the surplus of the regulated product and to set aside reserves against possible losses in marketing the surplus of the regulated product, and (vi) to use such licence fees to equalize or adjust returns received by producers of the regulated product."

Per Kerwin C.J. and Rand J.: This amendment as interpreted in the reasons is not *ultra vires*.

Per Taschereau, Fauteux and Abbott JJ.: Clauses (i) to (iv) are *intra vires* but clause (v), except to the extent that it authorizes the use of licence fees to pay the expenses of the local board, and the whole of clause (vi), are *ultra vires*.

Per Locke and Nolan JJ.: The amendment is *intra vires* except that that part of clause (v) which authorizes the imposition of license fees to provide moneys to pay for the losses referred to and to set up reserves and for the purposes referred to in clause (vi), is *ultra vires*.

Per Cartwright J.: Clauses (v) and (vi) are *ultra vires* but the other clauses are *intra vires*.

8. *Per curiam*: The Board would not have power under the proposed amendment to authorize a local board to impose licence fees and to use those licence fees to equalize or adjust returns to the producers.

15. Attorney-General for Manitoba v. Manitoba Egg and Poultry Association (Chicken & Egg Reference), 1971

~ The more pragmatic approach to the federal "trade and commerce" power did not usher in a new era of federal regulation of the Canadian economy. The *Carnation*[1] case in 1968 provided the only occasion in the 1960's on which the Supreme Court was called upon to consider the scope of the trade and commerce power. But in this case, Section 91(2), far from serving as a positive basis for federal power, was dismissed as grounds for objecting to provincial economic regulations which impinged on extra-provincial trade. The Quebec legislation in question authorized the province's Agricultural Marketing Board to fix the price of milk sold by Quebec dairy farmers to the Carnation Company, most of whose products were exported from the province. Justice Martland writing for a unanimous Court ruled that this indirect effect of the province's economic regulations on export trade did not constitute an invasion of federal jurisdiction over interprovincial and international trade.

But early in the 1970's the Supreme Court rendered two decisions, both of which expressed an inclination towards strengthening "trade and commerce" as a significant source of federal power. Both of these cases brought the Supreme Court as the nation's constitutional arbiter to the centre of major conflicts in federal-provincial politics.

At stake in the *Caloil* case[2] was a clash between a major element in the federal government's national energy policy and the economic development ambitions of Quebec. Caloil Inc. of Montreal had been importing petroleum from Algeria and Spain and selling its products through gasoline stations in Ontario and Quebec. But in May, 1970, the National Energy Board, with the aim of preserving the key Ontario market for petroleum produced in Western Canada, moved to keep Caloil out of the Ontario market. Regulations were promulgated which would in effect have denied Caloil a licence to

[1] *Carnation Co. Ltd.* v. *The Quebec Agricultural Marketing Board et al.* [1968] S.C.R. 238.

[2] *Caloil Inc.* v. *Attorney General of Canada*, [1971] S.C.R. 543.

import petroleum if it sold *any* gasoline west of a line running down the Ontario-Quebec border and through the Ottawa valley. Caloil successfully challenged the constitutional validity of these regulations before the Exchequer Court. Immediately the federal authorities amended the regulations so that the conditions required for obtaining a licence to import petroleum were more explicitly stated and any restriction on selling oil within provincial markets applied only to imported petroleum. The Exchequer Court reviewed these amended regulations and found them valid. The Supreme Court "in view of the urgency of a matter involving an interference with important business operations"[3] heard the appeal from this judgment a few weeks later and also found the Energy Board regulations valid.

In the *Caloil* case the Supreme Court was again unanimous. Justice Pigeon, the newest Quebec appointee, wrote the principal opinion. He found the Supreme Court's earlier decision in the Murphy case[4] an apt precedent for bringing the impugned legislation within the federal trade and commerce power. In his view "the true character" of the enactment was the control of imports as part of the administration of an extra-provincial marketing scheme; in these circumstances the federal government could validly interfere with local trade in a province. Immediately following the decision, at a press conference in Montreal, Quebec economist Jacques Parizeau announced that some of Caloil's 1,200 workers might lose their jobs and the Montreal refinery close as a result of the Supreme Court decision.[5]

The second decision, the "Chicken and Egg" Reference which is reported below, was an episode in another economic struggle involving Quebec, this time with some of her sister provinces. Quebec, a major importer of eggs, had granted powers to FEDCO, the province's egg marketing agency, enabling it to restrict egg imports in order to protect Quebec producers. The major provinces affected by the regulations were Ontario and Manitoba which supply most of Quebec's egg imports. On the chicken side, the situation was reversed: here Quebec, a major exporter of broilers, soon found that a number of provinces were retaliating against her by restricting the importation of broilers into their provinces. Manitoba, the

[3] *Ibid.*, at p. 547.
[4] *Murphy* v. *C.P.R.* and *Attorney General of Canada* [1968] S.C.R. 626. See above p. 102.
[5] *Globe and Mail*, Nov. 26, 1970.

province most hurt by Quebec's restrictions on egg imports and least assisted by the retaliatory measures protecting broilers, propelled the Chicken and Egg War into the courts by initiating a reference case in its own Court of Appeal. The regulations referred to the Court were drawn up to resemble Quebec's egg marketing scheme. The question of their constitutional validity was hypothetical in the extreme: not only were they not put into force but Manitoba in fact is not an importer of eggs. Nonetheless, the Manitoba Court found the regulations beyond provincial competence and this decision was upheld on appeal by the Supreme Court of Canada.

Justice Martland, whose decision was supported by five other justices, considered that a scheme such as that drafted by Manitoba must be designed to protect Manitoba egg producers from imported eggs. Hence it could be characterized as legislation made primarily in relation to inter-provincial trade, a field reserved to the federal legislature under the trade and commerce power in Section 91. The case also provided the occasion for Justice Bora Laskin's first major decision on the Canadian Constitution. Justice Laskin's concurring opinion carefully reviews the recent tendency in judicial interpretation to overcome the earlier "attenuation of the federal power in relation to S.91(2)" and establish a more balanced understanding of "trade and commerce" as a positive basis of federal power in regulating and integrating national economic life. Although Justice Laskin expressed his dismay at being asked to decide such a constitutional case without any of the relevant empirical data, still he was able to find that the Manitoba scheme was aimed primarily at the regulation of imports and as such constituted an invasion of the federal trade and commerce power. But he, like all the other judges who participated in the case, refused to answer the final part of the Reference question which called upon the Court to define the degree to which a provincial marketing scheme could affect interprovincial trade without becoming unlawful. ∼

ATTORNEY-GENERAL FOR MANITOBA *v.*
MANITOBA EGG AND POULTRY ASSOCIATION ET AL.
In the Supreme Court of Canada [1971] *S.C.R. 689.*

The judgment of Fauteux C.J. and of Abbott, Martland, Judson, Ritchie and Spence J.J. was delivered by

MARTLAND J.: This is an appeal from an opinion pronounced, unanimously, by the Court of Appeal for Manitoba

([1971] 18 D.L.R. (3d) 326) on a matter referred to it by an Order of the Lieutenant-Governor-in-Council, dated November 5, 1970, as amended by a further Order-in-Council dated December 18, 1970. An appeal to this Court is permitted by s. 37 of the *Supreme Court of Canada Act*.

The Order-in-Council approved a recommendation of the Attorney-General for Manitoba for the submission to the Court of Appeal for its consideration of certain questions. The relevant portions of the Order-in-Council, as amended, are reproduced, as follows, with the answers given by the Court of Appeal to each of the questions:

~ The Order-in-Council refers to efforts by certain provinces to regulate the marketing of agricultural products imported from other provinces. It then asks the Court to consider the constitutional validity of Manitoba legislation authorizing a marketing scheme which would require all eggs sold in the province to be marketed through a Board elected by Manitoba producers. This Board could, among other things, establish quotas or prohibit the sale "of a particular regulated product." The Manitoba Court of Appeal held it was not within the legislative competence of Manitoba to authorize such a plan. ~

. . . The Plan . . . contemplates that it shall be applicable to all eggs marketed in Manitoba, whether or not they are produced in that province. While the provincial Legislature could not control, or permit the Producer Board (hereinafter referred to as "the Board") to control the production of eggs in another province, the terms of the Plan are applicable to the produce of another province once it is within Manitoba and available for marketing. . . .

We have, therefore, a Plan which is intended to govern the sale in Manitoba of all eggs, wherever produced, which is to be operated by and for the benefit of the egg producers of Manitoba, to be carried out by a Board armed with the power to control the sale of eggs in Manitoba, brought in from outside Manitoba, by means of quotas, or even outright prohibition.

The issue which has to be considered in this appeal is as to whether the Plan is *ultra vires* of the Manitoba Legislature because it trespasses upon the exclusive legislative authority of the Parliament of Canada to legislate on the matter of the regulation of trade and commerce conferred by s. 91(2) of *The British North America Act*.

When the Privy Council first addressed itself to the meaning of that provision it was stated that it included "regulation of trade in matters of interprovincial concern" (*Citizens Insurance Company of Canada* v. *Parsons*, (1881) 7 App. Cas. 96 at 113). That proposition has not since been challenged. However, the case went on to hold that the provision did not include the regulation of the contracts of a particular business or trade in a single province. . . .

The earlier authorities on the matter of provincial marketing regulation were considered by various members of this Court in the *Reference Respecting The Farm Products Marketing Act* ([1957] S.C.R. 198), which case, as well as some of those authorities, was reviewed in the judgment of this Court in *Carnation Company Limited* v. *The Quebec Agricultural Marketing Board* ([1968] S.C.R. 238). It was said, in that case, at p. 253:

While I agree with the view of the four judges in the Ontario Reference *that a trade transaction, completed in a province, is not necessarily, by that fact alone, subject only to provincial control, I also hold the view that the fact that such a transaction incidentally has some effect upon a company engaged in interprovincial trade does not necessarily prevent its being subject to such control.*

Our conclusion was that each transaction and regulation had to be examined in relation to its own facts, and that, in determining the validity of the regulatory legislation in issue in that appeal, the issue was not as to whether it might affect the inter-provincial trade of the appellant company, but whether it was made in relation to the regulation of inter-provincial trade and commerce. There was cited the following passage from the reasons of Kerwin C.J. in the *Ontario Reference* (at p. 204):

Once a statute aims at "regulation of trade in matters of inter-provincial concern" it is beyond the competence of a Provincial Legislature.

It is my opinion that the Plan now in issue not only affects inter-provincial trade in eggs, but that it aims at the regulation of such trade. It is an essential part of this scheme, the purpose of which is to obtain for Manitoba producers the most advantageous marketing conditions for eggs, specifically to control and regulate the sale in Manitoba of imported eggs. It is designed to restrict or limit the free flow of trade between provinces as such. Because of that, it constitutes an invasion of the exclusive legislative authority of the Parliament of Canada over the matter of the regulation of trade and commerce.

That being so, I would hold that the Regulation and Order are not ones which are within the legislative competence of the Manitoba Legislature to authorize . . .

The judgment of Hall and Laskin J.J. was delivered by

LASKIN J.: The utility of the Reference as a vehicle for determining whether actual or proposed legislation is competent under the allocations of power made by the *British North America Act* is seriously affected in the present case because there is no factual underpinning for the issues that are raised by the Order of Reference. Marketing data to illuminate those issues might have been set out in the Order itself (as was done, for example, in the *Margarine* Reference ([1949] S.C.R. 1), or in an agreed statement of facts, or, indeed, might have been offered to the court to indicate the circumstances which prompted the questions addressed to it.

As it is, I know nothing of the nature of the market for eggs in Manitoba or outside of it, nothing of the production of eggs in that province, nothing of the uses to which the production is put, nothing of the number of producers in Manitoba, nothing of any problems that may have been created in relation to quality, price or otherwise by the entry of out-of-province eggs. I know only, and then in the broad terms set out in the first two recitals in the Order of Reference (and of which matters I could, in any event, have taken judicial notice) that (to quote them) "many Provinces of Canada, including the Province of Manitoba, have enacted legislation pertaining to the regulation and control of marketing of agricultural products" and "certain of the marketing agencies established under the afore-mentioned legislation in some of the Provinces assert the right to prohibit, regulate and control the marketing within a Province of agricultural products produced outside that Province".

A knowledge of the market in Manitoba, the extent to which it is supplied by Manitoba producers, and of the competition among them as it is reflected in supply, quality and price, would be of assistance in determining the application of the proposed legislative scheme. Thus, if out-of-province eggs were, to put an example, insignificant in the Manitoba market, this would be a factor bearing on a construction of the scheme as operative only in respect of Manitoba producers, retailers and consumers in production, distribution and consumption in Manitoba. Conversely, if such eggs were significant in the Manitoba market, the legislative scheme, not being expressly confined to production distribution and consumption in Manitoba, could properly be regarded as directed to the out-of-province eggs. In this respect, the issue would be one of its validity or invalidity, and not one of construing it to be applicable only to the distribution and consumption within the province of eggs produced in the province.

The absence of what I regard as relevant data leaves the position as one where, on the face of the legislative scheme and in the light of the arguments thereon addressed to the court, the contemplated regulation and order purport to embrace out-of-province eggs sent or brought into the province. Moreover, the embrace would extend to out-of-province eggs of whatever quantity, and to whatever extent they might engulf the Manitoba retailer and consumer market. On this view of the situation, there is the naked constitutional question to be faced, namely; there being no federal regulatory legislation in force with the same thrust, is the proposed scheme offensive to the legislative power of Parliament in relation to "the regulation of trade and commerce" under s. 91(2) of the *B.N.A. Act*; and, if not or if so, is it, in any event offensive to the prescriptions of s. 121 of that Act?

Previous cases which have been concerned with the validity of provincial regulatory legislation as tested by the scope of s. 91(2) alone (and not also by the concurrent presence of federal regulatory legislation) cannot be dissociated from cases which have been concerned with the validity of federal regulatory legislation and which, accordingly, have dealt affirmatively with the scope of s. 91(2). These two classes are not necessarily opposite sides of the same coin, and hence, the frame of the legislation in each situation has central importance. On the provincial side, a comparison is apt of *Lawson* v. *Interior Tree Fruit and Vegetable Committee of Direction* ([1931] S.C.R. 357) with *Shannon* v. *Lower Mainland Dairy Products Board* ([1938] A.C. 708); and on the federal side, a comparison may be made of *Reference re Natural Products Marketing Act* ([1937] A.C. 377) with *Murphy* v. *C.P.R.* ([1958] S.C.R. 626).

I adopt the position put by Rand J. in *Reference re Ontario Farm Products Marketing Act* ([1957] S.C.R. 198 at 208-209), that there is a field of trade within provincial power, such power being a subtraction from that comprehended within s. 91(2). The subtraction is, to me, quite rational under the scheme of the *B.N.A. Act*, although stronger terms, referable to a necessary degree of provincial autonomy, have been used in the cases to support it. That there is such subtraction if a provincial regulatory field is to be recognized was obvious to this court in its earliest years. In the very first reported case on the distribution of legislative power, *Severn v. The Queen* ((1878), 2 S.C.R. 70), Strong J., in a dissenting judgment which favoured the validity of the provincial statute that was successfully challenged, pointed out (at p. 104) that, literally, "the regulation of trade and commerce in the Provinces, domestic and internal, as well as foreign and external, [was] by the British North America Act exclusively conferred upon the Parliament of the Dominion." A reduction of this all-embracing authority was effected by this Court in *Citizens Insurance Co. v. Parsons* ((1880), 4 S.C.R. 215), a decision affirmed by the Privy Council ((1881), 7 App. Cas. 96) but with *obiter* remarks that led over the years to almost as much an attenuation of the federal power in relation to s. 91(2) as its literal construction would have led to its aggrandizement. A necessary balance has been coming into view over the past two decades, as is evident from the judgments of this court in *Murphy* v. *C.P.R.*, already cited (and emphasized by the refusal of leave to appeal in *Regina* v. *Klassen* ((1959), 20 D.L.R. (2d) 406, [1959] S.C.R. IX)) and *Carnation Company Ltd.* v. *Quebec Agricultural Marketing Board* ([1968] S.C.R. 238).

What this balance points to is a more particular understanding of the meaning of the terms "trade" and "trade and commerce" as they relate respectively to the areas of provincial and federal competence. In *Montreal* v. *Montreal Street Railway* ([1912] A.C. 333 at 344), the Judicial Committee referred to s. 91(2) as expressing "two of the matters enumerated in s. 91." That provision is perhaps better seen as specifying a single class of subject in words that indicate a stronger source of authority than would be found if "trade" alone was used or "commerce" alone. This view is strengthened by the fact that it is unnecessary here to rely on s. 91(2) for transportation authority (having regard to ss. 92(10) (a) (b), 91(10) and 91(29)), in contra-distinction to the judicial history of the commerce power in the United States under clause 3 of Article I of its Constitution and to the evolution of the power of the Commonwealth Parliament under s. 51(i) of the Australian Constitution to make laws with respect to "trade and commerce with other countries and among the States". Etymologically, commerce refers to the buying and selling of goods, and trade has among its meanings (other than commerce) that of mercantile occupation. Although literal application is unthinkable, these meanings do indicate the capacity which inheres in s. 91(2).

Not too often in the history of the interaction of provincial and federal legislation with s. 9(2) have there been attempts to define its terms. . . . It has been put beyond doubt that Parliament's power under s. 91(2) is exclusive so far as concerns the prohibition or regulation of exports to and imports from other countries, and that a province may not, as legislator, prohibit or regulate the export of goods therefrom. This last-mentioned proposition . . . does not, however, mean that, in the absence of federal legislation, a province is incompetent to impose any regulation upon transactions in goods produced therein and between persons therein simply because the regulation may have an effect upon ultimate export of the goods from the province, whether in their original or in some processed form.

The stage of dealing at which the regulation is imposed and its purpose, on which economic data would be relevant, are important considerations in assessing provincial competence. This emerges clearly from *Carnation Milk Company Ltd.* v. *Quebec Agricultural Marketing Board, supra,* where this court rejected a contention that the regulatory scheme, as reflected in three challenged orders, constituted an unlawful invasion of federal power in relation to export. What was there involved was the fixing of prices, by arbitration if agreement could not otherwise be reached, at which milk and dairy products produced in the province were to be sold by provincial producers, operating under a joint marketing plan, to a distributor and processor in the province. The fact that the processed products were largely distributed and sold outside the province did not react upon the validity of the scheme whose purpose was to improve the bargaining position in the province of provincial producers in their dealings with manufacturers or processors in the province. The regulatory scheme under attack did not involve a marketing control which extended through the various stages of production, distribution and consumption.

What was raised in the *Carnation Milk* case was the meaning, for constitutional purposes, of an intraprovincial transaction where the issue was seen in the context of goods leaving the province. The present Reference raises this question in the context of goods entering the province and their subjection, in consequence, to the same regulatory scheme that operates upon like goods produced in the province. This was a matter which had been considered in the *Shannon* case, *supra*, and in *Home Oil Distributors Ltd.* v. *Attorney-General of British Columbia* ([1940] S.C.R. 444), in both of which the impugned schemes were held to be within provincial legislative competence.

There is a passage in the reasons of the Judicial Committee in the *Shannon* case which has a bearing on this Reference. Lord Atkin said this (at pp. 718-719 of [1938] A.C.):

It is sufficient to say upon the first ground that it is apparent that the legislation in question is confined to regulating transactions that take place wholly within the Province, and are therefore within the sovereign powers granted to the Legislature in that respect by s. 92 of the British North America Act. *Their Lordships do not accept the view that natural products as defined in the Act are confined to natural products produced in British Columbia. There is no such restriction in the Act, and the limited construction would probably cause difficulty if it were sought at some future time to cooperate with a valid Dominion scheme. But the Act is clearly confined to dealings with such products as are situate within the Province.*

The second sentence in this passage must be read in the light of the history of marketing legislation as it evolved in that period. Parliament and provincial legislatures had enacted what they thought was dovetailing legislation only to find that the central piece, the federal enactment, had over-reached in attempting to encompass purely intra-provincial transactions in products grown and marketed in the province, this element of the scheme being founded on the fact that some portion of the product might be exported: see *Attorney-General of British Columbia* v. *Attorney-General of Canada* ([1937] A.C. 377). The Privy Council appeared to think in the *Shannon* case that effective cooperation in marketing could better be ensured if the small extra-provincial element was an appendage of provincial legislation. The decision did not foresee the later developments in this area through such legislation as the *Motor Vehicle Transport Act* 1954 (Can.), c. 59 and the *Agricultural Products Marketing Act*, R.S.C. 1952, c. 6, as amended by 1957 (Can.), c. 15.

In my opinion, the *Shannon* case cannot today have the effect which a literal application of the second sentence of the quoted passage would suggest. Moreover, the fourth and last sentence indicates that the legislation did not purport to apply to out-of-province producers. However, I find this difficult to reconcile with the second sentence unless it be taken that the marketing scheme did not apply to out-of-province products on their mere entry into the province or that any such application was *de minimis* and not an aim of the scheme. If so, the scheme in the *Shannon* case differs from that involved in this Reference.

Home Oil Distributors Ltd. v. *Attorney-General of British Columbia* ([1940] S.C.R. 444) concerned not a marketing scheme of the type involved in the *Shannon* case or in the present case, but rather a price fixing scheme, embracing both maximum and minimum prices for coal and petroleum products sold at wholesale or retail in the province or for use in the province. It was urged that the legislation was intended to protect local industry from outside competition and, indeed, was aimed at extra-territorial sources of supply and at an integrated interprovincial and international industry. The challenge to the validity of the legislation was made by companies operating refineries in the province who sold to persons in the province, but whose raw supplies came from outside. There was no attempt to control the entry of their oil which, when refined in the province, was marketed therein, save as that control resulted from the price fixing authority. In these circumstances, the legislation was upheld on the principle of the *Shannon* case.

I cannot see in the *Home Oil* case any parallel with the marketing scheme which the Order of Reference put before the Manitoba Court of Appeal. In saying this, I reserve my opinion on a question not dealt with in the reasons of this court in the *Home Oil* case; that is, whether it would have made any difference if under the power given to "fix schedules of prices for different qualities, quantities, standards, grades and kinds of coal and petroleum products" imported goods were treated discriminatorily simply because they were imported. . . .

The *Ontario Farm Products Marketing Act* Reference, although refining the meaning of an intra-provincial transaction, did not expressly address itself to the position of an extra-provincial producer, or a purchaser from him, seeking to bring his production into a province free of a regulatory scheme applicable to local produce. Fauteux J. as he then was, noted in that Reference that the hog marketing scheme which was the subject of the court's concern did not cover hogs produced outside the province nor were producers outside the province affected thereby. "In the result," he said, "any one in Ontario is free to import therein and one beyond its boundaries to export thereto the regulated product" (at p. 254 of [1957] S.C.R.). This is, however, precisely the issue that must be faced in the present Reference.

It must be faced under a scheme which, as set out in the proposed measures attached to the Order of Reference, has the following elements:

(1) A Producer Board is established through which all eggs to be marketed in Manitoba must be sold.

(2) All such eggs must go to grading and packing stations which are to be operated by persons under contract with the Board.

(3) All such eggs must be graded, packed and marked in the grading and packing stations.

(4) They are to be packed in containers provided by the Board which are to bear inscriptions of the grade, station number, grading date, place of origin of the eggs and the Board trade mark.

(5) Only authorized collectors may take delivery of eggs from a producer.

(6) Production and marketing quotas may be allotted to producers by the Board.

(7) The Board may establish quotas for production and sale and also fix the time and place of marketing and, equally, may prohibit marketing otherwise or in violation of established quotas or standards.

(8) The Board may contract with distributors as its intermediaries in sales to retailers.

(9) Weekly prices for each grade of egg are to be set by the Board and distributors are entitled to buy at those prices.

Although the emphasis is on control of the Manitoba producers and distributors in order (as stated in the proposed measures) "to obtain for producers the most advantageous marketing conditions" and "to avoid overproduction", the scheme brings into its grasp "persons" as well as producers, that is, those outside the province who are either producers or distributors seeking to enter the Manitoba market or those inside the province who are not themselves producers but who bring in out-of-province eggs for disposition in Manitoba. This view is reinforced by the provision for indicating the origin of eggs, including eggs other than those produced in Manitoba.

There may be a variety of reasons which impel a province to enact regulatory legislation for the marketing of various products. For example, it may wish to secure the health of the inhabitants by establishing quality standards; it may wish to protect consumers against exorbitant prices; it may wish to equalize the bargaining or competitive position of producers or distributors or retailers, or all three classes; it may wish to ensure an adequate supply of certain products. These objects may not all nor always be realizable through legislation which fastens on the regulated product as being within the province. That is no longer, if it ever was, the test of validity. Just as the province may not, as a general rule, prohibit an owner of goods from sending them outside the province, so it may not be able to subject goods to a regulatory scheme upon their entry into the province. This is not to say that goods that have come into a province may not, thereafter, be subject to the same controls in, for example, retail distribution to consumers as apply to similar goods produced in the province.

Assuming such controls to be open to a province, the scheme before this court is not so limited. It embraces products which are in the current of interprovincial trade and, as noted at the beginning of these reasons, it embraces them in whatever degree they seek to enter the provincial market. It begs the question to say that out-of-province producers who come in voluntarily (certainly they cannot be compelled by Manitoba) must not expect to be treated differently from local producers. I do not reach the question of discriminatory standards applied to out-of-province producers or distributors (that is, the question of a possibly illegal administration of the scheme as bearing on its validity) because I am of opinion that the scheme is on its face an invasion of federal power in relation to s. 91(2).

There are several grounds upon which I base this conclusion. The proposed scheme has as a direct object the regulation of the importation of eggs, and it is not saved by the fact that the local market is under the same regime. Anglin J. said in *Gold Seal Ltd.* v. *Dominion Express Co.* ((1921), 62 S.C.R. 424 at 465) that "it is common ground that the prohibition of importation is beyond the legislative jurisdiction of the province". Conversely, the general limitation upon provincial authority to exercise of its powers within or in the province precludes it from intercepting either goods moving into the province or goods moving out, subject to possible exceptions, as in the case of danger to life or health. Again, the Manitoba scheme cannot be considered in isolation from similar schemes in other provinces; and to permit each province to seek its own advantage, so to speak, through a figurative sealing of its borders to entry of goods from others would be to deny one of the objects of Confederation, evidenced by the catalogue of federal powers and by s. 121, namely, to form an economic unit of the whole of Canada: see the *Lawson* case ([1931] S.C.R. 357 at 373). The existence of egg marketing schemes in more than one province, with objectives similar to the proposed Manitoba scheme, makes it clear that interprovincial trade in eggs is being struck at by the provincial barriers to their movement into various provincial markets. If it be thought necessary or desirable to arrest such movement at any provincial border then the aid of the Parliament of Canada must be sought, as was done through Part V of the *Canada Temperance Act*, R.S.C. 1952, c. 30, in respect of provincial regulation of the sale of intoxicating liquor.

I do not find it necessary in this case to invoke s. 121, and hence say nothing about its applicabiilty to the marketing scheme under review. . . .

~ Justice Pigeon also wrote a brief concurring opinion and agreed with Justice Martland's opinion. ~

PART THREE

16. In re Regulation and Control of Aeronautics in Canada, *1932*

~ An important issue is any federal system is the way in which the federal state's capacity for participating in international agreements is affected by its internal division of powers between national and local governments. Basic to this question is the distinction between the power of entering into treaties with other states and the power of implementing such treaties through changes in the domestic legal system. In Canada, as in the United States and Australia, the power to contract international obligations is now held to be the exclusive preserve of the federal government. It is only in connection with the implementation or enforcement of such international undertakings that the division of legislative powers might impose limitations on the national legislature.

In Canada the only direct reference which the B.N.A. Act makes to the field of foreign affairs is Section 132 which grants to the national Parliament and government all the powers necessary for carrying out obligations which Canada assumes as a result of treaties concluded between the British Empire and foreign states. Clearly when this section was draughted in 1867 there was no anticipation of a time when Canada would conduct her own external affairs. All that Section 132 provided for was that the Canadian Parliament should have the power of enacting any legislation required in Canada for the implementation of treaties negotiated by the Imperial Government. As long as Canada's relations with other states were carried on under the aegis of the Imperial Government, the treaty-implementing power raised no serious constitutional problems. It would appear that under Section 132 Parliament's power of enforcing British Empire treaties could even override the normal division of powers in Sections 91 and 92 of the B.N.A. Act. For instance, a few years before this *Aeronautics Reference* both the Supreme

Court and the Privy Council had ruled invalid a British Columbia Act which barred Japanese and Chinese from certain kinds of employment on the grounds that it violated an Act passed by the Dominion Parliament implementing a 1913 treaty made between Great Britain and Japan.[1] But in the 1920's and 1930's as Canada came to assume the status of an independent nation the question of treaty implementation emerged in an entirely different context: now that Canada entered into international agreements on her own as an autonomous nation and not as a subordinate part of the British Empire, would the national Parliament find adequate powers under the Constitution for implementing such treaties?

The *Aeronautics Reference* did not force the courts to squarely face this issue. The questions submitted by the federal government to the Supreme Court concerned the validity of the Dominion's Aeronautics Act and Air Regulations establishing a comprehensive system of control over aerial navigation in Canada. The main components of this scheme had been enacted with a view to performing Canada's obligations which arose out out of a Convention ratified on behalf of the British Empire in 1922. Thus Lord Sankey had no difficulty in finding support in Section 132 for the Dominion enactments. It should be noted, however, that the Canadian Supreme Court had not been willing to construe Section 132 as granting to the Dominion *exclusively* the power of implementing British Empire treaties and was unanimous in giving a negative answer to the first question in the reference.

Although Lord Sankey did not deal directly with the effect of Dominion autonomy on the treaty enforcement power, the concluding words of his judgment did point to one possible solution to this problem. He applied the national aspect test to the question, suggesting that the regulation of aerial navigation, the subject matter of an international agreement, was a matter of such general concern to the whole body politic of Canada that it could be brought under Parliament's power of making laws for the peace, order and good government of Canada. ~

---

[1] *In re Employment of Aliens* (1922), 63 S.C.R. 293 and *A.-G. B.C.* v. *A.-G. Canada* [1924] A.C. 204.

IN RE REGULATION AND CONTROL OF
AERONAUTICS IN CANADA
In the Privy Council. [*1932*] *A.C. 54; II Olmsted 709.*

The judgment of their Lordships was delivered by

LORD SANKEY L.C. This appeal raises an important question
as between the Dominion and the Provinces of Canada regarding the right to control and regulate aeronautics, including the
granting of certificates to persons to act as pilots, the inspection
and licensing of aircraft, and the inspection and licensing of
aerodromes and air-stations. The question is whether the subject
is one on which the Dominion Parliament is alone competent to
legislate, or whether it is in each Province so related to Provincial property and civil rights and local matters as to exclude the
Dominion from any (or from more than a very limited)
jurisdiction in respect of it.

The Supreme Court of Canada has decided the question in
its several branches adversely to the claims of the Dominion,
and has held in effect that while the Dominion has a considerable
field of jurisdiction in the matter under various heads of s. 91
of the British North America Act, 1867, there is also a local
field of jurisdiction for the Provinces, and that the Dominion
jurisdiction does not extend so far as to permit it to deal with
the subject in the broad way in which it has attempted to deal
with it in the legislation under consideration.

During the sittings of the peace conference in Paris at the
close of the European war, a convention relating to the regulation of aerial navigation, dated October 13, 1919, was drawn
up by a Commission constituted by the Supreme Council of the
peace conference. That convention was signed by the representatives of the allied and associated powers, including Canada,
and was ratified by His Majesty on behalf of the British Empire
on June 1, 1922. It is now in force between the British Empire
and seventeen other States.

With a view to performing her obligations as part of the
British Empire under this convention, which was then in course
of preparation, the Parliament of Canada enacted the Air
Board Act, c. 11 of the Statutes of Canada, 1919 (1st session),
which with an amendment thereto, was consolidated in the
Revised Statutes of Canada, 1927, as c. 43, under the title the
Aeronautics Act. It is to be noted, however, that the Act does
not by reason of its reproduction in the Revised Statutes take
effect as a new law. The Governor-General in Council, on

December 31, 1919, pursuant to the Air Board Act, issued detailed "Air Regulations" which, with certain amendments, are now in force. By the National Defence Act, 1922, the Minister of National Defence thereafter exercised the duties and functions of the Air Board.

By these statutes and the Air Regulations, and the amendments thereto, provision is made for the regulation and control in a general and comprehensive way of aerial navigation in Canada, and over the territorial waters thereof. In particular, s. 4 of the Aeronautics Act purports to give the Minister of National Defence a general power to regulate and control, subject to approval by the Governor in Council (with statutory force and under the sanction of penalties on summary conviction), aerial navigation over Canada and her territorial waters, including power to regulate the licensing of pilots, aircraft, aerodromes and commercial services; the conditions under which aircraft may be used for goods, mails and passengers, or their carriage over any part of Canada; the prohibition (absolute or conditional) of flying over prescribed areas; aerial routes, and provision for safe and proper flying.

Their Lordships were told during the course of the argument that no Provincial Legislature had passed any such legislation, but that this had not prevented the progress of aeronautical development in the Provinces. It appears, for example, that in Ontario there has been established subject to these Regulations one of the most complete survey services in the Empire, and that it is working most harmoniously. Their Lordships are not aware that any practical difficulty has arisen in consequence of the general control of flying being in the hands of the Dominion, but at a conference at Ottawa between representatives of the Dominion Government and of the several Provincial Governments in November, 1927, a question was raised by the representatives of the Province of Quebec as to the legislative authority of the Parliament of Canada to sanction regulations for the control of aerial navigation generally within Canada – at all events in their application to flying operations carried on within a Province – and it was agreed that the question so raised was proper to be determined by the Supreme Court of Canada. Thereupon four questions were referred by His Excellency, the Governor-General in Council, under an Order dated April 15, 1929, to the Supreme Court for hearing and consideration, pursuant to s. 55 of the Supreme Court Act, R.S. Can., 1927, c. 35, touching the respective powers under the British North America Act, 1867, of the Parliament and Government of

Canada and of the Legislatures of the Provinces in relation to the regulation and control of aeronautics in Canada.

The determination of these questions depends upon the true construction of ss. 91, 92 and 132 of the British North America Act. Sect. 132 provides as follows: "The Parliament and Government of Canada shall have all powers necessary or proper for performing the obligations of Canada or of any province thereof, as part of the British Empire, towards foreign countries, arising under treaties between the Empire and such foreign countries." It is not necessary to set out at length the familiar ss. 91 and 92 which deal with the distribution of legislative powers. Sect. 91 tabulates the subjects to be dealt with by the Dominion, and s. 92 the subjects to be dealt with exclusively by the Provincial legislatures, but it will not be forgotten that s. 91, in addition, authorizes the King by and with the advice and consent of the Senate and House of Commons of Canada to make laws for the peace, order and good government of Canada in relation to all matters not coming within the classes of subjects by this Act assigned exclusively to the legislatures of the Provinces, and further provides that any matter coming within any of the classes of subjects enumerated in the section shall not be deemed to come within the classes of matters of a local and private nature comprised in the enumeration of classes of subjects assigned by s. 92 exclusively to the legislatures of the Provinces.

The four questions addressed to the Court are as follows:

(1) Have the Parliament and Government of Canada exclusive legislative and executive authority for performing the obligation entitled "Convention relating to the Regulation of Aerial Navigation?"

(2) Is legislation of the Parliament of Canada providing for the regulation and control of aeronautics generally within Canada, including flying operations carried on entirely within the limits of a Province, necessary or proper for performing the obligations of Canada or of any Province thereof, under the convention aforementioned within the meaning of s. 132 of the British North America Act, 1867?

(3) Has the Parliament of Canada legislative authority to enact, in whole or in part, the provisions of s. 4 of the Aeronautics Act, c. 3, Revised Statutes of Canada, 1927?

(4) Has the Parliament of Canada legislative authority to sanction the making and enforcement, in whole or in part, of the regulations contained in the Air Regulations, 1920, respecting:

(a) The granting of certificates or licences authorizing persons to act as pilots, navigators, engineers or inspectors of aircraft and the suspension or revocation of such licences; (b) the regulation, identification, inspection, certification, and licensing of all aircraft; and (c) the licensing, inspection and the regulation of all aerodromes and air stations? . . .

. . . To question 1, and retaining the word "exclusive," the Board's answer is "Yes."

~ The Judicial Committee was not asked to review the Supreme Court's answer to question 2. ~

To question 3, their answer is also "Yes."

To question 4, their answer is again "Yes."

Before discussing the several questions individually, it is desirable to make some general observations upon ss. 91 and 92, and 132.

With regard to ss. 91 and 92, the cases which have been decided on the provisions of these sections are legion. Many inquests have been held upon them, and many great lawyers have from time to time dissected them.

Under our system decided cases effectively construe the words of an Act of Parliament and establish principles and rules whereby its scope and effect may be interpreted. But there is always a danger that in the course of this process the terms of the statute may come to be unduly extended and attention may be diverted from what has been enacted to what has been judicially said about the enactment.

To borrow an analogy; there may be a range of sixty colours, each of which is so little different from its neighbour that it is difficult to make any distinction between the two, and yet at the one end of the range the colour may be white and at the other end of the range black. Great care must therefore be taken to consider each decision in the light of the circumstances of the case in view of which it was pronounced, especially in the interpretation of an Act such as the British North America Act, which was a great constitutional charter, and not to allow general phrases to obscure the underlying object of the Act, which was to establish a system of government upon essentially federal principles. Useful as decided cases are, it is always advisable to get back to the words of the Act itself and to remember the object with which it was passed.

Inasmuch as the Act embodies a compromise under which the original Provinces agreed to federate, it is important to keep in mind that the preservation of the rights of minorities was a condition on which such minorities entered into the federation, and the foundation upon which the whole structure was subsequently erected. The process of interpretation as the years go on ought not to be allowed to dim or to whittle down the provisions of the original contract upon which the federation was founded, nor is it legitimate that any judicial construction of the provisions of ss. 91 and 92 should impose a new and different contract upon the federating bodies.

But while the Courts should be jealous in upholding the charter of the Provinces as enacted in s. 92 it must no less be borne in mind that the real object of the Act was to give the central Government those high functions and almost sovereign powers by which uniformity of legislation might be secured on all questions which were of common concern to all the Provinces as members of a constituent whole.

While the decisions which the Board has pronounced in the many constitutional cases which have come under their consideration from the Dominion must each be regarded in the light of the facts involved in it, their Lordships recognize that there has grown up around the British North America Act a body of precedents of high authority and value as guides to its interpretation and application. The useful and essential task of taking stock of this body of authority and reviewing it in relation to the original text has been undertaken by this Board from time to time and notably, for example, in *Attorney-General for Ontario* v. *Attorney-General for Canada* ([1896] A.C. 348); *Attorney-General for Canada* v. *Attorney-General for Ontario* ([1898] A.C. 700); *City of Montreal* v. *Montreal Street Ry.* ([1912] A.C. 333); and in the same year *Attorney-General for Ontario* v. *Attorney-General for Canada* ([1912] A.C. 571). In all these four cases the scope of the two sections was carefully considered, but it is not necessary to cite them at length because so recently as last year this Board reviewed them in the case of *Attorney-General for Canada* v. *Attorney-General for British Columbia* ([1930] A.C. 111, 118), and laid down four propositions relative to the legislative competence of Canada and the Provinces respectively as established by the decisions of the Judicial Committee. These propositions are as follows:

1. The legislation of the Parliament of the Dominion, so long as it strictly relates to subjects of legislation expressly enumerated in s. 91, is of paramount authority, even though it trenches upon matters assigned to the Provincial legislatures by s. 92.

2. The general power of legislation conferred upon the Parliament of the Dominion by s. 91 of the Act in supplement of

the power to legislate upon the subjects expressly enumerated must be strictly confined to such matters as are unquestionably of national interest and importance, and must not trench on any of the subjects enumerated in s. 92, as within the scope of Provincial legislation, unless these matters have attained such dimensions as to affect the body politic of the Dominion.

3. It is within the competence of the Dominion Parliament to provide for matters which, though otherwise within the legislative competence of the Provincial legislature, are necessarily incidental to effective legislation by the Parliament of the Dominion upon a subject of legislation expressly enumerated in s. 91.

4. There can be a domain in which Provincial and Dominion legislation may overlap, in which case neither legislation will be ultra vires if the field is clear, but if the field is not clear and the two legislations meet the Dominion legislation must prevail.

Their Lordships particularly emphasize the second and third of these categories, and refer to the remarks made by Lord Watson in *Attorney-General for Ontario* v. *Attorney-General for Canada, supra,* p. 361, where he says: "Their Lordships do not doubt that some matters, in their origin local and provincial, might attain such dimensions as to affect the body politic of the Dominion, and to justify the Canadian Parliament in passing laws for their regulation or abolition in the interest of the Dominion. But great caution must be observed in distinguishing between that which is local and provincial, and therefore within the jurisdiction of the provincial legislatures, and that which has ceased to be merely local or provincial, and has become matter of national concern in such sense as to bring it within the jurisdiction of the Parliament of Canada." Further, their Lordships desire to refer to *Fort Frances Pulp and Power Co.* v. *Manitoba Free Press Co.* ([1923] A.C. 695, 704, 706), where it was held that the Canadian War Measures Act, 1914, and certain Orders in Council made thereunder during the War were intra vires of the Dominion. Lord Haldane there said: "The general control of property and civil rights for normal purposes remains with the Provincial Legislatures. But questions may arise by reason of the special circumstances of the national emergency which concern nothing short of the peace, order and good government of Canada as a whole." These remarks must again be taken subject to the situation then prevailing, for he adds later: "It may be that it has become clear that the crisis which arose is wholly at an end and that there is no justification for the continued exercise of an exceptional interference which becomes ultra vires when it is no longer called for. In such a case the law as laid down for the distribution of powers in the ruling instrument would have to be invoked."

It is obvious, therefore, that there may be cases of emergency where the Dominion is empowered to act for the whole. There may also be cases where the Dominion is entitled to speak for the whole, and this not because of any judicial interpretation of ss. 91 and 92, but by reason of the plain terms of s. 132, where Canada as a whole, having undertaken an obligation, is given the power necessary and proper for performing that obligation.

During the course of the argument, learned counsel on either side endeavoured respectively to bring the subject of aeronautics within s. 91 or s. 92. Thus, the appellant referred to s. 91, item 2 (the regulation of trade and commerce); item 5 (postal services); item 9 (beacons); item 10 (navigation and shipping). Their Lordships do not think that aeronautics can be brought within the subject navigation and shipping, although undoubtedly to a large extent, and in some respects, it might be brought under the regulation of trade and commerce, or the postal services. On the other hand, the respondents contended that aeronautics as a class of subject came within item 13 of s. 92 (property and civil rights in the Provinces) or item 16 (generally all matters of a merely local and private nature in the Provinces). Their Lordships do not think that aeronautics is a class of subject within property and civil rights in the Provinces, although here again, ingenious arguments may show that some small part of it might be so included.

In their Lordships' view, transport as a subject is dealt with in certain branches both of s. 91 and of s. 92, but neither of those sections deals specially with that branch of transport which is concerned with aeronautics.

Their Lordships are of opinion that it is proper to take a broader view of the matter rather than to rely on forced analogies or piecemeal analysis. They consider the governing section to be s. 132, which gives to the Parliament and Government of Canada all powers necessary or proper for performing the obligations towards foreign countries arising under treaties between the Empire and such foreign countries. As far as s. 132 is concerned, their Lordships are not aware of any decided case which is of assistance on the present occasion. It will be observed, however, from the very definite words of the section, that it is the Parliament and Government of Canada who are to have all powers necessary or proper for performing the obligations of Canada, or any Province thereof. It would therefore appear to follow that any Convention of the character under discussion necessitates Dominion legislation in order that it may be carried out. It is only necessary to look at the Convention itself to see what wide powers are necessary for performing the obligations arising thereunder. By article 1 the high contracting parties recognize that every Power (which includes Canada) has complete and exclusive sovereignty over the air space above its territory; by article 40, the British Dominions and India are deemed to be States for the purpose of the Convention.

~ Lord Sankey then listed the principal obligations undertaken by Canada as part of the British Empire under the stipulations of the Convention. ~

It is therefore obvious that the Dominion Parliament, in order duly and fully to "perform the obligations of Canada or of any Province thereof" under the Convention, must make provision for a great variety of subjects. Indeed, the terms of the Convention include almost every conceivable matter relating to aerial navigation, and we think that the Dominion Parliament not only has the right, but also the obligation, to provide by statute and by regulation that the terms of the Convention shall be duly carried out. With regard to some of them, no doubt, it would appear to be clear that the Dominion has power to legislate, for example, under s. 91, item 2, for the regulation of trade and commerce, and under item 5 for the postal services, but it is not necessary for the Dominion to piece together its powers under s. 91 in an endeavour to render them co-extensive with its duty under the Convention when s. 132 confers upon it full power to do all that is legislatively necessary for the purpose.

To sum up, having regard (a) to the terms of s. 132; (b) to the terms of the Convention which covers almost every conceivable matter relating to aerial navigation; and (c) to the fact that further legislative powers in relation to aerial navigation reside in the Parliament of Canada by virtue of s. 91, items 2, 5 and 7, it would appear that substantially the whole field of legislation in regard to aerial navigation belongs to the Dominion. There may be a small portion of the field which is not by virtue of specific words in the British North America Act vested in the Dominion; but neither is it vested by specific words in the Provinces. As to that small portion it appears to the Board that it must necessarily belong to the Dominion under its power to make laws for the peace, order and good government of Canada. Further, their Lordships are influenced by the facts that the subject of aerial navigation and the fulfilment of Canadian obligations under s. 132 are matters of national interest and importance; and that aerial navigation is a class of subject which has attained such dimensions as to affect the body politic of the Dominion.

For these reasons their Lordships have come to the conclusion that it was competent for the Parliament of Canada to pass the Act and authorize the Regulations in question, and that questions 1, 3 and 4, which alone they are asked to answer, should be answered in the affirmative.

17. In re Regulation and Control of Radio Communication in Canada, *1932*

~ The question of Parliament's capacity to implement international agreements entered into by Canada as an independent nation was the central issue in the *Radio* case of 1932. In 1927, Canada with seventy-nine other countries had signed the international Radio Telegraph Convention. This Convention was ratified by the Canadian government without any reference to the British Empire. To implement its provisions Parliament subsequently enacted the Radio Telegraph Act. This reference initiated by the federal government was designed to test the Dominion's general capacity for regulating radio communications in Canada.

In the crucial paragraph of the Judicial Committee's judgment which refers to the treaty implementing power, Viscount Dunedin rejected the argument of Quebec's counsel that the power to implement international agreements such as the Radio Convention must be subject to the division of powers as provided for in Sections 91 and 92 of the B.N.A. Act. In Lord Dunedin's view the power of ensuring that Canadian citizens do not violate undertakings which Canada has made with other states must be undivided and rests exclusively with the national Parliament. Further, he acknowledged that with the achievement of autonomy Canada's obligations to foreign states could no longer be construed in terms of the British Empire treaties envisaged by Section 132. But the implementation of Canadian treaties must, in his view, be considered a new matter not explicitly provided for in either Section 91 or Section 92 and therefore one that should be brought under Parliament's residual power.

Hence the outcome of Viscount Dunedin's decision was that the power of implementing treaties lay exclusively with Parliament and indeed the Dominion would acquire authority over a subject normally under provincial jurisdiction if legislation was required to carry out an international obligation dealing with that subject. This decision did much to encourage the Bennett government in the belief that Canada's participation in the conventions of the International Labour Organization could provide grounds for enacting a wide-sweeping program of labour legislation. It was this legislation which gave rise to the next major case dealing with the question of implementing treaties – a case which in effect cut in exactly the opposite direction from the *Radio Reference*. ~

IN RE REGULATION AND CONTROL OF
RADIO COMMUNICATION IN CANADA
In the Privy Council. [1932] *A.C. 304; III Olmsted 18.*

The judgment of their Lordships was delivered by

VISCOUNT DUNEDIN. This is an appeal from a judgment of the Supreme Court of Canada, answering questions referred to it by His Excellency the Governor-General in Council, for hearing and consideration, pursuant to the authority of s. 55 of the Supreme Court Act (R.S. Can., 1927, c. 35), touching the jurisdiction of the Parliament of Canada to regulate and control radio communication.

The questions so referred were as follows:

1. Has the Parliament of Canada jurisdiction to regulate and control radio communication, including the transmission and reception of signs, signals, pictures and sounds of all kinds by means of Hertzian waves, and including the right to determine the character, use and location of apparatus employed?

2. If not, in what particular or particulars or to what extent is the jurisdiction of Parliament limited?

The answers of the Chief Justice and the other judges of whom the Court was composed were as follows:

THE CHIEF JUSTICE: Question No. 1. In view of the present state of radio science as submitted. Yes. Question No. 2. No answer.

NEWCOMBE J.: Question No. 1. Should be answered in the affirmative. Question No. 2. No answer.

RINFRET J.: Question No. 1. Construing it as meaning "jurisdiction in every respect" the answer is in the negative. Question No. 2. The answer should be ascertained from the reasons certified by the learned judge.

LAMONT J.: Question No. 1. Not exclusive jurisdiction. Question No. 2. The jurisdiction of Parliament is limited as set out in the learned judge's reasons.

SMITH J.: Question No. 1. Should be answered in the affirmative. Question No. 2. No answer.

The learned Chief Justice and Rinfret J. expressed their regret that at the time of delivering judgment they had not had the advantage of knowing what was the conclusion reached by this Board on the question referred as to aviation. It is however unnecessary to speculate as to what would have been the result had the learned judges known as we know now that the judgment of this Board (*In re Regulation and Control of Aeronautics in Canada* (p. 54 ante. (A.C.))), delivered on October 22, 1931) settled that the regulation of aviation was a matter for the Dominion. It would certainly only have confirmed the majority in their opinions. And as to the minority, though it is true that reference is made in their opinions to the fact that as the case then stood aviation had been decided not to fall within the exclusive jurisdiction of the Dominion, yet had they known the eventual judgment it is doubtful whether that fact would have altered their opinion. For this must at once be admitted; the leading consideration in the judgment of the Board was that the subject fell within the provisions of s. 132 of the British North America Act, 1867, which is as follows: "The Parliament and Government of Canada shall have all powers necessary or proper for performing the obligations of Canada or of any Province thereof as part of the British Empire towards foreign countries arising under treaties between the Empire and such foreign countries." And it is said with truth that, while as regards aviation there was a treaty, the convention here is not a treaty between the Empire as such and foreign countries, for Great Britain does not sign as representing the Colonies and Dominions. She only confirms the assent which had been signified by the Colonies and Dominions who were separately represented at the meetings which drafted the convention. But while this is so, the aviation case in their Lordships' judgment cannot be put on one side.

Counsel for the Province felt this and sought to avoid any general deduction by admitting that many of the things provided by the convention and the regulations thereof fell within various special heads of s. 91. For example, provisions as to beacon signals he would refer to head 10 of s. 91 – navigation and shipping. It is unnecessary to multiply instances, because the real point to be considered is this manner of dealing with the subject. In other words the argument of the Province comes to this: Go through all the stipulations of the convention and each one you can pick out which fairly falls within one of the enumerated heads of s. 91, that can be held to be appropriate for Dominion legislation; but the residue belongs to the Province under the head either of head 13 of s. 92 – property and civil rights, or head 16 – matters of a merely local or private nature in the Province.

Their Lordships cannot agree that the matter should be so dealt with. Canada as a Dominion is one of the signatories to the convention. In a question with foreign powers the persons who might infringe some of the stipulations in the convention would not be the Dominion of Canada as a whole but would be individual persons residing in Canada. These persons must so to speak be kept in order by legislation and the only legislation that can deal with them all at once is Dominion legislation. This idea of Canada as a Dominion being bound by a convention equivalent to a treaty with foreign powers was quite unthought of in 1867. It is the outcome of the gradual development of the position of Canada *vis-à-vis* to the mother country, Great Britain, which is found in these later days expressed in the Statute of Westminster. It is not, therefore, to be expected that such a matter should be dealt with in explicit words in either s. 91 or s. 92. The only class of treaty which would bind Canada was thought of as a treaty by Great Britain, and that was provided for by s. 132. Being, therefore, not mentioned explicitly in either s. 91 or s. 92, such legislation falls within the general words at the opening of s. 91 which assign to the Government of the Dominion the power to make laws "for the peace, order and good government of Canada in relation to all matters not coming within the classes of subjects by this Act assigned exclusively to the legislatures of the Provinces." In fine, though agreeing that the Convention was not such a treaty as is defined in s. 132, their Lordships think that it comes to the same thing. On August 11, 1927, the Privy Council of Canada with the approval of the Governor-General chose a body to attend the meeting of all the powers to settle international agreements as to wireless. The Canadian body attended and took part in deliberations. The deliberations ended in the convention with general regulations appended being signed at Washington on November 25, 1927, by the representatives of all the powers who had taken part in the conference, and this convention was ratified by the Canadian Government on July 12, 1928.

The result is in their Lordships' opinion clear. It is Canada as a whole which is amenable to the other powers for the proper carrying out of the convention; and to prevent individuals in Canada infringing the stipulations of the convention it is necessary that the Dominion should pass legislation which should apply to all the dwellers in Canada.

At the same time, while this view is destructive of the view urged by the Province as to how the observance of the international convention should be secured, it does not, they say, dispose of the whole of the question. They say it does not touch the consideration of inter-Provincial broadcasting. Now, much the same might have been said as to aeronautics. It is quite possible to fly without going outside the Province, yet that was not thought to disturb the general view, and once you come to the conclusion that the convention is binding on Canada as a Dominion, there are various sentences of the Board's judgment in the aviation case which might be literally transcribed to this. The idea pervading that judgment is that the whole subject of aeronautics is so completely covered by the treaty ratifying the convention between the nations, that there is not enough left to give a separate field to the Provinces as regards the subject. The same might at least very easily be said on this subject, but even supposing that it were possible to draw a rigid line between inter-Provincial and Dominion broadcasting, there is something more to be said. It will be found that the argument for the Provinces really depends on a complete difference being established between the operations of the transmitting and the receiving instruments. The Province admits that an improper use of a transmitting instrument could by invasion of a wavelength not assigned by international agreement to Canada bring into effect a breach of a clause of the convention. But it says this view does not apply to the operation of a receiving instrument. Now it is true that a dislocation of a receiving instrument will not in usual cases operate a disturbance beyond a comparatively limited circular area; although their Lordships understand that a receiving instrument could be so manipulated as to make its area of disturbance much larger than what is usually thought of.

But the question does not end with the consideration of the convention. Their Lordships draw special attention to the provisions of head 10 of s. 92. These provisions, as has been explained in several judgments of the Board, have the effect of reading the excepted matters into the preferential place enjoyed by the enumerated subjects of s. 91, and the exceptions run that the works or undertakings are to be other than such as are of the following classes:

(a) Lines of steam or other ships, railways, canals, telegraphs, and other works and undertakings connecting the Province with any other or others of the Provinces, or extending beyond the limits of the Province; (b) Lines of steamships between the Province and any British or foreign country; (c) Such works as, although wholly situate within the Province, are before or after their execution declared by the Parliament of Canada to be for the general advantage of Canada or for the advantage of two or more of the Provinces. Now, does broadcasting fall within the excepted matters? Their Lordships are of opinion that it does, falling in (a) within both the word "telegraphs" and the general words "undertakings connecting the Province with any other or others of the Provinces or extending beyond the limits of the Province."

The argument of the Province really depends on making, as already said, a sharp distinction between the transmitting and the receiving instrument. In their Lordships' opinion this cannot be done. Once it is conceded, as it must be, keeping in view the duties under the convention, that the transmitting instrument must be so to speak under the control of the Dominion, it follows in their Lordships' opinion that the receiving instrument must share its fate. Broadcasting as a system cannot exist without both a transmitter and a receiver. The receiver is indeed useless without a transmitter and can be reduced to a nonentity if the transmitter closes. The system cannot be divided into two parts, each independent of the other. . . .

. . . Upon the whole matter, therefore, their Lordships have no hesitation in holding that the judgment of the majority of the Supreme Court was right, and their Lordships will therefore humbly advise His Majesty that the appeal should be dismissed. No costs will be awarded, this being a question to be decided between the Dominion and the Provinces.

Although the question had obviously to be decided on the terms of the statute, it is a matter of congratulation that the result arrived at seems consonant with common sense. A divided control between transmitter and receiver could only lead to confusion and inefficiency.

18. Attorney-General for Canada v.
Attorney-General for Ontario
(Labour Conventions Case), *1937*

~ The Canadian government first faced the question of whether it could "invade" provincial jurisdiction in order to carry out international labour conventions when Canada became a member of the International Labour Organization after World War I. At that time it took the cautious course and, following the advice of the federal Department of Justice, left the implementation of five of the six conventions adopted at the first session of the International Labour Conference to the provinces. This procedure was approved by the Supreme Court in 1925 when it was asked to review the proper method of implementing Canada's obligations as a participant in the International Labour Conference.[1] But in 1935 the Bennett government, emboldened by the outcome of the *Radio* case, tried to base an integral part of its "New Deal" program on the treaty implementing capacity of Parliament. Early in the 1935 session Parliament ratified Draft Conventions of the International Labour Organization dealing with hours of work, weekly rest and minimum wages and, later in the session, to give effect to these Conventions it passed the three Acts referred to in this case.

The Privy Council refused to accept the treaty implementing power as a constitutional support for the impugned labour legislation. Section 132 was ruled out on the grounds that even though the Treaty of Versailles was without question a British Empire treaty it had not obliged Canada to accede to the Conventions authorized by the labour part of the treaty. The Canadian government had acted on its own in deciding to ratify these Conventions. Lord Atkin who delivered the judgment also denied the interpretation of the *Radio* case that would justify characterizing the enforcement of independently negotiated treaties as a novel class of legislative matter and therefore subject to the Dominion's residual power. The regulation of radio communications as a new subject might rightly be regarded as

[1] *In re Legislative Jurisdiction over Hours of Labour* [1925] S.C.R. 505.

falling under the residual power but legislation implementing Canadian treaties was not to be treated in the same way. On the contrary, the proper authority for enforcing a Canadian treaty would depend entirely on the subject matter of the treaty. If the treaty dealt with a subject that was normally under Section 92, then legislation giving effect to it could only be enacted by the provincial legislatures.

Lord Atkin's judgment dealt a lethal blow to the doctrine that the national Parliament had a plenary power of implementing treaties. The federal legislature emerged from this decision subject to much more severe limitations on its power of performing international obligations than the federal constitutions of the United States or Australia impose on their central legislatures. Lord Atkin's approach in essence rendered the power of enforcing treaties thoroughly subject to the general division of powers in Canadian federalism. In effect this means that Canada cannot become a party to an international agreement which requires legislative action beyond the ambit of Section 91 unless the prior approval of the provinces is first secured. While this has not prevented the Canadian government from participating in such important and extensive international undertakings as the United Nations Charter, still when an international arrangement such as the Universal Declaration of Rights has referred to matters which clearly come under Section 92 of the B.N.A. Act, Canadian spokesmen have had to set appropriate qualifications to Canadian participation.

Most of those who have studied this area of Canadian constitutional law have found it difficult, if not impossible, to square Lord Atkin's judgment in the *Labour Conventions* case with Viscount Dunedin's in the *Radio* case. Certainly the fact that the composition of the Judicial Committee was completely different in the two cases did not contribute to continuity. Further, there is some evidence of a serious cleavage within the Judicial Committee on this case. In a speech published in 1955, Lord Wright, who had been a member of the Board which decided the *Labour Conventions* case, in a rare disclosure of dissent within the Privy Council, reported that there had been opposition to Lord Atkin's treatment of the treaty implementing power.[2] Finally it should be noted that the Supreme Court's only post-1949 references to the treaty implementation question give some indication of a willingness to deviate from Lord Atkin's position. In *Johannesson* v. *West St. Paul* the favour-

---

[2] (1955) 33 *Canadian Bar Review* 1123.

able references by a number of judges to Viscount Dunedin's reasoning in the *Radio* case has already been noted.[3] In addition, Chief Justice Kerwin in *Francis* v. *The Queen*[4] qualified his approval of the *Labour Conventions* case by stating that the case might have to be reconsidered in the future.

The question of the relationship between the executive power to enter into treaties on behalf of Canada and legislative competence to implement treaties was reopened in a remarkably casual fashion by the Supreme Court in the *Offshore Minerals* Reference in 1967.[5] This case arose in the context of a hot political dispute between Ottawa and most of the provinces (8 of Canada's 10 provinces have salt-water coast lines) over the ownership and control of mineral resources, especially oil, in the land under Canada's offshore ocean waters. In the midst of this controversy the federal government decided to refer the question as it related to British Columbia's claims to the Supreme Court. The Court in an unanimous decision found in favour of the federal government. Most of the Court's decision was concerned with British Columbia's claim that the land under the territorial sea immediately adjacent to her coast belonged to British Columbia. After carefully sifting through the conflicting legal authorities, the Court came to the conclusion that this sea bed was not provincial territory. The decision might well have stopped there as British Columbia could not claim to have an extra-territorial jurisdiction, and federal authority could be asserted on the basis of the residual power in section 91 or section 91(1A) "The Public Debt and Property."

But as we have earlier noted the Court went on to employ the national aspect application of "peace, order and good government" as a further basis of federal authority.[6] But it took a further and, apparently, a brasher step in establishing federal rights. In answering the questions both about the territorial seabed and the continental shelf the Court referred to international treaties which Canada had signed relating to these areas. It then argued that ". . . the rights in the territorial sea arise by international law and depend upon recognition by other sovereign states. Legislative jurisdiction in relation to the lands in question belong to Canada which is a sovereign state recognized by international law and thus able to enter

---

[3] See above, pp. 57-58.

[4] [1956] S.C.R. 618, at p. 621.

[5] *Reference Re: Offshore Mineral Rights*, [1967] S.C.R. 792.

[6] See above, p. 59.

into arrangements with other states respecting the rights in the territorial sea.''[7] If the Court thought this was germane to the issue at stake in this case – the division of jurisdiction between provincial and federal authorities *within* Canada – it was presumably implying that the federal power to enter into treaties must be matched by federal legislative power. The Court's failure to comment further on this point leaves it unclear as to whether it has at least partially reversed the Labour Convention's decision or whether it was simply confused. ～

ATTORNEY-GENERAL FOR CANADA
***v*. ATTORNEY-GENERAL FOR ONTARIO**
In the Privy Council. [1937] *A.C. 327; III Olmsted 180.*

The judgment of their Lordships was delivered by

LORD ATKIN. This is one of a series of cases brought before this Board on appeal from the Supreme Court of Canada on references by the Governor-General in Council to determine the validity of certain statutes of Canada passed in 1934 and 1935. Their Lordships will deal with all the appeals in due course, but they propose to begin with that involving The Weekly Rest in Industrial Undertakings Act, The Minimum Wages Act and The Limitation of Hours of Work Act, both because of the exceptional importance of the issues involved and because it affords them an opportunity of stating their opinion upon some matters which also arise in the other cases. At the outset they desire to express their appreciation of the valuable assistance which they have received from counsel, both for the Dominion and for the respective Provinces. No pains have been spared to place before the Board all the material both as to the facts and the law which could assist the Board in their responsible task. The arguments were cogent and not diffuse. The statutes in question in the present case were passed, as their titles recite, in accordance with conventions adopted by the International Labour Organization of the League of Nations in accordance with the Labour Part of the Treaty of Versailles of June 28, 1919. It was admitted at the bar that each statute affects property and civil rights within each Province; and that it was for the Dominion to establish that nevertheless the statute was validly enacted under the legislative powers given to the

[7] *Reference Re: Offshore Mineral Rights.* [1967] S.C.R. 792, at p. 817.

Dominion Parliament by the British North America Act, 1867. It was argued for the Dominion that the legislation could be justified either (1) under s. 132 of the British North America Act as being legislation "necessary or proper for performing the obligations of Canada, or of any Province thereof, as part of the British Empire, towards foreign countries, arising under treaties between the Empire and such foreign countries," or (2) under the general powers, sometimes called the residuary powers, given by s. 91 to the Dominion Parliament to make laws for the peace, order and good government of Canada in relation to all matters not coming within the classes of subjects by this Act assigned exclusively to the Legislatures of the Provinces.

The Provinces contended:

As to (1) − (a) That the obligations, if any, of Canada under the labour conventions did not arise under a treaty or treaties made between the Empire and foreign countries: and that therefore s. 132 did not apply. (b) That the Canadian Government had no executive authority to make any such treaty as was alleged. (c) That the obligations said to have been incurred, and the legislative powers sought to be exercised, by the Dominion were not incurred and exercised in accordance with the terms of the Treaty of Versailles.

As to (2), that if the Dominion had to rely only upon the powers given by s. 91, the legislation was invalid, for it related to matters which came within the classes of subjects exclusively assigned to the Legislatures of the Provinces − namely, property and civil rights in the Province.

In order to indicate the opinion of the Board upon these contentions it will be necessary briefly to refer to the Treaty of Versailles, Part XIII, Labour; to the procedure prescribed by it for bringing into existence labour conventions: and to the procedure adopted in Canada in respect thereto. The Treaty of Peace, signed at Versailles on June 28, 1919, was made between the Allied and Associated Powers of the one part and Germany of the other part. The British Empire was described as one of the Principal Allied and Associated Powers, and the High Contracting Party for the British Empire was His Majesty the King, represented generally by certain of his English Ministers, and represented for the Dominion of Canada by the Minister of Justice and the Minister of Customs, and for the other Dominions by their respective Ministers. The treaty began with Part I of the covenant of the League of Nations, by which the high contracting parties agreed to the covenant, the effect of which was that the signatories named in the annex to the covenant were to be the original members of the League of Nations. The Dominion of Canada was one of the signatories and so became an original member of the League. The treaty then proceeds in a succession of parts to deal with the agreed terms of peace, stipulations, of course, entered into not between members of the League, but between the high contracting parties, i.e., for the British Empire, His Majesty the King. Part XIII, entitled "Labour," after reciting that the object of the League of Nations is the establishment of universal peace, and that such a peace can only be established if it is based on social justice, and that social justice requires the improvement of conditions of labour throughout the world, provides that the high contracting parties agree to the establishment of a permanent organization for the promotion of the desired objects, and that the original and future members of the League of Nations shall be the members of this organization. The organization is to consist of a general conference of representatives of the members and an International Labour Office. After providing for meetings of the conference and for its procedure the treaty contains arts. 405 and 407:

~ Lord Atkin then set out the two articles. ~

In accordance with the provisions of Part XIII draft conventions were adopted by general conferences of the International Labour Organization as follows:

October 29–November 29, 1919, Conference.

Draft Convention limiting the hours of work in industrial undertakings.

October 25–November 19, 1921, Conference.

Draft Convention concerning the application of the weekly rest in industrial undertakings.

May 30–June 16, 1928, Conference.

Draft Convention concerning the creation of minimum wage-fixing machinery.

Each of the conventions included stipulations purporting to bind members who ratified it to carry out its provisions, the first two conventions by named dates – namely, July 1, 1921, and January 1, 1924, respectively. These three conventions were in fact ratified by the Dominion of Canada, Hours of Work on March 1, 1935, Weekly Rest on March 1, 1935, and Minimum Wages on April 12, 1935.

In each case in February and March, 1935, there had been passed resolutions of the Senate and House of Commons of Canada approving them. The ratification was approved by order of the Governor-General in Council, was recorded in an instrument of ratification executed by the Secretary of State for External Affairs for Canada, Mr. Bennett, and was duly communicated to the Secretary-General of the League of Nations. The statutes, which in substance give effect to the draft conventions, were passed by the Parliament of Canada and received the Royal Assent, "Hours of Work," on July 5, 1935, to come into force three months after assent; "Weekly Rest," on April 4, 1935, to come into force three months after assent; "Minimum Wage," on July 28, 1935, to come into force, so far as the convention provisions are concerned, when proclaimed by the Governor in Council, an event which has not yet happened. In 1925 the Governor-General in Council referred to the Supreme Court questions as to the obligations of Canada under the provisions of Part XIII of the Treaty of Versailles, and as to whether the Legislatures of the Provinces were the authorities within whose competence the subject-matter of the conventions lay. The answers to the reference, which are to be found in *In re Legislative Jurisdiction over Hours of Labour* ([1925] Can. S.C.R. 505), were that the Legislatures of the Provinces were the competent authorities to deal with the subject-matter, save in respect of Dominion servants, and the parts of Canada not within the boundaries of any Province: and that the obligation of Canada was to bring the convention before the Lieutenant-Governor of each Province to enable him to bring the appropriate subject-matter before the Legislature of his Province, and to bring the matter before the Dominion Parliament in respect of so much of the convention as was within their competence. This advice appears to have been accepted, and no further steps were taken until those which took place as stated above in 1935.

Their Lordships, having stated the circumstances leading up to the reference in this case, are now in a position to discuss the contentions of the parties which were summarized earlier in this judgment. It will be essential to keep in mind the distinction between (1) the formation, and (2) the performance, of the obligations constituted by a treaty, using that word as comprising any agreement between two or more sovereign States. Within the British Empire there is a well-established rule that the making of a treaty is an executive act, while the performance of its obligations, if they entail alteration of the existing domestic law, requires legislative action. Unlike some other countries, the stipulations of a treaty duly ratified do not within the Empire, by virtue of the treaty alone, have the force of law. If the national executive, the government of the day, decide to incur the obligations of a treaty which involve alteration of law they have to run the risk of obtaining the assent of Parliament to the necessary statute or statutes. To make themselves as secure as possible they will often in such cases before final ratification seek to obtain from Parliament an expression of approval. But it has never been suggested, and it is not the law, that such an expression of approval operates as law, or that in law it precludes the assenting Parliament, or any subsequent Parliament, from refusing to give its sanction to any legislative proposals that may subsequently be brought before it. Parliament, no doubt, as the Chief Justice points out, has a constitutional control over the executive: but it cannot be disputed that the creation of the obligations undertaken in treaties and the assent to their form and quality are the function of the executive alone. Once they are created, while they bind the State as against the other contracting parties, Parliament may refuse to perform them and so leave the State in default. In a unitary State whose Legislature possesses unlimited powers the problem is simple. Parliament will either fulfil or not treaty obligations imposed upon the State by its executive. The nature of the obligations does not affect the complete authority of the Legislature to make them law if it so chooses. But in a State where the Legislature does not possess absolute authority, in a federal State where legislative authority is limited by a constitutional document, or is divided up between different Legislatures in accordance with the classes of subject-matter submitted for legislation, the problem is complex. The obligations imposed by treaty may have to be performed, if at all, by several Legislatures; and the executive have the task of obtaining the legislative assent not of the one Parliament to whom they may be responsible, but possibly of several Parliaments to whom they stand in no direct relation. The question is not how is the obligation formed, that is the function of the executive; but how is the obligation to be performed, and that depends upon the authority of the competent Legislature or Legislatures. . . .

. . . The first ground upon which counsel for the Dominion sought to base the validity of the legislation was s. 132. So far as it is sought to apply this section to the conventions when ratified the answer is plain. The obligations are not obligations of Canada as part of the British Empire, but of Canada, by virtue of her new status as an international person, and do not arise under a treaty between the British Empire and foreign countries. This was clearly established by the decision in the *Radio* case ([1932] A.C. 304), and their Lordships do not think that the proposition admits of any doubt. It is unnecessary, therefore, to dwell upon the distinction between legislative powers given to the Dominion to perform obligations imposed upon Canada as part of the Empire by an Imperial executive responsible to and controlled by the Imperial Parliament, and the legislative power of the Dominion to perform obligations created by the Dominion executive responsible to and controlled by the Dominion Parliament. While it is true, as was pointed out in the *Radio* case, that it was not contemplated in 1867 that the Dominion would possess treaty-making powers, it is impossible to strain the section so as to cover the uncontemplated event. A further attempt to apply the section was made by the suggestion that while it does not apply to the conventions, yet it clearly applies to the Treaty of Versailles itself, and the obligations to perform the conventions arise "under" that treaty because of the stipulations in Part XIII. It is impossible to accept this view. No obligation to legislate in respect of any of the matters in question arose until the Canadian executive, left with an unfettered discretion, of their own volition acceded to the conventions, a novus actus not determined by the treaty. For the purposes of this legislation the obligation arose under the conventions alone. It appears that all the members of the Supreme Court rejected the contention based on s. 132, and their Lordships are in full agreement with them.

If, therefore, s. 132 is out of the way, the validity of the legislation can only depend upon ss. 91 and 92. Now it had to be admitted that normally this legislation came within the classes of subjects by s. 92 assigned exclusively to the Legislatures of the Provinces, namely – property and civil rights in the Province. This was in fact expressly decided in respect of these same conventions by the Supreme Court in 1925. How, then, can the legislation be within the legislative powers given by s. 91 to the Dominion Parliament? It is not within the enumerated classes of subjects in s. 91: and it appears to be expressly excluded from the general powers given by the first words of the section. It appears highly probable that none of the members of the Supreme Court would have departed from their decision in 1925 had it not been for the opinion of the Chief Justice that the judgments of the Judicial Committee in the *Aeronautics* case ([1932] A.C. 54) and the *Radio* case constrained them to hold that jurisdiction to legislate for the purpose of performing the obligation of a treaty resides exclusively in the Parliament of Canada. Their Lordships cannot take this view of those decisions. The *Aeronautics* case concerned legislation to perform obligations imposed by a treaty between the Empire and foreign countries. Sect. 132, therefore, clearly applied, and but for a remark at the end of the judgment, which in view of the stated ground of the decision was clearly obiter, the case could not be said to be an authority on the matter now under discussion. The judgment in the *Radio* case appears to present more difficulty. But when that case is examined it will be found that the true ground of the decision was that the convention in that case dealt with classes of matters which did not fall within the enumerated classes of subjects in s. 92, or even within the enumerated classes in s. 91. Part of the subject-matter of the convention, namely – broadcasting, might come under an enumerated class, but if so it was under a heading "Inter-provincial Telegraphs," expressly excluded from s. 92. Their Lordships are satisfied that neither case affords a warrant for holding that legislation to perform a Canadian treaty is exclusively within the Dominion legislative power.

For the purposes of ss. 91 and 92, i.e., the distribution of legislative powers between the Dominion and the Provinces, there is no such thing as treaty legislation as such. The distribution is based on classes of subjects; and as a treaty deals with a particular class of subjects so will the legislative power of performing it be ascertained. No one can doubt that this distribution is one of the most essential conditions, probably the most essential condition, in the inter-provincial compact to which the British North America Act gives effect. If the position of Lower Canada, now Quebec, alone were considered, the existence of her separate jurisprudence as to both property and civil rights might be said to depend upon loyal adherence to her constitutional right to the exclusive competence of her own Legislature in these matters. Nor is it of less importance for the other Provinces, though their law may be based on English jurisprudence, to preserve their own right to legislate for themselves in respect of local conditions which may vary by as great a distance as separate the Atlantic from the Pacific. It would be remarkable that while the Dominion could not initiate legislation, however desirable, which affected civil rights in the Provinces, yet its Government not responsible to the Provinces nor controlled by Provincial Parliaments need only agree with a foreign country to enact such legislation, and its Parliament would be forthwith clothed with authority to affect Provincial rights to the full extent of such agreement. Such a result would appear to undermine the constitutional safeguards of Provincial constitutional autonomy.

It follows from what has been said that no further legislative competence is obtained by the Dominion from its accession to international status, and the consequent increase in the scope of its executive functions. It is true, as pointed out in the judgment of the Chief Justice, that as the executive is now clothed with the powers of making treaties so the Parliament of Canada, to which the executive is responsible, has imposed upon it responsibilities in connection with such treaties, for if it were to disapprove of them they would either not be made or the Ministers would meet their constitutional fate. But this is true of all executive functions in their relation to Parliament. There is no existing constitutional ground for stretching the competence of the Dominion Parliament so that it becomes enlarged to keep pace with enlarged functions of the Dominion executive. If the new functions affect the classes of subjects enumerated in s. 92 legislation to support the new functions is in the competence of the Provincial Legislatures only. If they do not, the competence of the Dominion Legislature is declared by s. 91 and existed ab origine. In other words, the Dominion cannot, merely by making promises to foreign countries, clothe itself with legislative authority inconsistent with the constitution which gave it birth.

But the validity of the legislation under the general words of s. 91 was sought to be established not in relation to the treaty-making power alone, but also as being concerned with matters of such general importance as to have attained "such dimensions as to affect the body politic," and to have "ceased to be merely local or provincial," and to have "become matter of national concern.". . .

It is only necessary to call attention to the phrases in the various cases, "abnormal circumstances," "exceptional conditions," "standard of necessity" (*Board of Commerce* case ([1922] 1 A.C. 191)), "some extraordinary peril to the national life of Canada," "highly exceptional," "epidemic of pestilence" (*Snider's* case ([1925] A.C. 396)), to show how far the present case is from the conditions which may override the normal distribution of powers in ss. 91 and 92. . . .

It must not be thought that the result of this decision is that Canada is incompetent to legislate in performance of treaty obligations. In totality of legislative powers, Dominion and Provincial together, she is fully equipped. But the legislative powers remain distributed, and if in the exercise of her new functions derived from her new international status Canada incurs obligations they must, so far as legislation be concerned, when they deal with Provincial classes of subjects, be dealt with by the totality of powers, in other words by co-operation between the Dominion and the Provinces. While the ship of state now sails on larger ventures and into foreign waters she still retains the watertight compartments which are an essential part of her original structure. The Supreme Court was equally divided and therefore the formal judgment could only state the opinions of the three judges on either side. Their Lordships are of opinion that the answer to the three questions should be that the Act in each case is ultra vires of the Parliament of Canada, and they will humbly advise His Majesty accordingly.

19. Bank of Toronto *v*. Lambe, *1887*

~ There is one element in the division of powers about which
the intentions of the framers of the Constitution seem reasonably clear: in the allocation of financial powers the main sources
of revenue were to be assigned to 'the federal government.
While the B.N.A. Act restricts the provinces to "direct taxation
within the province" (Section 92[2]), it grants the central government the power to raise funds "by any mode or system of
taxation" (Section 91[3]). Section 122 explicitly brings customs
and excise duties under the control of the Dominion. Thus, of
the three main tax sources which existed in 1867, customs
duties, excise duties and property taxes, the B.N.A. Act left only
the latter field open to the provinces. However with the expansion of the role of government in general and of provincial
responsibilities in particular there was increasing pressure on
the provinces to develop new forms of taxation. This search for
more revenue lead provincial governments not only into such
fields of taxation as income taxes and succession duties which
were obviously direct but also into other areas of taxation such
as corporation and sales taxes which were of more dubious
constitutional propriety. These efforts gave rise to a series of
challenges to the constitutional validity of provincial taxation
measures. In most of these cases the question of whether or not
the provincial tax was direct constituted the most serious test of
its validity.

In *Bank of Toronto* v. *Lambe* it was a Quebec tax on corporations, passed in 1882, which was challenged on a number
of grounds, including the charge that the tax was an indirect one.
The Privy Council, overruling the Quebec Court of Queen's
Bench, declared the tax a direct one and hence *intra vires*. In
reaching this conclusion Lord Hobhouse, speaking for the
Judicial Committee, presented what turned out to be the classic
formula for distinguishing a direct from an indirect tax. Follow-

ing the suggestion of Mr. Kerr, the appellant's counsel in the case, the Privy Council adopted the distinction as stated by John Stuart Mill in his *Principles of Political Economy*. According to Mill's definition a direct tax is one which is demanded from the very person who it is intended should pay it; whereas an indirect tax is one which is imposed on one person in the expectation that he will reimburse himself at the expense of another. But Lord Hobhouse stressed that the judiciary could not attempt to apply this economist's test of directness as an economist would by carefully tracing the real effects of the tax in order to ascertain its ultimate incidence. Instead, Mill's criterion was to be applied as a verbal formula to the language of taxing statutes. The mere possibility that someone subject to a tax might pass the burden on to someone else would in itself not constitute grounds for calling the tax indirect. A tax could only to be characterized as an indirect tax if it had the general tendency of shifting the burden of taxation in an obviously traceable way to someone other than the actual taxpayer.

In succeeding cases Mill's definitions, offered at first with some diffidence as an indication of what the Fathers of Confederation must have had in mind in 1867, hardened into a firm principle of constitutional law. As a test of directness Mill's formula was qualified only by the rule that species of taxation which according to the common understanding in 1867 would obviously have been considered direct or indirect must continue to bear the same legal character. It was on the basis of this principle that a local "business" tax was upheld as a direct tax by the Privy Council in 1928.[1]~

BANK OF TORONTO *v.* LAMBE

In the Privy Council. (1887), 12 App. Cas. 575;
1 Olmsted 222.

The judgment of their Lordships was delivered by

LORD HOBHOUSE. These appeals raise one of the many difficult questions which have come up for judicial decision under those provisions of the British North America Act, 1867, which apportion legislative powers between the parliament of the Dominion and the legislatures of the Provinces. It is undoubtedly a case of great constitutional importance, as the appellants' counsel have earnestly impressed upon their Lordships. But

[1] *Halifax* v. *Estate of Fairbanks*, [1928] A.C. 117.

questions of this class have been left for the decision of the ordinary Courts of law, which must treat the provisions of the Act in question by the same methods of construction and exposition which they apply to other statutes. A number of incorporated companies are resisting payment of a tax imposed by the legislature of Quebec, and four of them are the present appellants. It will be convenient first to deal with the case of the Bank of Toronto, which was argued first.

In the year 1882 the Quebec legislature passed a statute entitled "An Act to impose certain direct taxes on certain commercial corporations." It is thereby enacted that every bank carrying on the business of banking in this province; every insurance company accepting risks and transacting the business of insurance in this province; every incorporated company carrying on any labour, trade, or business in this province; and a number of other specified companies, shall annually pay the several taxes thereby imposed upon them. In the case of banks the tax imposed is a sum varying with the paid-up capital, and an additional sum for each office or place of business.

The appellant bank was incorporated in the year 1855 by an Act of the then parliament of Canada. Its principal place of business is at Toronto, but it has an agency at Montreal. Its capital is said to be kept at Toronto, from whence are transmitted the funds necessary to carry on the business at Montreal. The amount of its capital at present belonging to persons resident in the province of Quebec, and the amount disposable for the Montreal agency, are respectively much less than the amount belonging to other persons and the amount disposable elsewhere.

The bank resists payment of the tax in question on the ground that the Quebec legislature had no power to pass the statute which imposes it. Mr. Justice Rainville sitting in the Superior Court took that view, and dismissed an action brought by the government officer, who is the respondent. The Court of Queen's Bench, by a majority of three judges to two, took the contrary view, and gave the plaintiff a decree. The case comes here on appeal from that decree of the Court of Queen's Bench.

The principal grounds on which the Superior Court rested its judgment were as follows: That the tax is an indirect one; that it is not imposed within the limits of the province; that the parliament has exclusive power to regulate banks; that the provincial legislature can tax only that which exists by their authority or is introduced by their permission; and that if the power to tax such banks as this exists, they may be crushed out by it, and so the power of the parliament to create them may be nullified. The grounds stated in the decree of the Queen's Bench are two, viz., that the tax is a direct tax, and that it is also a matter of a merely local or private nature in the province, and so falls within class 16 of the matters of provincial legislation. It has not been contended at the bar that the provincial legislature can tax only that which exists on their authority or permission. And when the appellants' counsel were proceeding to argue that the tax did not fall within class 16, their Lordships intimated that they would prefer to hear first what could be said in favour of the opposite view. All the other grounds have been argued very fully, and their Lordships must add very ably, at the bar.

To ascertain whether or no the tax is lawfully imposed, it will be best to follow the method of inquiry adopted in other cases. First, does it fall within the description of taxation allowed by class 2 of sect. 92 of the Federation Act, viz., "Direct taxation within the province in order to the raising of a revenue for provincial purposes?" Secondly, if it does, are we compelled by anything in sect. 91 or in the other parts of the Act so to cut down the full meaning of the words of sect. 92 that they shall not cover this tax?

First, is the tax a direct tax? For the argument of this question the opinions of a great many writers on political economy have been cited, and it is quite proper, or rather necessary, to have careful regard to such opinions, as has been said in previous cases before this Board. But it must not be forgotten that the question is a legal one, viz., what the words mean, as used in this statute; whereas the economists are always seeking to trace the effect of taxation throughout the community, and are apt to use the words "direct," and "indirect," according as they find that the burden of a tax abides more or less with the person who first pays it. This distinction is illustrated very clearly by the quotations from a very able and clear thinker, the late Mr. Fawcett, who, after giving his tests of direct and indirect taxation, makes remarks to the effect that a tax may be made direct or indirect by the position of the taxpayers or by private bargains about its payment. Doubtless, such remarks have their value in an economical discussion. Probably it is true of every indirect tax that some persons are both the first and the final payers of it; and of every direct tax that it affects persons other than the first payers; and the excellence of an economist's definition will be measured by the accuracy with which it contemplates and embraces every incident of the thing defined. But that very excellence impairs its value for the purposes of the lawyer. The legislature cannot possibly have meant to give a power of taxation valid or invalid according to its actual results in particular cases. It must have contemplated some tangible dividing line referable to and ascertainable by the general tendencies of the tax and the common understanding of men as to those tendencies.

After some consideration Mr. Kerr chose the definition of John Stuart Mill as the one he would prefer to abide by. That definition is as follows:

"Taxes are either direct or indirect. A direct tax is one which is demanded from the very persons who it is intended or desired should pay it. Indirect taxes are those which are demanded from one person in the expectation and intention that he shall indemnify himself at the expense of another; such are the excise or customs.

"The producer or importer of a commodity is called upon to pay a tax on it, not with the intention to levy a peculiar contribution upon him, but to tax through him the consumers of the commodity, from whom it is supposed that he will recover the amount by means of an advance in price."

It is said that Mill adds a term – that to be strictly direct a tax must be general; and this condition was much pressed at the Bar. Their Lordships have not thought it necessary to examine Mill's works for the purpose of ascertaining precisely what he does say on this point; nor would they presume to say whether for economical purposes such a condition is sound or unsound; but they have no hesitation in rejecting it for legal purposes. It would deny the character of a direct tax to the income tax of this country, which is always spoken of as such, and is generally looked upon as a direct tax of the most obvious kind; and it would run counter to the common understanding of men on this subject, which is one main clue to the meaning of the legislature.

Their Lordships then take Mill's definition above quoted as a fair basis for testing the character of the tax in question, not only because it is chosen by the Appellant's counsel, nor only because it is that of an eminent writer, nor with the intention that it should be considered a binding legal definition, but because it seems to them to embody with sufficient accuracy for this purpose an understanding of the most obvious indicia of direct and indirect taxation, which is a common understanding, and is likely to have been present to the minds of those who passed the Federation Act.

Now whether the probabilities of the case or the frame of the Quebec Act are considered, it appears to their Lordships that the Quebec legislature must have intended and desired that the very corporations from whom the tax is demanded should pay and finally bear it. It is carefully designed for that purpose. It is not like a customs' duty which enters at once into the price of the taxed commodity. There the tax is demanded of the importer, while nobody expects or intends that he shall finally bear it. All scientific economists teach that it is paid, and scientific financiers intend that it shall be paid, by the consumer; and even those who do not accept the conclusions of the economists maintain that it is paid, and intend it to be paid, by the foreign producer. Nobody thinks that it is, or intends that it shall be, paid by the importer from whom it is demanded. But the tax now in question is demanded directly of the bank apparently for the reasonable purpose of getting contributions for provincial purposes from those who are making profits by provincial business. It is not a tax on any commodity which the bank deals in and can sell at an enhanced price to its customers. It is not a tax on its profits, nor on its several transactions. It is a direct lump sum, to be assessed by simple reference to its paid-up capital and its places of business. It may possibly happen that in the intricacies of mercantile dealings the bank may find a way to recoup itself out of the pockets of its Quebec customers. But the way must be an obscure and circuitous one, the amount of recoupment cannot bear any direct relation to the amount of tax paid, and if the bank does manage it, the result will not improbably disappoint the intention and desire of the Quebec Government. For these reasons their Lordships hold the tax to be direct taxation within class 2 of sect. 92 of the Federation Act. . . .

. . . The next question is whether the tax is taxation within the province. It is urged that the bank is a Toronto corporation, having its domicil there, and having its capital placed there; that the tax is on the capital of the bank; that it must therefore fall on a person or persons, or on property, not within Quebec. The answer to this argument is that class 2 of sect. 92 does not require that the persons to be taxed by Quebec are to be domiciled or even resident in Quebec. Any person found within the province may legally be taxed there if taxed directly. The bank is found to be carrying on business there, and on that ground alone it is taxed. There is no attempt to tax the capital of the bank, any more than its profits. The bank itself is directly ordered to pay a sum of money; but the legislature has not chosen to tax every bank, small or large, alike, nor to leave the amount of tax to be ascertained by variable accounts or any uncertain standard. It has adopted its own measure, either of that which it is just the banks should pay, or of that which they have means to pay, and these things it ascertains by reference to facts which can be verified without doubt or delay. The banks are to pay so much, not according to their capital, but according to their paid-up capital, and so much on their places of business. Whether this method of assessing a tax is sound or unsound, wise or unwise, is a point on which their Lordships have no opinion, and are not called on to form one, for as it does not carry the taxation out of the province it is for the Legislature and not for Courts of Law to judge of its expediency.

Then is there anything in sect. 91 which operates to restrict the meaning above ascribed to sect. 92? Class 3, certainly is in literal conflict with it. It is impossible to give exclusively to the Dominion the whole subject of raising money by any mode of taxation, and at the same time to give to the provincial legislatures, exclusively or at all, the power of direct taxation for provincial or any other purposes. This very conflict between the two sections was noticed by way of illustration in the case of *Parsons* (7 App. Cas. 96). Their Lordships there said (7 App. Cas. 108): "So 'the raising of money by any mode or system of taxation' is enumerated among the classes of subjects in sect. 91; but, though the description is sufficiently large and general to include 'direct taxation within the province, in order to the raising of a revenue for provincial purposes,' assigned to the provincial legislatures by sect. 92, it obviously could not have been intended that, in this instance also, the general power should override the particular one." Their Lordships adhere to that view, and hold that, as regards direct taxation within the province to raise revenue for provincial purposes, that subject falls wholly within the jurisdiction of the provincial legislatures.

It has been earnestly contended that the taxation of banks would unduly cut down the powers of the parliament in relation to matters falling within class 2, *viz.* the regulation of trade and commerce; and within class 15, *viz.*, banking, and the incorporation of banks. Their Lordships think that this contention gives far too wide an extent to the classes in question. They cannot see how the power of making banks contribute to the public objects of the provinces where they carry on business can interfere at all with the power of making laws on the subject of banking, or with the power of incorporating banks. The words "regulation of trade and commerce" are indeed very wide, and in *Severn's* case (2 Sup. Court of Canada, 70) it was the view of the Supreme Court that they operated to invalidate the licence duty which was there in question. But since that case was decided the question has been more completely sifted before the Committee in *Parson's* case, and it was found absolutely necessary that the literal meaning of the words should be restricted, in order to afford scope for powers which are given exclusively to the provincial legislatures. It was there thrown out that the power of regulation given to the parliament meant some general or interprovincial regulations. No further attempt to define the subject need now be made, because their Lordships are clear that if they were to hold that this power of regulation prohibited any provincial taxation on the persons or things regulated, so far from restricting the expressions, as was found necessary in *Parson's* case, they would be straining them to their widest conceivable extent.

Then it is suggested that the legislature may lay on taxes so heavy as to crush a bank out of existence, and so to nullify the power of parliament to erect banks. But their Lordships cannot conceive that when the Imperial Parliament conferred wide powers of local self-government on great countries such as Quebec, it intended to limit them on the speculation that they would be used in an injurious manner. People who are trusted with the great power of making laws for property and civil rights may well be trusted to levy taxes. There are obvious reasons for confining their power to direct taxes and licences, because the power of indirect taxation would be felt all over the Dominion. But whatever power falls within the legitimate meaning of classes 2 and 9, is, in their Lordships' judgment, what the Imperial Parliament intended to give; and to place a limit on it because the power may be used unwisely, as all powers may, would be an error, and would lead to insuperable difficulties, in the construction of the Federation Act. . . .

20. The King v. Caledonian Collieries Limited, 1928

~ This case simply provides an example of how the application of the criterion of directness put forward in *Bank of Toronto* v. *Lambe* could cut down a provincial tax. The Alberta Mine Owners Tax Act which was challenged in this case was imposed on producers rather than consumers of coal. Consequently both the Supreme Court and the Privy Council concluded that the tax was indirect, for the producers could easily shift the burden of the tax by adding it on to the price they charged their consumers. This decision should be compared with the Privy Council's decision a few years later in *Attorney-General for British Columbia* v. *Kingcome Navigation Co. Ltd.*,[1] which pointed to a way in which a provincial tax on commodities might avoid the constitutional ban against indirect provincial taxes. In this case a British Columbia Act which imposed a tax on consumers of fuel-oil according to the amount consumed was held direct on the grounds that it was demanded from the very persons who the legislature intended should pay it.

The frequency with which the question of constitutional limitations on provincial taxation powers came up in cases before both the Supreme Court and the Privy Council reflected the continuing uncertainty in Canada over the financial powers of the provinces. In the 1930's the impact of the depression on traditional sources of revenue increased the provinces' interest in imposing retail sales taxes. But there were still grave doubts concerning the provinces' capacity under the B.N.A. Act for effectively entering the retail sales tax field. To remove these doubts the Dominion government, at the unanimous request of the provinces, agreed to seek an amendment to Section 92 (2) of the B.N.A. Act which would allow the provinces to impose a retail tax in the form of an indirect tax on the vendor. The resolution calling for this amendment was, however, defeated in the Senate. The attack on it was led by Arthur Meighen who argued that the power of imposing a sales tax would enable the provinces to erect what would amount to provincial tariff walls.

This proposal of a constitutional amendment to allow the provinces to impose an indirect sales tax has been revived

[1] [1934] A.C. 45.

during the Dominion-Provincial negotiations on the amendment of the B.N.A. Act which have gone on since World War II. But the urgency of this proposal has been greatly reduced by the provinces' success in draughting sales taxes which have satisfied the judiciary's standard of directness. Indeed, following the Privy Council's approval of the statutory device tested in the *Atlantic Smoke Shops* case,[2] it would appear that the only purpose of amending the Constitution now would be to simplify the tasks of those responsible for draughting and administering provincial sales taxes. ~

THE KING *v*. CALEDONIAN COLLIERIES LTD.
In the Privy Council. [1928] *A.C. 358; II Olmsted 569.*

The judgment of their Lordships was delivered by

LORD WARRINGTON OF CLYFFE. The question raised by this appeal is whether the Mine Owners Tax Act, 1923, of the Province of Alberta, which imposes upon mine owners as therein defined a percentage tax upon the gross revenues of their coal mines is ultra vires the Province as an attempt to impose indirect taxation.

The question whether a tax is direct or indirect has on many occasions been the subject of decision by this Board, but it is unnecessary to refer to any of these decisions except that of *Bank of Toronto* v. *Lambe* (12 App. Cas. 575, 581, 582), in which Lord Hobhouse, in delivering the judgment of the Board, made some useful observations as to the mode in which the question should be approached.

The passage has often been cited, but it is worth while citing it again: "First, is the tax a direct tax? For the argument of this question the opinions of a great many writers on political economy have been cited, and it is quite proper, or, rather necessary, to have careful regard to such opinions, as has been said in previous cases before this Board. But it must not be forgotten that the question is a legal one, *viz.*, what the words mean, as used in this statute; whereas the economists are always seeking to trace the effect of taxation throughout the community, and are apt to use the words 'direct,' and 'indirect,' according as they find that the burden of a tax abides more or less with the person who first pays it. This distinction is illustrated very

---

[2] *Atlantic Smoke Shops Ltd.* v. *Conlon and A.-G. Canada*, [1943] A.C. 550. See below p. 157.

clearly by the quotations from a very able and clear thinker, the late Mr. Fawcett, who, after giving his tests of direct and indirect taxation, makes remarks to the effect that a tax may be made direct or indirect by the position of the taxpayers or by private bargains about its payment. Doubtless, such remarks have their value in an economical discussion. Probably it is true of every indirect tax that some persons are both the first and the final payers of it; and of every direct tax that it affects persons other than the first payers; and the excellence of an economist's definition will be measured by the accuracy with which it contemplates and embraces every incident of the thing defined. But that very excellence impairs its value for the purposes of the lawyer. The Legislature cannot possibly have meant to give a power of taxation valid or invalid according to its actual results in particular cases. It must have contemplated some tangible dividing line referable to and ascertainable by the general tendencies of the tax and the common understanding of men as to those tendencies."

What then is the general tendency of the tax now in question?

First, it is necessary to ascertain the real nature of the tax. It is not disputed that, though the tax is called a tax on "gross revenue," such gross revenue is in reality the aggregate of sums received from sales of coal, and is indistinguishable from a tax upon every sum received from the sale of coal.

The respondents are producers of coal, a commodity the subject of commercial transactions. Their Lordships can have no doubt that the general tendency of a tax upon the sums received from the sale of the commodity which they produce and in which they deal is that they would seek to recover it in the price charged to a purchaser. Under particular circumstances the recovery of the tax may, it is true, be economically undesirable or practically impossible, but the general tendency of the tax remains.

It is said on behalf of the appellant that at the time a sale is made the tax has not become payable, and therefore cannot be passed on. Their Lordships cannot accept this contention; the tax will have to be paid, and there would be no more difficulty in adding to the selling price the amount of the tax in anticipation than there would be if it had been actually paid.

Their Lordships therefore agree with the views expressed by the judges of the Supreme Court that the tax in question is not a direct tax.

Some attempt was made in argument to support the tax on the ground that it is analogous to an income tax, which has always been regarded as the typical example of a direct tax; but there are marked distinctions between a gross revenue and a tax on income, which for taxation purposes means gains and profits. There may be considerable gross revenues, but no income taxable by an income tax in the accepted sense.

For these reasons their Lordships are of opinion that the appeal should be dismissed with costs, and they will humbly advise His Majesty accordingly.

21. Atlantic Smoke Shops Limited v. Conlon, *1943*

~ This case provided a crucial test of the efficacy of provincial draughting techniques in framing retail sales taxes which could avoid being classified as indirect by the courts. The New Brunswick tax challenged in this case was one imposed on anyone who purchased tobacco, by himself or through an agent, for his own consumption. It was also imposed on anyone who imported tobacco into New Brunswick for his own consumption. To obviate the charge that the burden of this tax, which was in effect a retail sales tax, would be shifted by the retailer to the purchaser, it had been so designed that the retailer became the tax-collector, collecting the tax directly from the consumer. A majority of the Supreme Court, while willing to uphold the tax as direct when levied on the actual consumer, ruled that it was indirect when imposed on the consumer's agent. The Privy Council denied the significance of this distinction and upheld the tax as direct and valid in all of its aspects.

Although this case had originated in private litigation between a retail tobacco company which had raised constitutional objections to the tax and the Tax Commissioner responsible for administering the tax, the federal government and most of the provinces intervened and supported their respective sides of the case before the Judicial Committee. The outcome was undoubtedly a victory for the provinces. In effect it reduced the provinces' difficulties in entering the retail sales tax field to one of shrewd draughtsmanship.

The result of this case which confirmed that it was possible to impose a tax on products imported into the province seemed, to some, to make a mockery of Section 121 of the B.N.A. Act, which requires that the goods of any province be admitted free into each of the other provinces. But it should be noted that while, as a revenue-raising measure, a tax such as the one upheld in the *Atlantic Smoke Shops* case might perform the function of a customs duty, it could hardly perform the protective function of a tariff. Given the principle that the regulation of interprovincial trade is a matter of federal trade and commerce subject exclusively to Dominion jurisdiction,[1] it is unlikely that

[1] See *Reference re Farm Products Marketing Act (Ontario)*, [1957] S.C.R. 198. See above, p. 101.

the courts would uphold a provincial tax imposed only on products imported into the province so as to protect domestic provincial production.

In 1960 the Supreme Court of Canada demonstrated that it was prepared to follow the course charted by the Privy Council. In *Cairns Construction Ltd.* v. *Government of Saskatchewan*[2] the Court upheld a Saskatchewan tax which employed the same technique as the one tested in the *Atlantic Smoke Shops* case, except that here the tax was applied not to consumable goods but to non-consumable tangible personal property. ~

ATLANTIC SMOKE SHOPS LTD. v. CONLON
In the Privy Council. [1943] *A.C. 550; III Olmsted 403.*

The judgment of their Lordships was delivered by

VISCOUNT SIMON L.C. This appeal from a judgment of the Supreme Court of Canada raises the important and difficult question whether the Tobacco Act of New Brunswick, 1940 (4 Geo. 6, c. 44), and the regulations made thereunder are within the powers of the provincial legislature as constituting "direct taxation within the province," or whether, on the contrary, all or any part of these provisions must be held to be ultra vires having regard to the distribution of legislative powers effected by the British North America Act, 1867, and to the bearing of ss. 121 and 122 of the Act on provincial taxing powers.

The New Brunswick Tobacco Tax Act is entitled "An Act to provide for imposing a tax on the consumption of tobacco." [His Lordship referred to ss. 2 to 10 of the Act and continued:] There are thus four applications of the tax provided for by ss. 4 and 5: (*a*) In its main and simplest form the tax is to be paid by anyone who purchases tobacco, as defined, for his own consumption (or for the consumption of other persons at his expense) from a retail vendor in the province. The tax amounts to ten per cent on the retail price charged on the sale. By regulations made under s. 20 of the Act it is to be collected by the retail vendor, who is constituted an agent of the minister for the collection of the tax, and has to give a receipt for the tax to the customer and account to the Tobacco Tax Commissioner for the tax thus collected, subject to the allowance of three per cent as remuneration. (*b*) If the purchase from the retail

[2] [1960] S.C.R. 619.

vendor is made by an agent acting for a principal, who desires to acquire such tobacco for his own consumption (or for the consumption of other persons at his expense), the tax is payable by the agent. It is, however, clear that if the agent has not already been put in funds by his principal, he will be entitled to be indemnified by his principal for the tax, no less than for the purchase price. In both cases ((a) and (b)) the tax is payable at the time of making the purchase. (c) If a person residing or ordinarily resident or carrying on business in New Brunswick brings into the province such tobacco, or receives delivery of it in the province, for his own consumption (or for the consumption of other persons at his expense), he is to report the matter to the minister, with any invoice and other information required, and he becomes liable to pay the same tax as would have been payable if the tobacco had been purchased at a retail sale in the province. (d) Lastly, if such a person as is last described brings the tobacco into the province, or receives delivery there, as agent for a principal who desires to acquire it for his own consumption (or for the consumption of other persons at his expense), the agent is put under a similar obligation to report and to pay an equivalent tax. It may be noted that in this last case the principal is not in express terms limited to a principal within the province. This is perhaps implied, but, in any event, the instance of an agent within the province acting for a principal outside can seldom occur.

A striking difference of opinion has disclosed itself in the Canadian courts as to the validity of this taxing legislation. In the Supreme Court of New Brunswick, Baxter C.J. and his two colleagues, Grimmer and Richards J.J., held that the tax was valid. Applying the definition of a direct tax which was used by Lord Hobhouse in *Bank of Toronto* v. *Lambe* (12 App. Cas. 575, 582), and which is derived from John Stuart Mill's "Principles of Political Economy" (bk. V. c. 3) as "one which is demanded from the very persons who it is intended or desired should pay it," they held that the tax in all its forms was a direct tax and within the power of the provincial legislature to impose. On appeal to the Supreme Court of Canada, conflicting views were expressed, and these need to be carefully analysed.

~ His Lordship then stated the conclusions reached by the individual judges. ~

. . . In the result, therefore, the majority of the Supreme Court of Canada decided that the tax in the forms (a) and (c) was valid, but that it was invalid in the forms (b) and (d), since these latter forms involved taxation of an agent, whereas the burden of the taxation would fall on his principal. The arguments addressed to the Board, which included arguments on behalf of the Attorney-General for Canada supporting the appellants, and of other interveners representing Quebec and five other provinces supporting the respondents, ranged over all aspects of the tax, and their Lordships are requested to reach a conclusion as to the validity or non-validity of the tax in all its forms.

Their Lordships must first consider whether the tax in the form (a) is a valid exercise of provincial legislative powers. It has been long and firmly established that, in interpreting the phrase "direct taxation" in head 2 of s. 92 of the Act of 1867, the guide to be followed is that provided by the distinction between direct and indirect taxes which is to be found in the treatise of John Stuart Mill. The question, of course, as Lord Herchell said in *Brewers and Maltsters' Association of Ontario* v. *Attorney-General for Ontario* ([1897] A.C. 231, 236), is not what is the distinction drawn by writers on political economy, but in what sense the words were employed in the British North America Act. Mill's *Political Economy* was first published in 1848, and appeared in a popular edition in 1865. Its author became a member of parliament in this latter year and commanded much attention in the British House of Commons. Having regard to his eminence as a political economist in the epoch when the Quebec Resolutions were being discussed and the Act of 1867 was being framed, the use of Mill's analysis and classification of taxes for the purpose of construing the expression now under review is fully justified. In addition to the definition from Mill's *Political Economy* already quoted, citation may be made of two other passages as follows: "Direct taxes are either on income or on expenditure. Most taxes on expenditure are indirect, but some are direct, being imposed not on the producer or seller of an article, but immediately on the consumer" (bk. V. ch. 3). And again, in ch. 6, in discussing the comparative merits of the two types of tax, he takes as the essential feature of direct taxation that "under it everyone knows how much he really pays." Their Lordships, therefore, consider that this tobacco tax in the form they have called (a) would fall within the conception of a "direct" tax, and ought so to be treated in applying the British North America Act. It is a tax which is to be paid by the last purchaser of the article, and, since there is no question of further re-sale, the tax cannot be passed on to any other person by subsequent dealing. The money for the tax is found by the individual who finally bears the burden of it. It is unnecessary to consider the refinement which might arise if the taxpayer who has purchased the tobacco for his own consumption subsequently changes his mind and in fact re-sells it. If so, he would, for one thing, require a retail vendor's licence. But the instance is exceptional and farfetched, while for the purpose of classifying the tax, it is the general tendency of the impost which has to be considered. So regarded, it completely satisfies Mill's test for direct taxation. Indeed, the present instance is a clearer case of direct taxation than the tax on the consumer of fuel oil in *Attorney-General for British Columbia* v. *Kingcome Navigation Co.* ([1934] A.C. 45), for fuel oil may be consumed for the purpose of manufacture and transport, and the tax on the consumption of fuel oil might, as one would suppose, be sometimes passed on in the price of the article manufactured or transported. Yet the Privy Council held that the tax was direct. In the case of tobacco, on the other hand, the consumer produces nothing but smoke. Mr. Pritt argued that the tax is a sales tax, and that a sales tax is indirect because it can be passed on. The ordinary forms of sales taxes are, undoubtedly, of this character, but it would be more accurate to say that a sales tax is indirect when in the normal course it can be passed on. If a tax is so devised that (as Mill expresses it) the taxing authority is not indifferent as to which of the parties to the transaction ultimately bears the burden, but intends it as a "peculiar contribution" on the particular party selected to pay the tax, such a tax is not proved to be indirect by calling it a sales tax. Previous observations by this Board as to the general character of sales taxes, or of taxes on commercial dealings, ought not to be understood as denying the possibility of this exception.

There remains, on this first head, the question whether, notwithstanding that the tax in the form (*a*) is "direct" within Mill's test, it is none the less beyond the powers of the province to impose as being in the nature of "excise" in the sense that the attempted imposition would be an alteration of the "excise laws" of New Brunswick which the provincial legislature is debarred from affecting under s. 122 of the British North America Act. "Excise" is a word of vague and somewhat ambiguous meaning. Dr. Johnson's famous definition in his dictionary is distinguished by acerbity rather than precision. The word is usually (though by no means always) employed to indicate a duty imposed on home-manufactured articles in the course of manufacture before they reach the consumer. So regarded, an excise duty is plainly

PART IV: TAXATION – 179

indirect. A further difficulty in the way of the precise application of the word is that many miscellaneous taxes, at any rate in this country, are classed as "excise" merely because they are for convenience collected through the machinery of the Board of Excise – the tax on owning a dog, for example. Their Lordships do not find it necessary in the present case to determine whether this tobacco tax in the form (a) is for any purpose analogous to an excise duty, for it is enough to accept and apply the proposition laid down on behalf of this Board by Lord Thankerton in the *Kingcome* case, namely, "that if the tax is demanded from the very persons who it is intended or desired should pay it, the taxation is direct, and that it is none the less direct, even if it might be described as an excise tax" ([1934] A.C. 45, 55). . . . With the greatest respect to the view of the Chief Justice of Canada, their Lordships are unable to take the view that a valid distinction is to be found between the directness of the tax in the *Kingcome* case and the quality of the tax in the present instance on the ground that in the former case the tax was on every person who had consumed fuel oil whereas the tax in the present case is on every person who buys tobacco in order to consume it. In both instances the circumstance which makes the tax direct is the same, namely, that the person who pays the tax is the person who actually bears it, and this arises necessarily from the circumstance that purchase for re-sale is not taxed. Their Lordships, therefore, conclude that the tax in form (a) is valid.

Next comes the question whether the tax, though "direct" when the principal deals personally with the retail vendor across the counter, ceases to be "direct" if the purchase is made by an agent acting for his principal. Their Lordships have already pointed out that in this case also the person who bears the tax is really the principal, either because he has already given his agent the money to pay it or because he is bound forthwith to repay his agent for the expense incurred with his authority and on his behalf. This indemnification does not follow because there is any fresh transaction analogous to re-sale after the purchase by the agent has been made. It is part and parcel of a single transaction. The agent pays the tax for and on behalf of his principal. If, indeed, the agent gave the name of his principal to the vendor the contract of sale would be with the principal. If there was anything to complain of in the quality of the article it would be the principal, whether named or not, who might have a remedy against the vendor. It is said that the tax in this second form is not direct because the agent, who is personally liable for the tax and has to pay it when receiving the tobacco, is distinct from the principal who bears the burden of the duty, but, in their Lordships' opinion, this circumstance does not, according to the distinction laid down by Mill, prevent the tax from being a direct tax. There is an obvious distinction between an indirect tax, like an ordinary customs or excise duty, which enters into the cost of an article at each stage of its subsequent handling or manufacture, and an impost laid on the final consumer, as "the particular party selected to pay the tax," who produces the money which his agent pays over. This is mere machinery, and resembles the requirement in British income tax that in certain cases A is assessed for tax which B really bears – a circumstance which does not make income tax "indirect." The test for indirect taxation which Mill prescribed is the passing on of the burden of a duty by the person who first pays it through subsequent transactions to future recipients in the process of dealing with the commodity, or, at any rate, the tendency so to pass on the burden. Here the position is quite different. It is really the principal who in this case also both pays the tax and bears it. Their Lordships find it impossible to suppose that, in applying the economic distinction which is at the bottom of Mill's contrast, it would be correct to call this tax "direct" if a man bought a packet of cigarettes over the counter by putting his hand in his pocket and paying price and tax himself to the vendor, but "indirect" if he stood outside the shop and gave his wife the necessary amount to get the cigarettes and pay the tax for him. . . . Their Lordships, therefore, take the view that the tax imposed by s. 4 of the Act is valid both in the form (a) and in the form (b).

For the same reasons, and apart from other considerations which apply only to s. 5, their Lordships are of opinion that the tax is valid in the forms (c) and (d), but the tax imposed by s. 5 raises difficulties of a different order. It is manifest that s. 5 is enacted merely as a supplementary provision, to guard against the methods of avoidance of s. 4 which might otherwise remain available. At the same time, the validity of s. 5 must be judged according to its terms, and, if its enactment by the provincial legislature be beyond the powers of that legislature, it cannot be justified on the ground that it is needed to make the whole scheme watertight. Objection is taken to the validity of s. 5 on the alleged ground that it offends against ss. 121 and 122 of the British North America Act. When the scheme of Canadian federation is considered as a whole, the purpose and effect of these two sections seem plain enough. Previous to the date of

cherche à y trouver un motif qui serait celui, qu'il avait déjà allégué dans sa déclaration, "que ce règlement avait été passé spécialement dans le but de limiter les activités du demandeur et des Témoins de Jéhovah."

Il est à remarquer que le règlement lui-même ne dit rien de tel; il s'applique à tous, quelle que soit leur nationalité, leur doctrine ou leur religion. Mais, en plus, le juge de première instance a décidé en fait qu'il "n'a pas été prouvé que ce règlement avait été passé spécialement dans ce but." D'autre part, en matière d'excès de pouvoirs, c'est toujours au mérite ("pith and substance") de la législation qu'il faut s'arrêter. Ce que le règlement vise est uniquement l'usage des rues pour fins de distribution. En outre que, ainsi que l'a décidé le juge de la Cour Supérieure, aucun motif, aucune arrière-pensée n'a été dévoilée par la preuve faite à l'enquête, c'est une idée erronée que de chercher à attribuer un motif à une loi qui n'en mentionne pas. Un règlement peut être valide même si le but du conseil municipal est mauvais. . . .

. . . La seule question que les tribunaux ont à examiner est celle de savoir si la Cité de Québec avait le pouvoir d'adopter ce règlement. Nous n'avons pas à chercher derrière le texte qu'elle a adopté pour voir quel a pu être son but en ce faisant. J'irai même plus loin et je dirai que l'usage des rues d'une municipalité est indiscutablement une question du domaine municipal et une question locale. Je cherche encore en vertu de quoi on pourrait prétendre que cette matière ne tombe pas exclusivement dans la catégorie des sujets attribués aux provinces en vertu de l'article 92 de l'Acte de l'Amérique britannique du Nord; et, dans ce cas, même s'il est admis que le droit de culte est du domaine fédéral, le pouvoir de contrôle des rues municipales, étant un sujet spécifiquement attribué aux provinces, il aurait préséance sur le pouvoir supposé du Parlement fédéral de légiférer en matière de culte. Il est de jurisprudence constante que du moment qu'un sujet est spécialement attribué au domaine provincial par l'article 92, il a préséance et priorité sur tout pouvoir que prétendrait exercer le fédéral, en vertu des pouvoirs généraux mentionnés dans l'article 91. . . .

. . . Ironie du sort, les Témoins de Jéhovah qui, dans leurs publications, affirment catégoriquement non seulement qu'ils ne constituent pas une religion, mais qu'ils sont opposés à toute religion et que les religions sont une invention du démon, sont maintenant devant les tribunaux du Canada pour demander protection au nom de la religion; et, à cette fin, à l'encontre de la constitutionnalité des lois municipales de la province de

directly." Their Lordships agree with the majority of the Supreme Court that this is not a duty of customs.

Similar considerations dispose of the contention that, as applied to the recipient of tobacco manufactured in another province, the tax offends s. 121. Here again, it is important to remember the special feature of the tax that it is imposed as a direct tax on the consumer. Sect. 121 was the subject of full and careful exposition by the Supreme Court of Canada in *Gold Seal, Ltd.* v. *Attorney-General for Alberta* ([1921] 62 S.C.R. [Can.] 424, 439), where the question arose whether the parliament of Canada could validly prohibit the importation of intoxicating liquor into those provinces where its sale for beverage purposes was forbidden by provincial law. The meaning of s. 121 cannot vary according as it is applied to dominion or to provincial legislation, and their Lordships agree with the interpretation put on the section in the *Gold Seal* case. Duff J. held that "the phraseology adopted, when the contest is considered in which the section is found, shows, I think, that the real object of the clause is to prohibit the establishment of customs duties affecting interprovincial trade in the products of any province of the union" (Ibid. 456 (A.C.)). Anglin J. said: "The purpose of that section is to insure that articles of the growth, produce or manufacture of any province shall not be subjected to any customs duty when carried into any other province" ([1934] A.C. 45). Mignault J. described the purpose of the section as being to secure that admission of the articles described should be "without any tax or duty imposed as a condition of their admission" (Ibid. 59 (A.C.)). These considerations make it clear that if s. 5 of the Tobacco Tax Act is not obnoxious to s. 122 of the British North America Act, it is also free from objection on the score of s. 121. That the tax is taxation within the province is, their Lordships think, clear for the reasons given by Taschereau J.

Their Lordships will humbly advise His Majesty that the appeal fails and that the Tobacco Tax Act, 1940, is in all respects a valid exercise of the powers of the legislature of the province of New Brunswick. The order of the Supreme Court must, therefore, be varied by omitting the words "with the exception of the provisions thereof making the agent liable for the tax."

PART FIVE

CIVIL LIBERTIES

22. Reference re Alberta Statutes, *1938*

~ The Canadian Constitution, unlike that of the United States, contains nothing like a Bill of Rights protecting a list of fundamental civil liberties from legislative encroachment. There are, of course, certain provisions of the B.N.A. Act which, to the extent that they cannot be amended unilaterally by either level of government, are guaranteed. But beyond this restriction on the amending power, Parliament and the legislatures would appear to be supreme within their allotted spheres. Nor did the Canadian Bill of Rights do anything to alter this situation. The Bill of Rights as an ordinary statute is not part of the written Constitution. It does not refer at all to the provinces and it leaves the federal Parliament free to set the Bill aside at its will. Also, since its enactment in 1960, the courts, at all levels, have shown almost a total unwillingness to apply the Bill effectively to federal legislation which is alleged to violate its provisions.

The only significant possibilities for constitutional guarantees of basic freedoms arise out of a series of decisions by the Supreme Court of Canada cutting down some illiberal provincial statutes. These decisions point to two ways in which the B.N.A. Act might safeguard fundamental freedoms. One approach would protect basic freedoms only from provincial encroachment by ruling that the power to limit such freedoms as speech and worship by criminal sanctions lies exclusively with Parliament under its "criminal law" power. The second approach would go much further and draw from those phrases in the B.N.A. Act which call for a parliamentary system of government in Canada the implication that the political and communicative freedoms essential to that system are not to be diminished by the provinces nor even, possibly, by the national Parliament.

In the *Reference re Alberta Statutes* both of these approaches were present in the reasons given by Chief Justice Duff and Justice Cannon for declaring The Accurate News and Information Act invalid. The federal government had asked the Supreme contenaient la doctrine des Témoins de Jéhovah, en ajoutant: "They comprise the official view, doctrines and principles advocated and taught by Jehovah's Witnesses at the date of publication of each of such books." Or, dans toutes ces publications, il est affirmé que les Témoins de Jéhovah ne sont pas une religion; que, au contraire, leur but est de combattre toutes les religions et que la religion est une invention du démon. . . .

. . . Pour ce qui est du deuxième point ci-dessus mentionné, il faut réitérer que l'article 2 du chapitre 307 ne permet pas la jouissance et le libre exercice du culte d'une profession religieuse d'une façon absolue. Il faut que cela ne "serve pas d'excuse à la licence, ni à des pratiques incompatibles avec la paix et la sûreté de la province." C'est le texte même de la loi.

Si donc, à l'encontre de la preuve, il fallait décider que les Témoins de Jéhovah pratiquent un culte, il n'en faudrait pas moins, en vertu du texte de la Loi concernant la liberté des cultes, que la province ou la municipalité ait le droit de contrôler cet exercice "de manière à ne pas servir d'excuse à la licence, ni à autoriser des pratiques incompatibles avec la paix et la sûreté de la province."

Puisque les Témoins de Jéhovah prétendent que leur profession religieuse consiste à distribuer des tracts religieux, il s'ensuit que la province ou la municipalité, à laquelle la province délègue ce pouvoir, a le droit d'examiner les pamphlets religieux que l'on entend distribuer, de façon à en autoriser ou non la distribution.

A cet égard, je le répète, les Témoins de Jéhovah, ayant pris la position qu'ils ne demanderaient pas l'autorisation et qu'ils ne soumettraient pas la littérature qu'ils voulaient distribuer, nous n'avons aucune preuve au dossier susceptible de nous permettre de savoir si cette littérature tombait ou non dans les exceptions prévues par l'article 2 du chapitre 307. Mais, si nous nous croyions justifiés de prendre pour acquit que cette littérature serait de la même nature que les livres et les tracts qui ont été produits au dossier, ou encore qu'elle contiendrait les déclarations faites par le vice-président Covington, il serait inconcevable qu'une municipalité ne put empêcher la circulation dans ses rues de cette littérature que son conseil pourrait certainement considérer comme constituant de la licence ou des pratiques incompatibles avec la paix et la sûreté de la province; et, dès lors, comme tombant dans l'exception exprimée dans l'article 2.

Voici, en effet, ce qu'on trouve dans le témoignage de M. Covington:

P 202

Q. Are you informed that the religion of a greater part of the people in this province and in this city is Roman Catholic? – A. Yes, I have that information.

En fait, il est notoire que 90 pour cent de la population de la Cité de Québec est catholique romaine et 45 pour cent de la population du Canada appartient à la même religion.

On lui demande alors de lire les passages suivants des publications des Témoins de Jéhovah:

. . . Religion is the adulteress and idolatress that befriends and commits religious fornication with the political and commercial elements. She is the lover of this world and blesses the world from the balcony of the Vatican and in the pulpits. Religion, whose most powerful representative has ruled from Rome for sixteen centuries, traces her origin all the way back to Babylon of Nimrod's founding, and organized religion deservedly bears the name Babylon. . . . I will shew unto thee the judgment of the great whore (or idolatress) that sitteth upon many waters: with whom the kings of the earth have committed fornication, and the inhabitants of the earth have been made drunk with the wine of her fornication . . . full of abominations and filthiness of her fornication; and upon her forehead was a name written, MYSTERY, BABYLON THE GREAT, THE MOTHER OF HARLOTS AND ABOMINATIONS OF THE EARTH.

Les citations qui précèdent sont tirées de l'exhibit D-49, aux pages 345 et 346.

Après avoir mis le témoin Covington en présence des extraits ci-dessus, l'avocat de la Cité de Québec lui demande:

Q. Do you consider that writing such books with such insults against another religion, in fact the religion practised by the people of this province or city, a proper means of preaching the gospel? – A. I do.

Et au cours de cette réponse, il dit:

. . . history abundantly attests to the fact that the Roman Catholic Hierarchy has had relationship with the world and has had part tacitly in the wars between the nations and the destruction of nations.

Un peu plus loin:

Q. Do you consider necessary for your organization to attack the other religions, in fact, the Catholic, the Protestant electors, and by the electors themselves of their responsibilities in the election of their representatives.

The right of public discussion is, of course, subject to legal restrictions; those based upon considerations of decency and public order, and others conceived for the protection of various private and public interests with which, for example, the laws of defamation and sedition are concerned. In a word, freedom of discussion means, to quote the words of Lord Wright in *James* v. *Commonwealth* ([1936] A.C. 578, at 627), "freedom governed by law."

Even within its legal limits, it is liable to abuse and grave abuse, and such abuse is constantly exemplified before our eyes; but it is axiomatic that the practice of this right of free public discussion of public affairs, notwithstanding its incidental mischiefs, is the breath of life for parliamentary institutions.

We do not doubt that (in addition to the power of disallowance vested in the Governor-General) the Parliament of Canada possesses authority to legislate for the protection of this right. That authority rests upon the principle that the powers requisite for the protection of the constitution itself arise by necessary implication from The British North America Act as a whole (*Fort Frances Pulp & Power Co. Ltd.* v. *Manitoba Free Press Co. Ltd.* ([1923] A.C. 695)); and since the subject-matter in relation to which the power is exercised is not exclusively a provincial matter, it is necessarily vested in Parliament.

But this by no means exhausts the matter. Any attempt to abrogate this right of public debate or to suppress the traditional forms of the exercise of the right (in public meeting and through the press) would, in our opinion, be incompetent to the legislatures of the provinces, or to the legislature of any one of the provinces, as repugnant to the provisions of The British North America Act, by which the Parliament of Canada is established as the legislative organ of the people of Canada under the Crown, and Dominion legislation enacted pursuant to the legislative authority given by those provisions. The subject matter of such legislation could not be described as a provincial matter purely; as in substance exclusively a matter of property and civil rights within the province, or a matter private or local within the province. It would not be, to quote the words of the judgment of the Judicial Committee in *Great West Saddlery Co.* v. *The King* ([1921] 2 A.C. 91, at 122), "legislation directed solely to the purposes specified in section 92"; and it would be invalid on the principles enunciated in that judgment and adopted in *Caron* v. *The King* ([1924] A.C. 999, at 1005-6).

The question, discussed in argument, of the validity of the legislation before us, considered as a wholly independent enactment having no relation to the Alberta Social Credit Act, presents no little difficulty. Some degree of regulation of newspapers everybody would concede to the provinces. Indeed, there is a very wide field in which the provinces undoubtedly are invested with legislative authority over newspapers; but the limit, in our opinion, is reached when the legislation effects such a curtailment of the exercise of the right of public discussion as substantially to interfere with the working of the parliamentary institutions of Canada as contemplated by the provisions of The British North America Act and the statutes of the Dominion of Canada. Such a limitation is necessary, in our opinion, "in order," to adapt the words quoted above from the judgment in *Bank of Toronto* v. *Lambe* ((1887) 12 A.C. 575), "to afford scope" for the working of such parliamentary institutions. In this region of constitutional practice, it is not permitted to a provincial legislature to do indirectly what cannot be done directly (*Great West Saddlery Co.* v. *The King*).

Section 129 of The British North America Act is in these words:

129. Except as otherwise provided by this Act, all Laws in force in Canada, Nova Scotia or New Brunswick, at the Union, and all Courts of Civil and Criminal Jurisdiction, and all legal Commissions, Powers, and Authorities, and all Officers, Judicial, Administrative, and Ministerial, existing therein at the Union, shall continue in Ontario, Quebec, Nova Scotia, and New Brunswick respectively, as if the Union had not been made; subject nevertheless (except with respect to such as are enacted by or exist under Acts of the Parliament of Great Britain or of the Parliament of the United Kingdom of Great Britain and Ireland), to be repealed, abolished, or altered by the Parliament of Canada, or by the Legislature of the respective Province, according to the Authority of the Parliament or of that Legislature under this Act.

The law by which the right of public discussion is protected existed at the time of the enactment of The British North America Act and, as far as Alberta is concerned, at the date on which the Alberta Act came into force, the 1st of September, 1905. In our opinion (on the broad principle of the cases mentioned which has been recognized as limiting the scope of general words defining the legislative authority of the Dominion) the Legislature of Alberta has not the capacity under section 129 to alter that law by legislation obnoxious to the principle stated.

The legislation now under consideration manifestly places in the hands of the Chairman of the Social Credit Commission autocratic powers which, it may well be thought, could, if arbitrarily wielded, be employed to frustrate in Alberta these rights of the Crown and the people of Canada as a whole. We do not, however, find it necessary to express an opinion upon the concrete question whether or not this particular measure is invalid as exceeding the limits indicated above.

The answer to the question concerning this Bill is that it is *ultra vires*.

CANNON J.:

~ The learned judge first examined The Bank Taxation Act and The Credit of Alberta Regulation Act and concluded that both were *ultra vires*. ~

The third question put to us is the following:

Is Bill No. 9, entitled "An Act to ensure the Publication of Accurate News and Information," or any of the provisions thereof and in what particular or particulars or to what extent intra vires *of the legislature of the province of Alberta? . . .*

The preamble of the bill, which I will hereafter call the "Press bill" recites that it is

expedient and in the public interest that the newspapers published in the Province should furnish to the people of the Province statements made by the authority of the Government of the Province as to the true and exact objects of the policy of the Government and as to the hindrances to or difficulties in achieving such objects to the end that the people may be informed with respect thereto.

Section 3 provides that any proprietor, editor, publisher or manager of any newspaper published in the province shall, when required to do so by the Chairman of the Board constituted by section 3 of the Alberta Social Credit Act, publish in that newspaper any statement furnished by the Chairman which has for its object the correction or amplification of any statement relating to any policy or activity of the government of the province published by that newspaper within the next preceding thirty-one days.

And section 4 provides that the proprietor, etc., of any newspaper upon being required by the Chairman in writing shall within twenty-four hours after the delivery of the requirement *make a return in writing setting out every source from which any information emanated, as to any statement contained in any issue of the newspaper published within sixty days of the making of the requirement and the names, addresses and occupations of all persons by whom such information was furnished to the newspaper and the name and address of the writer of any editorial, article or news item contained in any such issue of the newspaper.*

Section 5 denies any action for libel on account of the publication of any statement pursuant to the Act.

Section 6 enacts that in the event of a proprietor, etc., of any newspaper being guilty of any contravention of any of the provisions of the Act, the Lieutenant-Governor-in-Council, upon a recommendation of the Chairman, may by order prohibit,

(a) *the publication of such newspaper either for a definite time or until further order;*

(b) *the publication in any newspaper of anything written by any person specified in the order;*

(c) *the publication of any information emanating from any person or source specified in the order.*

Section 7 provides for penalties for contraventions or defaults in complying with any requirement of the Act.

The policy referred to in the preamble of the Press bill regarding which the people of the province are to be informed from the government standpoint, is undoubtedly the Social Credit policy of the government. The administration of the bill is in the hands of the Chairman of the Social Credit Board who is given complete and discretionary power by the bill. "Social Credit," according to sec. 2(*b*) of ch. 3, 1937, second session, of The Alberta Social Credit Amendment Act is

the power resulting from the belief inherent within society that its individual members in association can gain the objectives they desire;

and the objectives in which the people of Alberta must have a firm and unshaken belief are the monetization of credit and the creation of a provincial medium of exchange instead of money to be used for the purposes of distributing to Albertans loans without interest, per capita dividends and discount rates to purchase goods from retailers. This free distribution would be based on the unused capacity of the industries and people of the province of Alberta to produce goods and services, which capacity remains unused on account of the lack or absence of purchasing power in the consumers in the province. The purchasing power would equal or absorb this hitherto unused capacity to produce goods and services by the issue of Treasury Credit certificates against a Credit Fund or Provincial credit account established by the Commission each year representing the monetary value of this "unused capacity" – which is also called "Alberta credit."

It seems obvious that this kind of credit cannot succeed unless every one should be induced to believe in it and help it along. The word "credit" comes from the latin: *credere*, to believe. It is, therefore, essential to control the sources of information of the people of Alberta, in order to keep them immune from any vacillation in their absolute faith in the plan of the government. The Social Credit doctrine must become, for the people of Alberta, a sort of religious dogma of which a free and uncontrolled discussion is not permissible. The bill aims to control any statement relating to any policy or activity of the government of the province and declares this object to be a matter of public interest. The bill does not regulate the relations of the newspapers' owners with private individual members of the public, but deals exclusively with expressions of opinion by the newspapers concerning government policies and activities. The pith and substance of the bill is to regulate the press of Alberta from the viewpoint of public policy by preventing the public from being misled or deceived as to any policy or activity of the Social Credit Government and by reducing any opposition to silence or bring upon it ridicule and public contempt.

I agree with the submission of the Attorney-General for Canada that this bill deals with the regulation of the press of Alberta, not from the viewpoint of private wrongs or civil injuries resulting from any alleged infringement or privation of civil rights which belong to individuals, considered as individuals, but from the viewpoint of public wrongs or crimes, i.e., involving a violation of the public rights and duties to the whole community, considered as a community, in its social aggregate capacity.

Do the provisions of this bill, as alleged by the Attorney-General for Canada, invade the domain of criminal law and trench upon the exclusive legislative jurisdiction of the Dominion in this regard?

The object of an amendment of the criminal law, as a rule, is to deprive the citizen of the right to do that, apart from the amendment, he could lawfully do. Sections 130 to 136 of the

Criminal Code deal with seditious words and seditious publications; and sect. 133 (*a*) reads as follows:

> No one shall be deemed to have a seditious intention only
> because he intends in good faith, –
> (a) to show that His Majesty has been misled or mistaken in
> his measures; or
> (b) to point out errors or defects in the government or constitution of the United Kingdom, or of any part of it, or of
> Canada or any province thereof, or in either House of Parliament of the United Kingdom or of Canada, or in any legislature,
> or in the administration of justice; or to excite His Majesty's
> subjects to attempt to procure, by lawful means, the alteration
> of any matter of state; or
> (c) to point out, in order to their removal, matters which are
> producing or have a tendency to produce feelings of hatred and
> ill-will between different classes of His Majesty's subjects.

It appears that in England, at first, criticism of any government policy was regarded as a crime involving severe penalties and punishable as such; but since the passing of Fox's Libel Act in 1792, the considerations now found in the above article of our criminal code that it is not criminal to point out errors in the Government of the country and to urge their removal by lawful means have been admitted as a valid defence in a trial for libel.

Now, it seems to me that the Alberta legislature by this retrograde Bill is attempting to revive the old theory of the crime of seditious libel by enacting penalties, confiscation of space in newspapers and prohibitions for actions which, after due consideration by the Dominion Parliament, have been declared innocuous and which, therefore, every citizen of Canada can do lawfully and without hindrance or fear of punishment. It is an attempt by the legislature to amend the Criminal Code in this respect and to deny the advantage of sect. 133 (*a*) to the Alberta newspaper publishers.

Under the British system, which is ours, no political party can erect a prohibitory barrier to prevent the electors from getting information concerning the policy of the government. Freedom of discussion is essential to enlighten public opinion in a democratic State; it cannot be curtailed without affecting the right of the people to be informed through sources independent of the government concerning matters of public interest. There must be an untrammelled publication of the news and political opinions of the political parties contending for ascendancy. As stated in the preamble of The British North America Act, our constitution is and will remain, unless radically changed, "similar in principle to that of the United Kingdom." At the time of Confederation, the United Kingdom was a democracy. Democracy cannot be maintained without its foundation: free public opinion and free discussion throughout the nation of all matters affecting the State within the limits set by the criminal code and the common law. Every inhabitant in Alberta is also a citizen of the Dominion. The province may deal with his property and civil rights of a local and private nature within the province; but the province cannot interfere with his status as a Canadian citizen and his fundamental right to express freely his untrammelled opinion about government policies and discuss matters of public concern. The mandatory and prohibitory provisions of the Press Bill are, in my opinion, *ultra vires* of the provincial legislature. They interfere with the free working of the political organization of the Dominion. They have a tendency to nullify the political rights of the inhabitants of Alberta, as citizens of Canada, and cannot be considered as dealing with matters purely private and local in that province. The federal parliament is the sole authority to curtail, if deemed expedient and in the public interest, the freedom of the press in discussing public affairs and the equal rights in that respect of all citizens throughout the Dominion. These subjects were matters of criminal law before Confederation, have been recognized by Parliament as criminal matters and have been expressly dealt with by the criminal code. No province has the power to reduce in that province the political rights of its citizens as compared with those enjoyed by the citizens of other provinces of Canada. Moreover, citizens outside the province of Alberta have a vital interest in having full information and comment, favourable and unfavourable, regarding the policy of the Alberta government and concerning events in that province which would, in the ordinary course, be the subject of Alberta newspapers' news items and articles.

I would, therefore, answer the question as to Bill No. 9 in the negative.

~ Justice Davis concurred with Chief Justice Duff. Justices Kerwin, Crocket, and Hudson all concluded that the three bills were *ultra vires*. However their conclusion that the Press Bill was *ultra vires* was based not on the considerations regarding freedom of the press advanced by Chief Justice Duff and Justice Cannon, but on the much narrower grounds that the Act was ancillary to and dependent upon the Alberta Social Credit Act which was itself *ultra vires*. ~

23. Saumur *v.* Quebec and Attorney-General for Quebec, *1953*

~ In this case Saumur, a Jehovah's Witness, challenged the constitutional validity of a Quebec City by-law passed under the Charter of the City of Quebec, prohibiting the distribution in the streets of any book, pamphlet or tract without the permission of the Chief of Police. But the significance of this case went far beyond the immediate question of the validity of the Quebec City by-law. As far as the Jehovah's Witnesses were concerned it was designed to test the general competence of the provinces to restrict a Canadian citizen's rights to freedom of expression and freedom of religious practice. Saumur claimed that these rights were guaranteed by the Constitution, referring in particular to the preamble of the B.N.A. Act, and also by statute, referring here to a number of Acts including The Freedom of Worship Act, a pre-Confederation Canadian statute which had been re-enacted by the Quebec Legislature in 1941. Saumur's action was rejected in the Superior Court of Quebec and his appeal against this judgment had been dismissed by the Quebec Court of Queen's Bench.

Before the Supreme Court of Canada Saumur was more successful – at least on the immediate issue. By a five-to-four majority the Supreme Court ruled that the by-law did not operate so as to prevent Saumur from distributing his tracts. Four of the five judges who made up the majority (Justices Rand, Locke, Kellock, and Estey) rested their conclusion on the broad grounds that it was beyond the jurisdiction of a province to restrict freedom of religious expression. But the deciding vote was cast by Justice Kerwin and his decision was based on the very different grounds that the by-law, although *intra vires*, must not conflict with the Freedom of Worship Act. Contrary to the view of the other members of the majority, Justice Kerwin held that the matter of religious freedom (as well as freedom of the press) was subject to provincial jurisdiction. His opinion would consequently entitle the Quebec Legislature to so amend the Freedom of Worship Act as to exclude sects like the Jehovah's Witnesses from its protection. Indeed under the leadership of Premier Duplessis the Quebec Legislature lost little time in taking advantage of the loop-hole created by Justice Kerwin's opinion and shortly after this decision amended the Freedom of Worship Act so that it would not apply to the distribution of Jehovah's Witness literature.

Thus, on the larger issue of the constitutional status of civil liberties and of religious freedom in particular, Saumur, together with those who sought some clarification of this issue, were not successful. At best the outcome can be described as inconclusive. Three sharply contrasting views were expressed on the general relationship of civil liberties to the division of powers and not one of these views could command the support of a majority. At one extreme, three judges (Chief Justice Rinfret and Justices Taschereau and Kerwin) adopted the completely novel position that freedom of religious practice was subject to provincial jurisdiction, holding that religious freedom was a "civil right in the province" and hence as a subject matter of legislation fell under 92(13). In direct contradiction of this, four judges (Justices Rand, Locke, Kellock, and Estey) denied that the phrase "civil rights" in 92 (13) embraced such rights as the right to the free exercise of one's religion. On a number of grounds they held that the B.N.A. Act removed from the provinces the power of legislating for the purpose of curtailing religious freedom. All four of these judges cited the preamble of the B.N.A. Act in support of their conclusion and two (Justices Rand and Locke) explicitly associated freedom of religious expression with the rights which Chief Justice Duff in *Reference re Alberta Statutes* had deduced from the preamble. Justices Locke and Estey considered that the power of limiting religious freedom lay exclusively with Parliament under its "criminal law" power. Three members of this group also cited the safeguards provided by Section 93 of the B.N.A. Act against provincial infringement of the educational rights of religious denominations as implying that the provinces have no jurisdiction in relation to religious freedom. Finally an intermediate position adopted by Justices Cartwright and Fauteux would deny that a question of civil liberties might be considered to be the main ingredient of a piece of legislation for the purpose of bringing it under one of the heads of power in the B.N.A. Act. Restrictions on civil liberties might be incidental effects of laws but not their pith and substance. Thus both Parliament and the provinces could validly limit freedom of worship providing they did so in the course of legislating on some other subject which lay within their respective powers. ~

SAUMUR *v.* QUEBEC AND
ATTORNEY-GENERAL FOR QUEBEC
In the Supreme Court of Canada. [*1953*] *2 S.C.R. 299.*

RINFRET C.J. (dissenting): Dépouillée de son extravagante mise-en-scène et réduite à sa véritable dimension, cette cause, à mon avis, est vraiment très simple. Elle n'a sûrement pas l'ampleur et l'importance qu'ont tenté de lui donner les Témoins de Jéhovah par le truchement de M. Laurier Saumur, l'appelant, se désignant comme un missionnaire-évangéliste.

Il s'agit de la validité d'un règlement municipal et il y a probablement eu des centaines et des centaines de causes de ce genre depuis la Confédération. Si, par contre, cette catégorie de causes n'a pas été soumise très fréquemment à la Cour Suprême du Canada, c'est uniquement à raison de son peu d'importance relative et de son application restreinte, dans chaque cas, au territoire de la municipalité concernée.

Voici le texte du règlement attaqué:

Règlement n° 184

1° Il est, par le présent règlement, défendu de distribuer dans les rues de la Cité de Québec, aucun livre, pamphlet, brochure, circulaire, fascicule quelconque sans avoir au préalable obtenu pour ce faire la permission par écrit du Chef de Police.

2° Toute personne qui contreviendra au présent règlement sera passible d'une amende avec ou sans les frais, et à défaut du paiement immédiat de ladite amende avec ou sans les frais, selon le cas, d'un emprisonnement, le montant de ladite amende et le terme d'emprisonnement à être fixé par la Cour du Recorder de la Cité de Québec, à sa discrétion; mais ladite amende ne dépassera pas cent dollars, et l'emprisonnement n'excédera pas trois mois de calendrier; ledit emprisonnement cependant, devant cesser en tout temps avant l'expiration du terme fixé par le paiement de ladite amende et des frais, selon le cas; et si l'infraction est réitérée, cette récidive constituera, jour par jour, après sommation ou arrestation, une offense séparée.

L'appelant, invoquant sa qualité de sujet de Sa Majesté le Roi et de résident dans la Cité de Québec, alléguant en outre qu'il est un missionnaire-évangéliste et l'un des Témoins de Jéhovah, déclare qu'il considère de son devoir de prêcher la Bible, soit oralement, soit en distribuant des publications sous forme de livres, opuscules, périodiques, feuillets, etc., de maison en maison et dans les rues.

Il prétend que le règlement n° 184, reproduit plus haut, a pour effet de rendre illégale cette distribution de littérature sans l'approbation écrite du Chef de Police de la Cité de Québec. Il ajoute qu'en sa qualité de citoyen canadien il a un droit absolu à l'expression de ses opinions et que cela découle de son droit à la liberté de parole, la liberté de la presse et le libre exercice de son culte envers Dieu, tel que garanti par la Constitution britannique non écrite, par l'Acte de l'Amérique britannique du Nord généralement, et également par les Statuts de la province de Québec, spécialement la "Loi concernant la liberté des cultes et le bon ordre dans les églises et leurs alentours" (S.R.Q. 1941, c. 307).

Il allègue que la Cité de Québec et la province de Québec n'ont aucune juridiction, soit en loi, soit constitutionnellement, pour adopter un règlement tel que ci-dessus, et que ce dernier est *ultra vires*, inconstitutionnel, illégal et nul. . . .

. . . L'intimée, la Cité de Québec, a plaidé que le règlement n° 184 était une loi municipale légalement passée dans l'exercice des pouvoirs de réglementation de la Cité et conforme à son acte d'incorporation; que la loi de la province, en vertu de laquelle le règlement a été adopté, est constitutionnelle, légale et valide; que le règlement concerne la propreté, le bon ordre, la paix et la sécurité publiques, la prévention de troubles et émeutes et se rapporte à l'économie intérieure et au bon gouvernement local de la ville; que le demandeur a systématiquement contrevenu à ce règlement de façon délibérée et s'est obstinément refusé à s'y soumettre; qu'il n'a jamais demandé et, par conséquent, n'a pu obtenir de permis pour distribuer ses pamphlets dans la ville de Québec et qu'il a ignoré d'une manière absolue si le règlement est susceptible de le priver d'aucun de ses droits, ayant préféré y désobéir de son plein gré. Comme conséquence, l'appelant fut condamné suivant la loi par un tribunal compétent.

La plaidoirie écrite allègue, en outre, que l'appelant n'est pas un ministre du culte et que l'organisation dont il fait partie n'est pas une église ni une religion. Au contraire, les pamphlets ou tracts qu'elle insiste à distribuer sans autorisation ont un caractère provocateur et injurieux, ne sont pas des gestes religieux mais des actes anti-sociaux qui étaient et sont de nature à troubler la paix publique et la tranquillité et la sécurité des paisibles citoyens dans la Cité de Québec, où ils risquent de provoquer des désordres. Il est malvenu en fait et en droit d'invoquer des libertés de parole, de presse et de culte, qui ne sont aucunement concernées en l'occurrence; il n'a jamais été persécuté et, si la Cité de Québec a mis en vigueur son règlement, ce ne fut que pour remplir ses obligations envers le bien commun, l'ordre public exigeant que le règlement soit dûment appliqué dans la Cité.

Après une longue enquête et la production de quelque chose comme soixante-quinze exhibits, avec en plus des mémoires rédigés par l'abbé Gagné, le très révérend Doyen Evans, le rabbin Frank et M. Damien Jasmin, le juge de première instance a maintenu la défense et rejeté l'action de l'appelant. Ce jugement a été confirmé dans son intégrité par la Cour du Banc de la Reine (en appel) (Q.R. [1952] Q.B. 475), (les honorables juges Barclay, Marchand, Pratte et Hyde), l'honorable juge Bertrand se déclarant dissident. . . .

. . . Disons tout de suite que le règlement en litige n'est rien autre chose qu'un règlement de police; il est basé primordialement sur le fait que les rues ne doivent pas être utilisées pour fins de distribution de documents. . . .

. . . Faisons remarquer d'abord que la Charte de la Cité de Québec est antérieure à la Confédération (29-30 Vict. c. 57). La Cité n'est pas régie par la "Loi des Cités et Villes," S.R.Q. 1941, c. 233, mais il n'est pas hors de propos de référer à cette loi pour se rendre compte de l'étendue des pouvoirs qui y sont conférés pour la réglementation des rues.

~ The Chief Justice then listed the powers asserted in the Cities and Towns Act. These included the power of regulating the distribution of literature in the streets. ~

Il est non moins clair que l'Acte de l'Amérique britannique du Nord 1867, dans la distribution qu'elle fait des pouvoirs législatifs, aux paragraphes 91 et 92 attribue, dans chaque province, à la Législature, le pouvoir exclusif de faire des lois relatives aux institutions municipales dans la province (par. 8), à la propriété et les droits civils dans la province (par. 13) et généralement à toutes les matières d'une nature purement locale et privée dans la province (par. 16).

Il serait vraiment fantastique de prétendre que quelques-uns des pouvoirs ci-dessus mentionnés et que l'on trouve dans la "Loi des Cités et Villes" de la province de Québec, pourraient relever du domaine fédéral. Je ne me représente pas facilement le Parlement fédéral entreprenant d'adopter des lois sur aucune de ces matières (Voir le jugement du Conseil Privé dans *Hodge* v. *The Queen* ((1883) 9 App. Cas. 117, 131, 133, 134)).

Je ne comprends pas, d'ailleurs, que le procureur de l'appelant dirige son argumentation à l'encontre de ce principe général. Il demande à la Cour de s'écarter du texte du règlement et il cherche à y trouver un motif qui serait celui, qu'il avait déjà allégué dans sa déclaration, "que ce règlement avait été passé spécialement dans le but de limiter les activités du demandeur et des Témoins de Jéhovah."

Il est à remarquer que le règlement lui-même ne dit rien de tel; il s'applique à tous, quelle que soit leur nationalité, leur doctrine ou leur religion. Mais, en plus, le juge de première instance a décidé en fait qu'il "n'a pas été prouvé que ce règlement avait été passé spécialement dans ce but." D'autre part, en matière d'excès de pouvoirs, c'est toujours au mérite ("pith and substance") de la législation qu'il faut s'arrêter. Ce que le règlement vise est uniquement l'usage des rues pour fins de distribution. En outre que, ainsi que l'a décidé le juge de la Cour Supérieure, aucun motif, aucune arrière-pensée n'a été dévoilée par la preuve faite à l'enquête, c'est une idée erronée que de chercher à attribuer un motif à une loi qui n'en mentionne pas. Un règlement peut être valide même si le but du conseil municipal est mauvais. . . .

. . . La seule question que les tribunaux ont à examiner est celle de savoir si la Cité de Québec avait le pouvoir d'adopter ce règlement. Nous n'avons pas à chercher derrière le texte qu'elle a adopté pour voir quel a pu être son but en ce faisant. J'irai même plus loin et je dirai que l'usage des rues d'une municipalité est indiscutablement une question du domaine municipal et une question locale. Je cherche encore en vertu de quoi on pourrait prétendre que cette matière ne tombe pas exclusivement dans la catégorie des sujets attribués aux provinces en vertu de l'article 92 de l'Acte de l'Amérique britannique du Nord; et, dans ce cas, même s'il est admis que le droit de culte est du domaine fédéral, le pouvoir de contrôle des rues municipales, étant un sujet spécifiquement attribué aux provinces, il aurait préséance sur le pouvoir supposé du Parlement fédéral de légiférer en matière de culte. Il est de jurisprudence constante que du moment qu'un sujet est spécialement attribué au domaine provincial par l'article 92, il a préséance et priorité sur tout pouvoir que prétendrait exercer le fédéral, en vertu des pouvoirs généraux mentionnés dans l'article 91. . . .

. . . Ironie du sort, les Témoins de Jéhovah qui, dans leurs publications, affirment catégoriquement non seulement qu'ils ne constituent pas une religion, mais qu'ils sont opposés à toute religion et que les religions sont une invention du démon, sont maintenant devant les tribunaux du Canada pour demander protection au nom de la religion; et, à cette fin, à l'encontre de la constitutionnalité des lois municipales de la province de

Québec, ils sont contraints d'invoquer une loi de la province de Québec, à savoir: la Loi concernant la liberté des cultes et du bon ordre dans les églises et leurs alentours (c. 307, S.R.Q. 1941).

Cette loi, invoquée par eux, contient l'article suivant:

> 2. *La jouissance et le libre exercice du culte de toute profession religieuse, sans distinction ni préférence, mais de manière à ne pas servir d'excuse à la licence ni à autoriser des pratiques incompatibles avec la paix et la sûreté de la province, sont permis par la constitution et les lois de cette province à tous les sujets de Sa Majesté qui y vivent. S.R. 1925, c. 198, a. 2.*

C'est bien ainsi que l'appelant a posé le problème dans sa déclaration:

> ... *his unqualified right as a Canadian citizen to the expression of his views on the issues of the day and in employing thereby his right of freedom of speech, freedom of the press and free exercise of worship of Almighty God as guaranteed by the unwritten British Constitution, by the provisions of the British North America Act generally and, in particular, in its preamble and sections 91, 92 and 129, as well as by the statute of the Province of Quebec generally and in particular, by "An Act Respecting Peddlers," (R.S.Q. 1941, Chapter 230, especially section 8 thereof); and by "An Act Respecting Licences," (R.S.Q. 1941, Chapter 76, especially section 82 thereof); and by "An Act Respecting Freedom of Worship and the Maintenance of Good Order In and Near Places of Public Worship," (R.S.Q. 1941, Chapter 307, especially section 2 thereof);*

Il n'y a pas lieu de s'arrêter à la référence à la Loi concernant les colporteurs et à la Loi des licences.

Le procureur de l'appelant ne s'est pas non plus expliqué sur ce qu'il entend par "the unwritten British Constitution" comme gouvernant les pouvoirs respectifs du Parlement canadien et des Législatures provinciales (tels qu'ils sont définis dans les articles 91 et 92 de l'Acte de l'Amérique britannique du Nord). C'est cette loi qui contient la Constitution du Canada et le Conseil Privé, à plusieurs reprises, a déclaré que les pouvoirs ainsi distribués entre le Parlement et les législatures couvraient absolument tous les pouvoirs que pouvait exercer le Canada comme entité politique. Mais l'appelant prétend que la question de l'exercice du culte est exclusivement de la juridiction du Parlement fédéral et, en particulier, que les prescriptions du règlement attaqué seraient couvertes par le début de l'article 91 qui autorise l'adoption de "lois pour la paix, l'ordre et le bon gouvernement du Canada," ou la "Loi criminelle."

Au sujet de la première prétention, il suffit de poursuivre la lecture de l'article 91 pour constater que le pouvoir du Parlement fédéral relativement à la paix, l'ordre et le bon gouvernement du Canada se bornent à toutes les matières ne tombant pas dans les "catégories de sujets exclusivement assignés par le présent acte aux Législatures des provinces." Comme il a été invariablement décidé par le Conseil Privé et conformément, d'ailleurs, au texte précis que nous venons de citer, dès que la matière est couverte par l'un des paragraphes de l'article 92, elle devient du domaine exclusif des législatures de chaque province et elle est soustraite à la juridiction du Parlement fédéral. Naturellement, nous ne parlons plus ici du contrôle des rues municipales, car il est évident que, dans ce cas, les paragraphes 8, 13 et 16 de l'article 92 (comme d'ailleurs nous l'avons vu plus haut) attribuent cette juridiction exclusivement aux législatures. Mais, si nous comprenons bien la prétention, c'est que la garantie de l'exercice du culte doit venir du Parlement fédéral et n'appartient pas aux législatures. Nous disons bien qu'elle doit venir, car il est très certain que, pour le moment, elle n'existe pas ailleurs que dans la "Loi concernant la liberté des cultes" invoquée par l'appelant dans sa déclaration (S.R.Q. 1941, c. 307).

La difficulté qu'éprouve ici l'appelant résulte de plusieurs raisons:

Premièrement: – Son droit de distribuer des pamphlets religieux ne constitue pas l'exercice d'un culte d'une profession religieuse.

Deuxièmement: – A tout événement, la jouissance et le libre exercice du culte d'une profession religieuse ne jouit pas, en vertu du chapitre 307, S.R.Q. 1941, d'une autorisation absolue, mais il faut que ce culte s'exerce "de manière à ne pas servir d'excuse à la licence, ni à autoriser des pratiques incompatibles avec la paix et la sûreté de la province."

Troisièmement: – L'exercice du culte est un droit civil et, par conséquent, tombe sous le paragraphe 13 de l'article 92 de l'Acte de l'Amérique britannique du Nord. Il est donc du domaine provincial.

Le premier point ci-dessus depend d'une question de fait. Or, l'appelant a fait entendre comme témoin un monsieur Hayden C. Covington, qui s'est décrit comme "ordained minister of the gospel, and lawyer, 124 Columbia Heights, Brooklyn, New York." Au cours de ce témoignage, ce témoin a identifié un nombre considérable de publications dont il a déclaré qu'elles contenaient la doctrine des Témoins de Jéhovah, en ajoutant: "They comprise the official view, doctrines and principles advocated and taught by Jehovah's Witnesses at the date of publication of each of such books." Or, dans toutes ces publications, il est affirmé que les Témoins de Jéhovah ne sont pas une religion; que, au contraire, leur but est de combattre toutes les religions et que la religion est une invention du démon. . . .

. . . Pour ce qui est du deuxième point ci-dessus mentionné, il faut réitérer que l'article 2 du chapitre 307 ne permet pas la jouissance et le libre exercice du culte d'une profession religieuse d'une façon absolue. Il faut que cela ne "serve pas d'excuse à la licence, ni à des pratiques incompatibles avec la paix et la sûreté de la province." C'est le texte même de la loi.

Si donc, à l'encontre de la preuve, il fallait décider que les Témoins de Jéhovah pratiquent un culte, il n'en faudrait pas moins, en vertu du texte de la Loi concernant la liberté des cultes, que la province ou la municipalité ait le droit de contrôler cet exercice "de manière à ne pas servir d'excuse à la licence, ni à autoriser des pratiques incompatibles avec la paix et la sûreté de la province."

Puisque les Témoins de Jéhovah prétendent que leur profession religieuse consiste à distribuer des tracts religieux, il s'ensuit que la province ou la municipalité, à laquelle la province délègue ce pouvoir, a le droit d'examiner les pamphlets religieux que l'on entend distribuer, de façon à en autoriser ou non la distribution.

A cet égard, je le répète, les Témoins de Jéhovah, ayant pris la position qu'ils ne demanderaient pas l'autorisation et qu'ils ne soumettraient pas la littérature qu'ils voulaient distribuer, nous n'avons aucune preuve au dossier susceptible de nous permettre de savoir si cette littérature tombait ou non dans les exceptions prévues par l'article 2 du chapitre 307. Mais, si nous nous croyions justifiés de prendre pour acquit que cette littérature serait de la même nature que les livres et les tracts qui ont été produits au dossier, ou encore qu'elle contiendrait les déclarations faites par le vice-président Covington, il serait inconcevable qu'une municipalité ne pût empêcher la circulation dans ses rues de cette littérature que son conseil pourrait certainement considérer comme constituant de la licence ou des pratiques incompatibles avec la paix et la sûreté de la province; et, dès lors, comme tombant dans l'exception exprimée dans l'article 2.

Voici, en effet, ce qu'on trouve dans le témoignage de M. Covington:

Q. Are you informed that the religion of a greater part of the people in this province and in this city is Roman Catholic? – A. Yes, I have that information.

En fait, il est notoire que 90 pour cent de la population de la Cité de Québec est catholique romaine et 45 pour cent de la population du Canada appartient à la même religion.

On lui demande alors de lire les passages suivants des publications des Témoins de Jéhovah:

. . . Religion is the adulteress and idolatress that befriends and commits religious fornication with the political and commercial elements. She is the lover of this world and blesses the world from the balcony of the Vatican and in the pulpits. Religion, whose most powerful representative has ruled from Rome for sixteen centuries, traces her origin all the way back to Babylon of Nimrod's founding, and organized religion deservedly bears the name Babylon. . . . I will shew unto thee the judgment of the great whore (or idolatress) that sitteth upon many waters: with whom the kings of the earth have committed fornication, and the inhabitants of the earth have been made drunk with the wine of her fornication . . . full of abominations and filthiness of her fornication; and upon her forehead was a name written, MYSTERY, BABYLON THE GREAT, THE MOTHER OF HARLOTS AND ABOMINATIONS OF THE EARTH.

Les citations qui précèdent sont tirées de l'exhibit D-49, aux pages 345 et 346.

Après avoir mis le témoin Covington en présence des extraits ci-dessus, l'avocat de la Cité de Québec lui demande:

Q. Do you consider that writing such books with such insults against another religion, in fact the religion practised by the people of this province or city, a proper means of preaching the gospel? – A. I do.

Et au cours de cette réponse, il dit:

. . . history abundantly attests to the fact that the Roman Catholic Hierarchy has had relationship with the world and has had part tacitly in the wars between the nations and the destruction of nations.

Un peu plus loin:

Q. Do you consider necessary for your organization to attack the other religions, in fact, the Catholic, the Protestant

*and the Jews? − A. Indeed. The reason for that is because the
Almighty God commands that error shall be exposed and not
persons or nations.*

La Cour demande au même témoin:

*Q. You are the only witnesses of the truth? − A. Jehovah's
Witnesses are the only witnesses to the truth of Almighty God
Jehovah. . . .
Q. Is the Roman Catholic a true Church? − A. No.
Q. Is it an unclean woman? − A. It is pictured in the Bible as
a whore, as having illicit relationship with the nations of this
world, and history proves that fact, history that all have studied
in school.*

A un autre point de vue, ce même témoin déclare:

*If obedience to a law of the state or nation would compel
them (les Témoins de Jéhovah) to thereby violate God's law,
they will obey God rather than men.*

Ce que, d'ailleurs, il avait déjà affirmé peu de temps auparavant
au cours de son témoignage, à une demande de la Cour:

*Q. Notwithstanding the laws of the country to the contrary?
− A. Notwithstanding the laws of the country to the contrary.*

Qui oserait prétendre que des pamphlets contenant les déclarations qui précèdent, distribués dans une cité comme celle
de Québec, ne constitueraient pas une pratique incompatible
avec la paix et la sûreté de la Cité ou de la province? Quel
tribunal condamnerait un conseil municipal qui empêcherait
la circulation de pareilles déclarations? Et je n'ai choisi que
quelques passages dans des livres et des tracts qui fourmillent de
semblables affirmations. La décence, d'ailleurs, me commanderait de ne pas en citer davantage. Et cela ne me paraît pas nécessaire pour démontrer qu'une municipalité, dont 90 pour cent
de la population est catholique, a non seulement le droit, mais
le devoir, d'empêcher la dissémination de pareilles infamies.

Enfin, le dernier point c'est la question que l'exercice des
cultes est un droit civil qui relève de la juridiction des législatures provinciales. C'est ainsi que l'ont considéré les provinces
de la Saskatchewan et de l'Alberta, qui ont adopté des lois intitulées: An Act to Protect Certain Civil Rights (1947, 11 Geo.
VI, c. 35). L'objet de la loi est déclaré dans le préambule comme
étant "to protect certain civil rights" et l'article 3 de la Loi
stipule:

. . . Every person and every class of persons shall enjoy the right to freedom of conscience, opinion and belief, and freedom of religious association, teaching, practice and worship.

La province de l'Alberta a un statut semblable.

Il est intéressant, sur ce point, de référer à l'interprétation donnée par le Conseil Privé de l'expression "civil rights" dans l'Acte de Québec de 1774, dans la cause de *Citizens Insurance Company of Canada* v. *Parsons* ((1881) 7 App. Cas. 96) :

. . . It is to be observed that the same words, "Civil rights" are employed in the Act of 14 Geo. 3, c. 83, which made provision for the Government of the province of Quebec, Sect. 8 of that Act enacted that His Majesty's Canadian subjects within the province of Quebec should enjoy their property, usages, and other civil rights, as they had before done, and that in all matters of controversy relative to property and civil rights resort should be had to the laws of Canada, and be determined agreeably to the said laws. In this statute the words "property" and "civil rights" are plainly used in their largest sense; and there is no reason for holding that in the statute under discussion they are used in a different and narrower one.

Il suffit de signaler la contradiction de l'argumentation du procureur de l'appelant qui, d'une part, allègue l'inconstitutionnalité de la Charte de Québec, en invoquant, d'autre part, qu'elle est en conflit avec la "Loi concernant la liberté des cultes" (S.R.Q. 1941, c. 307) de cette même province de Québec. Il est indiscutable que la législature qui a adopté le chapitre 307 avait la compétence voulue pour adopter la Charte de la Cité de Québec, en vertu de laquelle le règlement 184 a été édicté. . . .

. . . Sur le tout, je n'ai donc aucune hésitation à dire que le règlement attaqué est légal, valide et constitutionnel et que les jugements qui l'ont déclaré tel doivent être confirmés, avec dépens.

KERWIN J.: . . . Counsel for the appellant declined to contend that the by-law was invalid because a discretion was delegated to the Chief of Police. Counsel for the respondent, the City of Quebec, and for the intervenant, the Attorney-General of Quebec, did not deal with the point and nothing is therefore said about it. However, an argument was advanced based upon a pre-Confederation statute of 1852 of the old Province of Canada, 14-15 Vict. c. 175, the relevant part of which provides:

the free exercise and enjoyment of Religious Profession and Worship, without discrimination or preference, so as the same be not made an excuse for acts of licentiousness, or a justification of practices inconsistent with the peace and safety of the Province, is by the constitution and laws of this Province allowed to all Her Majesty's subjects within the same.

Section 129 of the British North America Act, 1867, enacts:

129. Except as otherwise provided by this Act, all Laws in force in Canada, Nova Scotia, or New Brunswick at the Union, and all Courts of Civil and Criminal Jurisdiction, and all legal Commissions, Powers, and Authorities, and all Officers, Judicial, Administrative and Ministerial, existing therein at the Union, shall continue in Ontario, Quebec, Nova Scotia, and New Brunswick respectively, as if the Union had not been made; subject nevertheless (except with respect to such as are enacted by or exist under Acts of the Parliament of Great Britain or of the Parliament of the United Kingdom of Great Britain and Ireland) to be repealed, abolished, or altered by the Parliament of Canada, or by the Legislature of the respective Province, according to the Authority of the Parliament or of that Legislature under this Act.

By virtue of this section that part of the pre-Confederation statute extracted above continued to operate in the Province of Quebec at the time of the coming into force of the British North America Act. Since then the Quebec Legislature enacted legislation practically in the same words, and certainly to the same effect, which legislation has been continued from time to time and is now found in section 2 of R.S.Q. 1941, c. 307, The Freedom of Worship Act. Whether or not such legislation be taken to supersede the pre-Confederation enactment, no statutes such as the Quebec City Charter, in the general terms in which they are expressed, and whenever originally enacted, have the effect of abrogating the specific terms of the enactment providing for freedom of worship.

It appears from the material filed on behalf of the appellant that Jehovah's Witnesses not only do not consider themselves as belonging to a religion but vehemently attack anything that may ordinarily be so termed but in my view they are entitled to "the free exercise and enjoyment of (their) Religious Profession and Worship." The Witnesses attempt to spread their views by way of the printed and written word as well as orally and state that such attempts are part of their belief. Their attacks on religion generally, or on one in particular, do not bring them within the exception "so as the same be not made an excuse for licentiousness or a justification of practices inconsistent with the peace and safety of the Province." While several definitions of "licentious" appear in standard dictionaries, the prevailing sense of that term is said to be "libertine, lascivious, lewd." To certain biblical expressions the pamphlets, etc., of Jehovah's Witnesses which they desire to distribute attach a meaning which is offensive to a great majority of the inhabitants of the Province of Quebec. But, if they have a legal right to attempt to spread their beliefs, as I think they have, the expressions used by them in so doing, as exemplified in the exhibits filed, do not fall within the first part of the exception. Nor in my opinion are their attacks "inconsistent with the peace and safety of the Province" even where they are directed particularly against the religion of most of the Province's residents. The peace and safety of the Province will not be endangered if that majority do not use the attacks as a foundation for breaches of the peace.

Confined to the argument now under consideration, the above reasons do not justify a declaration that the by-law is *ultra vires* the City of Quebec since, if not otherwise objectionable, the by-law may have its effect in other cases and under other circumstances; but they do warrant a declaration that the by-law does not extend so as to prohibit the appellant as a member of Jehovah's Witnesses from distributing in the streets of Quebec any book, pamphlet, booklet, circular or tract of Jehovah's Witnesses included in the exhibits and an injunction restraining the City, its officers and agents from in any way interfering with such actions of the appellant.

The appellant further contended that the by-law should be declared illegal on the ground that the Provincial Legislature has not power to authorize the Council of the City of Quebec to pass a general by-law prohibiting the distribution of books, pamphlets, etc., in the City streets. At first he argued that the subject-matter of any such legislation and by-law falls under section 91 of the British North America Act and not section 92, but later changed his position by arguing that neither Parliament nor the Provincial Legislatures possessed the requisite power. I am unable to agree with either of these submissions. I do not find it helpful to refer to rights conferred by early treaties or sanctioned by Imperial Statutes dealing with the old colonies and subdivisions of what is now Canada since it is well-settled that the British North America Act has conferred all powers of legislation either upon Parliament or the Legislatures of the

Provinces and that there is no field in which the one or the others may not operate. . . .

. . . In my view the right to practise one's religion is a civil right in the Province under head 13 of section 92 of the British North America Act just as much as the right to strike or lock-out dealt with by the Judicial Committee in *Toronto Electric Commissioners* v. *Snider* ([1925] A.C. 396). . . .

. . . For the same reason I also think that freedom of the press is a civil right in the Province. In *Re Alberta Information Act* ([1938] S.C.R. 100), Sir Lyman Duff stated a short ground considered by him (and Davis J.) sufficient to dispose of the question as to whether Bill No. 9 of the Legislative Assembly of Alberta, "An Act to Ensure the Publication of Accurate News and Information" was *intra vires* the Legislature of that Province. With the greatest respect I am unable to agree with that part of his ensuing reasons for judgment commencing at the foot of page 132 and continuing to the end of page 135, and particularly the following statement: "Any attempt to abrogate this right of public debate or to express the traditional forms of the exercise of the right (in public meeting and through the press), would, in our opinion be incompetent to the Legislature of the Province." Also, with respect, I must dissent from the views of Cannon J. upon this topic as expressed in the same report.

We have not a Bill of Rights such as is contained in the United States Constitution and decisions on that part of the latter are of no assistance. While it is true that, as recited in the preamble to the British North America Act the three Provinces expressed a desire to be federally united with a constitution similar in principle to that of the United Kingdom, a complete division of legislative powers being effected by the Act, I assume as it was assumed in *Re Adoption Act* ([1938] S.C.R. 398), (with reference, it is true, to entirely different matters) that Provincial Legislatures are willing and able to deal with matters of importance and substance that are within their legislative jurisdiction. It is perhaps needless to say that nothing in the foregoing has reference to matters that are confined to Parliament. . . .

RAND J.: . . . As in all controversies of this nature, the first enquiry goes to the real nature and character of the by-law; in what substance and aspect of legislative matter is it enacted? and we must take its objects and purposes to be what its language fairly embraces. The by-law places no restriction on the discretion of the officer and none has been suggested. If, under cover of such a blanket authority, action may be taken which directly deals with matters beyond provincial powers, can the fact that the language may, at the same time, encompass action on matters within provincial authority preserve it from the taint of *ultra vires*? May a court enter upon a delineation of the limits and contours of the valid and invalid areas within it? Must the provision stand or fall as one or can it be severed or otherwise dealt with? These are the subsidiary questions to be answered.

What the practice under the by-law demonstrates is that the language comprehends the power of censorship. From its inception, printing has been recognized as an agency of tremendous possibilities, and virtually upon its introduction into Western Europe it was brought under the control and licence of government. At that time, as now in despotisms, authority viewed with fear and wrath the uncensored printed word: it is and has been the *bête noire* of dogmatists in every field of thought; and the seat of its legislative control in this country becomes a matter of the highest moment.

The Christian religion, its practices and profession, exhibiting in Europe and America an organic continuity, stands in the first rank of social, political and juristic importance. The Articles of Capitulation in 1760, the Treaty of Paris in 1763, and the Quebec Act of 1774, all contain special provisions placing safeguards against restrictions upon its freedom, which were in fact liberations from the law in force at the time in England. The Quebec Act, by sec. 5, declared that His Majesty's subjects,

> *professing the religion of the Church of Rome of and in the said Province of Quebec, may have, hold and enjoy, the free exercise of the religion of the Church of Rome, subject to the King's supremacy. . . .*

and, by sec. 15, that

> *no ordnance touching religion . . . shall be of any force or effect until the same shall have received His Majesty's approbation.*

This latter provision, in modified form, was continued by sec. 42 of the Constitutional Act of 1791:

> *whenever any act or acts shall . . . in any manner relate to or affect the enjoyment of or exercise of any religious form or mode of worship*

the proposed Act was to be laid before both Houses of Parliament and the assent of the Sovereign could be given only if within thirty days thereafter no address from either House to withhold assent had been presented: The Union Act of 1840, sec. 42, contained a like provision. In each of the latter Acts existing laws were continued by secs. 33 and 46 respectively. From 1760, therefore, to the present moment religious freedom has, in our legal system, been recognized as a principle of fundamental character; and although we have nothing in the nature of an established church, that the untrammelled affirmations of religious belief and its propagation, personal or institutional, remain as of the greatest constitutional significance throughout the Dominion is unquestionable. . . .

. . . The only powers given by sec. 92 of the Confederation Act which have been suggested to extend to legislation in relation to religion are nos. 13, Property and Civil Rights, and 16, Matters of a merely local or private nature in the province. The statutory history of the expression "Property and Civil Rights" already given exhibiting its parallel enactment with special provisions relating to religion shows indubitably that such matters as religious belief, duty and observances were never intended to be included within that collocation of powers. If it had not been so, the exceptional safeguards to Roman Catholics would have been redundant.

Strictly speaking, civil rights arise from positive law; but freedom of speech, religion and the inviolability of the person, are original freedoms which are at once the necessary attributes and modes of self-expression of human beings and the primary conditions of their community life within a legal order. It is in the circumscription of these liberties by the creation of civil rights in persons who may be injured by their exercise, and by the sanctions of public law, that the positive law operates. What we realize is the residue inside that periphery. Their significant relation to our law lies in this, that under its principles to which there are only minor exceptions, there is no prior or antecedent restraint placed upon them: the penalties, civil or criminal, attach to results which their exercise may bring about, and apply as consequential incidents. So we have the civil rights against defamation, assault, false imprisonment and the like, and the punishments of the criminal law; but the sanctions of the latter lie within the exclusive jurisdiction of the Dominion. Civil rights of the same nature arise also as protection against infringements of these freedoms.

That legislation "in relation" to religion and its profession is not a local or private matter would seem to me to be self-evident: the dimensions of this interest are nationwide; it is even today embodied in the highest level of the constitutionalism of Great Britain; it appertains to a boundless field of ideas, beliefs and faiths with the deepest roots and loyalties; a religious incident reverberates from one end of this country to the other, and there is nothing to which the "body politic of the Dominion" is more sensitive.

There is, finally, the implication of sec. 93 of the Confederation Act which deals with education. In this section appear the only references in the statute to religion. Subsec. (i) speaks of "Denominational Schools" and preserves their existing rights and privileges. Subsec. (ii) extends to the separate schools "of the Queen's Protestant and Roman Catholic subjects" in Quebec the same "powers, privileges and duties" then conferred and imposed upon the separate schools of the "Queen's Roman Catholic subjects" in Upper Canada. Subsec. (iii) provides for an appeal to the Governor-General in Council from any act or decision of a provincial authority "affecting any right or privilege of the Protestant or Roman Catholic minority of the Queen's subjects in relation to education." Subsec. (iv) declares that in the event of any failure on the part of the provincial authority to observe or enforce the provincial laws contemplated by the section, Parliament may provide for the execution of the provisions of the section. On the argument advanced, and apart from the question of criminal law, these vital constitutional provisions could be written off by the simple expedient of abolishing, as civil rights and by provincial legislation, the religious freedoms of minorities, and so, in legal contemplation, the minorities themselves.

So is it with freedom of speech. The Confederation Act recites the desire of the three provinces to be federally united into one Dominion "with a constitution similar in principle to that of the United Kingdom." Under that constitution, government is by parliamentary institutions, including popular assemblies elected by the people at large in both provinces and Dominion: government resting ultimately on public opinion reached by discussion and the interplay of ideas. If that discussion is placed under licence, its basic condition is destroyed: the government, as licensor, becomes disjoined from the citizenry. The only security is steadily advancing enlightenment, for which the widest range of controversy is the sine qua non.

In the *Reference re The Accurate News and Information Act of Alberta* ([1938] S.C.R. 100), Sir Lyman Duff deals with this matter. The proposed legislation did not attempt to prevent discussion of affairs in newspapers but rather to compel the publication of statements as to the true and exact objects of governmental policy and as to the difficulties of achieving them.

~ The learned Judge then quoted the reasons given by Chief Justice Duff and Justice Cannon in *Reference re Alberta Statutes* for ruling that the provinces cannot abrogate the right of public debate. ~

What is proposed before us is that a newspaper, just as a religious, political or other tract or handbill, for the purposes of sale or distribution through use of streets, can be placed under the uncontrolled discretion of a municipal officer; that is, that the province, while permitting all others, could forbid a newspaper or any writing of a particular colour from being so disposed of. That public ways, in some circumstances the only practical means available for any appeal to the community generally, have from the most ancient times been the avenues for such communications, is demonstrated by the Bible itself: in the 6th verse of ch. xi of Jeremiah these words appear: "Proclaim all these words in the cities of Judah, and in the streets of Jerusalem"; and a more objectionable interference, short of complete suppression, with that dissemination which is the "breath of life" of the political institutions of this country than that made possible by the by-law can scarcely be imagined.

But it is argued that the by-law relates not to religion or free speech at all but to the administration of streets. Undoubtedly the city may pass regulations for that purpose but within the general and neutral requirement of licence by the by-law a number of equally plausible objects may be conjectured. No purpose whatever is indicated much less specified by the language; its sole effect is to create and vest in a functionary a power, to be exercised for any purpose or reason he sees fit, disclosed or undisclosed. . . .

. . . It was urged by Mr. Beaulieu that the city as proprietor of the streets has authority to forbid or permit as it chooses, in the most unlimited and arbitrary manner, any action or conduct that takes place on them. The possibilities of such a proposition can be easily imagined. But it misconceives the relation of the province to the public highways. The public entitled to use them is that of the Dominion, whose citizens are not of this or that province but of Canada. What has been confided to the provinces is the regulation of their use by that public.

Conceding, as in the Alberta Reference, that aspects of the

activities of religion and free speech may be affected by provincial legislation, such legislation, as in all other fields, must be sufficiently definite and precise to indicate its subject matter. In our political organization, as in federal structures generally, that is the condition of legislation by any authority within it: the courts must be able from its language and its relevant circumstances, to attribute an enactment to a matter *in relation to which* the legislature acting has been empowered to make laws. That principle inheres in the nature of federalism; otherwise, authority, in broad and general terms, could be conferred which would end the division of powers. Where the language is sufficiently specific and can fairly be interpreted as applying only to matter within the enacting jurisdiction, that attribution will be made; and where the requisite elements are present, there is the rule of severability. But to authorize action which may be related indifferently to a variety of incompatible matters by means of the device of a discretionary licence cannot be brought within either of these mechanisms; and the Court is powerless, under general language that overlaps exclusive jurisdictions, to delineate and preserve valid power in a segregated form. If the purpose is street regulation, taxation, registration or other local object, the language must, with sufficient precision, define the matter and mode of administration; and by no expedient which ignores that requirement can constitutional limitations be circumvented.

I would, therefore, allow the appeal, direct judgment declaring the by-law invalid, and enjoin the respondent City from acting upon it.

Locke J.: The preamble to chapter 175 of the Statutes of the Province of Canada for the year 1851 reads as follows:

Whereas the recognition of legal equality amongst all Religious Denominations is an admitted principle of Colonial Legislation: And whereas in the state and condition of this Province, to which such a principle is peculiarly applicable, it is desirable that the same should receive the sanction of direct Legislative Authority recognizing and declaring the same as a fundamental principle of our civil polity: Be it therefore declared and enacted by the Queen's Most Excellent Majesty, by and with the advice and consent of the Legislative Council and of the Legislative Assembly of the Province of Canada constituted and assembled by virtue of and under the authority of an Act passed in the Parliament of the United Kingdom of Great Britain and Ireland,

and intituled, An Act to re-unite the Provinces of Upper and Lower Canada, and for the Government of Canada, and it is hereby declared and enacted by the authority of the same, That the free exercise and enjoyment of Religious Profession and Worship, without discrimination or preference, so as the same be not made an excuse for acts of licentiousness, or a justification of practices inconsistent with the peace and safety of the Province, is by constitution and laws of this Province allowed to all Her Majesty's subjects within the same.

The statute was reserved for the signification of Her Majesty's pleasure and the Royal assent given by Her Majesty in Council on May 15th, 1852.

This statute was in force when the British North America Act of 1867 was passed by the Imperial Parliament. It could not, in my opinion, be repealed by the Province of Quebec or by the Legislature of any other province of Canada (*Dobie* v. *Temporalities Board* ((1882) 7 App. Cas. 136)). Whether it would be *intra vires* Parliament to repeal the Act, in view of the language of the preamble to the British North America Act, is a matter to be decided when that question arises. It does not arise in the present case. Parliament has passed no legislation purporting to repeal the Act. . . .

. . . On behalf of the intervenant it has been contended before us that, assuming the belief of the Jehovah's Witnesses is one entitled otherwise to the protection of the Statute of 1852 or the Provincial Statute, he may be deprived of that right by or under the authority of a statute of the Provincial Legislature. The argument is based on the contention that the rights so given to the people of Canada to complete freedom in these matters is a civil right of which they may be deprived by appropriate legislation by the Province. It is further contended, though rather faintly, that the legislation may be justified under Head 16 as being a matter of a merely local or private nature in the province.

In the factum of the intervenant the matter is thus expressed:

Under our constitution there is no religious freedom except within the limits determined by the competent legislative authority. No such authority is known other than the provincial authority; religious teaching as a matter of fact is part of the realm of education reserved to the provinces; besides, religious freedom is one of the civil rights also reserved to the provinces.

The reference to rights reserved to the provinces in respect of religious teaching refers, of course, to the provisions of section 93 of the British North America Act. If the argument is sound, then the holding of religious services by the adherents of any faith designated by the Legislature may be prohibited.

This argument put forward, so far as I am aware, for the first time in any reported case in Canada since Confederation raises questions which are of profound importance to all of the people of this country. Not only the right of freedom of worship would be affected but the exercise of other fundamental rights, such as that of free speech on matters of public interest and to publicly disseminate news, subject only to the restraints imposed by the Criminal Code and to such civil liability as may attach to the publication of libelous matters, might be restrained or prohibited. The language of the by-law is perfectly general and if this contention of the intervenants be right the Chief of Police might forbid the distribution in the streets of circulars or pamphlets published by one political party while allowing such distribution by that party which he personally favoured. It is well, in my opinion, that it be made clear that this right is involved in the decision of this case. Once a right of censorship of the contents of religious publications is established, the dissemination of the political views of writers by circulars or pamphlets delivered on the streets may equally be prohibited or restrained. . . .

. . . The purpose of this by-law is to establish a censorship upon the distribution of written publications in the City of Quebec. It is not the distribution of all pamphlets, circulars or other publications in the streets which is prohibited but of those in respect of which the written permission of the Chief of Police has not been obtained.

In the preamble to the British North America Act the opening paragraph says:

> *Whereas the Provinces of Canada, Nova Scotia and New Brunswick have expressed their desire to be federally united into one Dominion under the Crown of the United Kingdom of Great Britain and Ireland with a constitution similar in principle to that of the United Kingdom.*

and, after reciting that such a union would conduce to the welfare of the provinces, it is said that it is expedient not only that the constitution of the legislative authority in the Dominion be provided for but also that the nature of the Executive Government therein be declared. At the time this Act was passed, the Act of 1852 declaring the right to freedom of religious belief and worship was in force in Canada and gave to the inhabitants of the provinces the same rights in that respect as were then enjoyed by the people of the United Kingdom.

It has, I think, always been accepted throughout Canada that, while the exercise of this right might be restrained under the provisions of the saving clause of the statute of 1852 by criminal legislation passed by Parliament under Head 27 of section 91, it was otherwise a constitutional right of all the inhabitants of this country. . . .

. . . Whether the right to religious freedom and the right to free public discussion of matters of public interest and the right to disseminate news, subject to the restrictions to which I have above referred to, differ in their nature, it is unnecessary to decide. The former of these rights is, however, certainly not the lesser of them in Canada. Unless they differ, had the powers of censorship vested by the by-law in the Chief of Police of the City of Quebec been exercised by preventing the distribution of the written views of a political party (and they may be so used) rather than the religious views of Saumur, the opinion of Sir Lyman Duff, C.J. in the *Reference* as to *The Accurate News and Information Act of the Province of Alberta* ([1938] S.C.R. 100 at 132), would be directly to the contrary of the argument advanced on behalf of the intervenant.

~ The learned Judge then quoted at length Chief Justice Duff's reasons for ruling the Accurate News and Information Act invalid. ~

With this opinion in its entirety I respectfully agree and I have heard no reasoned argument against any of its conclusions. It may be said, with at least equal and I think greater force, that the right to the free exercise and enjoyment of religious profession and worship without discrimination or preference, subject to the limitations expressed in the concluding words of the first paragraph of the Statute of 1852, existed at the time of the enactment of the British North America Act and was not a civil right of the nature referred to under Head 13 of section 92 of the British North America Act. . . .

CARTWRIGHT J. (*dissenting*): . . . It is first necessary to determine the proper construction of the by-law. In doing so we must give to the words used their plain meaning in everyday language and when this is done I think it clear that what is prohibited is the distribution, without the permission of the Chief of Police, of printed matter of the kind described in the by-law in the streets of the City. The distribution of such matter anywhere else, as for example in private houses is not affected by the by-law. There is evidence in the record to indicate that the officials charged with the enforcement of the by-law have not so construed it and have instituted proceedings against persons, as for an infraction of the by-law, on the ground that such persons had distributed written matter at private residences in the City. Such evidence does not seem to me to be relevant to the proper construction of the by-law. It is only if the words of the by-law are ambiguous that we may resort to extraneous aids in its interpretation and the words used appear to me to be clear and unambiguous. The fact, if be the fact, that the by-law has been misinterpreted, can affect neither its proper construction nor the question of its validity.

In my view, legislation authorizing the city to pass this by-law is *prima facie*, in relation to either or both of two subjects within the provincial power which may be conveniently described as (i) the use of highways, and (ii) police regulations and the suppression of conditions likely to cause disorder.

~ The learned Judge then cited a number of cases which in his view supported both grounds (i) and (ii) for finding the by-law valid. ~

It follows from these authorities that it is within the competence of the Legislature of the Province to prohibit or regulate the distribution, in the streets of the municipalities in the Province, of written matter having a tendency to insult or annoy the recipients thereof with the possible result of giving rise to disorder, and perhaps violence, in the streets.

It is said, however, if I have correctly apprehended the argument for the appellant, that even if the legislation in question appears *prima facie* to fall within the powers of the Provincial Legislature under the two heads with which I have dealt above it is in reality an enactment destructive of the freedom of the press and the freedom of religion both of which are submitted to be matters as to which the Province has no power to legislate. In support of such submission counsel referred to a large number of cases decided in the Courts of the United States of America but I am unable to derive any assistance from them as they appear to be founded on provisions in the Constitution limiting the power to make laws in relation to such matters. Under the British North America Act, on the other hand, the whole range of legislative power is committed either to Parliament or the Provincial Legislatures and competence to deal with any subject matter must exist in one or other of such bodies.

There are thus no rights possessed by the citizens of Canada which cannot be modified by either Parliament or the Legislature, but it may often be a matter of difficulty to decide which of such bodies has the legislative power in a particular case.

It will be convenient to first examine the appellant's argument in so far as it deals with the freedom of the press. In Blackstone's *Commentaries* (1769) Vol. 4, at pages 151 and 152 it is said:

The liberty of the press is indeed essential to the nature of a free state: but this consists in laying no previous restraints upon publications, and not in freedom from censure for criminal matter when published. Every free-man has an undoubted right to lay what sentiments he pleases before the public: to forbid this, is to destroy the freedom of the press: but if he publishes what is improper, mischievous, or illegal, he must take the consequence of his own temerity. To subject the press to the restrictive power of a licenser, as was formerly done, both before and since the revolution, is to subject all freedom of sentiment to the prejudices of one man, and make him the arbitrary and infallible judge of all controverted points in learning, religion, and government. But to punish (as the law does at present) any dangerous or offensive writings, which, when published, shall on a fair and impartial trial be adjudged of a pernicious tendency, is necessary for the preservation of peace and good order, of government and religion, the only solid foundations of civil liberty.

Accepting this as an accurate description of what is commonly understood by the expression "the liberty of the press," as heretofore enjoyed by the inhabitants of Canada, it is clear that By-law No. 184 does infringe such liberty to a limited extent. It does, to adapt the words of Blackstone, lay some previous restraint upon publication. So far as the by-law is concerned every individual is left free to print and publish any matter he pleases except that one particular method of publication is conditionally denied to him. He is forbidden to publish such matter by distributing it in the streets of the City of Quebec without having previously obtained for so doing the written permission of the Chief of Police. I will assume, as is argued for the appellant, that the by-law contemplates that the Chief of Police will examine the written matter in respect of which he is asked to grant a permit and that his decision, whether to grant or refuse it, will be based on the view which he takes of the contents of such matter; that if he regards it as harmless, he will grant the permit, and that if he thinks it is calculated to provoke disorder by annoying or insulting those to whom it is distributed he will refuse the permit. It is urged that power to restrict the liberty of the press even to the limited extent provided in the by-law, is committed exclusively to Parliament under the opening words of section 91 or under head 27 of that section and further that Parliament has fully occupied the field by enacting those provisions of the Criminal Code which deal with blasphemous libel, seditious libel, speaking seditious words, spreading false news, defamatory libel, and publishing obscene matter. If I have followed the argument correctly, it is that as Parliament has enacted that certain publications are to be deemed criminal it has by implication declared that all other publications are lawful and that consequently the Legislature has no power to deal with any other type of publication. I am unable to accept this conclusion.

In my view, freedom of the press is not a separate subject matter committed exclusively to either Parliament or the Legislatures. In some respects, Parliament, and in others, the Legislatures may validly deal with it. In some aspects it falls within the field of criminal law, but in others it has been dealt with by Provincial legislation, the validity of which is not open to question, as for example The Libel and Slander Act R.S.O. 1950 Cap. 204, and the similar acts in the other provinces. If the subject matter of a Provincial enactment falls within the class of subjects enumerated in section 92 of the British North America Act such enactment does not, in my opinion, cease to be *intra vires* of the legislature by reason of the fact that it has the effect of cutting down the freedom of the press. The question of legislative competence is to be determined not by inquiring whether the enactment lays a previous restraint upon publication or attaches consequences after publication has occurred but rather by inquiring whether in substance the subject matter dealt with falls within the Provincial power. I have already indicated my view that the Province has power under the two headings which I have discussed above to authorize the passing of the by-law in question.

It is next necessary to consider the argument that the by-law is invalid because, as it is alleged, it interferes with freedom of religion. While it was questioned before us, I will, for the purposes of this argument, assume that the system of faith and worship professed by the body to which the plaintiff belongs is a religion, and that the distribution of printed matter in the streets is a practice directed by its teachings.

It may well be that Parliament alone has power to make laws in relation to the subject of religion as such, that that subject is, in its nature, one which concerns Canada as a whole and so cannot be regarded as of a merely local or private nature in any province or as a civil right in any province; but we are not called upon to decide that question in this appeal and I express no opinion upon it. I think it clear that the provinces, legislating within their allotted sphere, may affect the carrying on of activities connected with the practice of religion. For example, there are many municipal by-laws in force in cities in Ontario, passed pursuant to powers conferred by the Provincial Legislature, which provide that no buildings other than private residences shall be erected on certain streets. Such by-laws are, in my opinion, clearly valid although they prevent any religious body from building a church or similar edifice on such streets. Another example of Provincial Legislation which might be said to interfere directly with the free exercise of religious profession is that under which the by-law considered in *Re Cribbin* v. *The City of Toronto* ((1891) 21 O.R. 325) was passed. That was a by-law of the City of Toronto which provided in part:

No person shall on the Sabbath-day, in any public park, square, garden, or place for exhibition in the city of Toronto, publicly preach lecture or declaim.

The by-law was attacked on the ground, *inter alia*, that it was unconstitutional but it was upheld by Galt C.J. and in my opinion, his decision was right. No useful purpose would be served by endeavouring to define the limits of the provincial power to pass legislation affecting the carrying on of activities connected with the practice of religion. The better course is, I think, to deal only with the particular legislation now before us.

For the appellant, reliance was placed upon the Statute of Canada (1851) 14-15 Victoria, Chapter 175, re-enacted in substantially identical terms as R.S.Q. 1941 Cap. 307. I will assume, for the purposes of the argument, that counsel for the appellant is right in his submission that it is to the pre-Confederation Statute that we should look. In the relevant portion of that Statute it is enacted:

That the free exercise and enjoyment of Religious Profession and Worship, without discrimination or preference, so as the same be not made an excuse for acts of licentiousness, or a justification of practices inconsistent with the peace and safety of the Province, is by the constitution and laws of this Province allowed to all Her Majesty's subjects within the same.

I do not think that, on a proper construction, this statute absolves a religious body or an individual member thereof from obedience to any Act of Parliament or of the Legislature which happens to conflict with the teachings of such body. To give an example, if I am right in my view that *Re Cribbin* v. *City of Toronto* (*supra*) was rightly decided I do not think that an individual could have successfully argued that the by-law, although otherwise valid, did not apply to him because it was one of his beliefs and a teaching of the body to which he belonged that he must preach not only in churches, chapels or meeting houses or on private property but also in parks and public places. . . .

. . . To summarize, I am of opinion that it was within the competence of the Legislature to authorize the passing of the by-law in question under its power to legislate in relation to (i) the use of highways, and (ii) police regulations and the suppression of conditions likely to cause disorder; and that such legislation is not rendered invalid because it interferes to the limited extents indicated above with either the freedom of the press or the freedom of religion. It follows that I would dismiss the appeal. . . .

~ Justices Kellock and Estey gave reasons similar to those advanced by Justices Rand and Locke for finding the by-law *ultra vires*. Justice Taschereau concurred with Chief Justice Rinfret, and Justice Fauteux concurred with Justice Cartwright. ~

24. Switzman v. Elbling and Attorney-General for Quebec, *1957*

~ The legislation challenged before the Supreme Court of Canada in this case was the *Act Respecting Communistic Propaganda*, the so-called Padlock Law, which the Quebec legislature had passed in 1937. As its title implies, the object of this Act was to prohibit the propagation of communist ideology in the Province of Quebec. The litigation which lead to this appeal began in 1949 when Switzman, the tenant of premises in Montreal, was sued by his landlord, Freda Elbling, for cancellation of the lease and damages on the grounds that the premises had been used by Switzman for the illegal purpose of propagating communism. In his defence Switzman pleaded that the Padlock Act was unconstitutional. The Attorney-General of Quebec intervened to defend the Act. Both the trial judge and the Quebec Court of Queen's Bench (Appeal Side) found the Act *intra vires*.

The Supreme Court of Canada with only Justice Taschereau dissenting declared the Act *ultra vires*. Among the eight Judges who made up the majority five, Chief Justice Kerwin and Justices Locke, Cartwright, Fauteux, and Nolan based their conclusion on the grounds that the Act by making the propagation of communism a crime was in pith and substance legislation in respect of criminal law and hence an invasion of Parliament's "criminal law" power. This invocation of the federal "criminal law" power to invalidate a provincial Act regulating the expression of political ideas followed a similar decision by the Court two years earlier in *Birks and Sons (Montreal) Ltd.* v. *Montreal.*[1] In the *Birks* case the Supreme Court unanimously ruled that a Quebec statute authorizing municipal by-laws for closing stores on Roman Catholic holy days was unconstitutional. Here too, the decision of six of the nine Judges was based on their view that legislation compelling the observance of religious practices was criminal law under Section 91 (27).

In the *Padlock Law* case as in the *Birks* case only three judges (Justices Rand, Kellock and Abbott)[2] looked upon

---

[1] [1955] S.C.R. 799.

[2] In the *Birks* case Justices Rand, Kellock, and Locke construed the issue in terms of a restriction of civil liberties.

the provincial Act as constituting a restriction of a fundamental civil liberty. Justice Rand in his judgment returned again to the theme that the B.N.A. Act, as is indicated by its preamble, requires that Canadian citizens enjoy the free circulation of opinions without which the parliamentary system of government contemplated by the Act would be impossible. While Justice Rand cited this doctrine here as grounds for invalidating a provincial statute restricting freedom of speech there is nothing in his judgment to suggest that he would not also apply it to a federal statute which attempted to do the same thing. Justice Abbott went even further and for the first time explicitly stated that the prescriptions of an open society implied by the preamble to the B.N.A. Act put the power of abrogating the right of discussion and debate beyond the federal Parliament as well as the provincial legislatures.

Although it is difficult to draw firm conclusions from this series of cases on civil liberties, at the very least it would seem safe to infer that they deny the provincial legislatures the power to legislate for the primary purpose of restricting freedom of speech or religious freedom. Furthermore, the accumulation of judgments by such eminent jurists as Duff, Rand, and Kellock would appear to provide future Courts with strong support for denying the federal Parliament too the power of abrogating those communicative freedoms necessary for the practice of parliamentary democracy. ~

SWITZMAN v. ELBLING AND
ATTORNEY-GENERAL FOR QUEBEC
In the Supreme Court of Canada. [1957] *S.C.R. 285.*

KERWIN C.J.: This Act may be cited as Act Respecting Communistic Propaganda.
Sections 3 and 12 read:

3. It shall be illegal for any person, who possesses or occupies a house within the Province, to use it or allow any person to make use of it to propagate communism or bolshevism by any means whatsoever.

12. It shall be unlawful to print, to publish in any manner whatsoever or to distribute in the Province any newspaper, periodical, pamphlet, circular, document or writing whatsoever propagating or tending to propagate communism or bolshevism.

Sections 4 to 11 provide that the Attorney-General, upon

satisfactory proof that an infringement of s. 3 has been committed, may order the closing of the house; authorize any peace officer to execute such order, and provide a procedure by which the owner may apply by petition to a judge of the Superior Court to have the order revised. Section 13 provides for imprisonment of anyone infringing or participating in the infringement of s. 12. In my opinion it is impossible to separate the provisions of ss. 3 and 12.

The validity of the statute was attacked upon a number of grounds, but, in cases where constitutional issues are involved, it is important that nothing be said that is unnecessary. In my view it is sufficient to declare that the Act is legislation in relation to the criminal law over which, by virtue of head 27 of s. 91 of the British North America Act, the Parliament of Canada has exclusive legislative authority. The decision of this Court in *Bédard* v. *Dawson et al* ([1923] S.C.R. 681) is clearly distinguishable. As Mr. Justice Barclay points out, the real object of the Act here under consideration is to prevent propagation of communism within the Province and to punish anyone who does so – with provisions authorizing steps for the closing of premises used for such object. The *Bédard* case was concerned with the control and enjoyment of property. . . . It is not necessary to refer to other authorities, because, once the conclusion is reached that the pith and substance of the impugned Act is in relation to criminal law, the conclusion is inevitable that the Act is unconstitutional. . . .

TASCHEREAU J. (*dissenting*): . . . Il ne fait pas de doute qu'en vertu de l'art. 91 de l'Acte de l'Amérique britannique du Nord (s. 27), le droit criminel est une matière qui relève exclusivement de l'autorité fédérale, sur laquelle cette dernière seule a le pouvoir de légiférer. Et dans un cas comme celui-là, la théorie dite de l'"unoccupied field" ne peut trouver son application, et ne peut justifier une législature provinciale de s'arroger un pouvoir que la constitution lui refuse. . . .

. . . La loi dite "Loi protégeant la province contre la propagande communiste" stipule qu'il est illégal pour toute personne qui possède ou occupe une maison dans la province, de l'utiliser ou de permettre à une personne d'en faire usage pour propager le communisme ou bolchévisme par quelque moyen que ce soit. La loi autorise le procureur général, sur preuve satisfaisante d'une infraction, d'ordonner la fermeture de la maison pour une période n'excédant pas une année. Le recours conféré par la loi au propriétaire de la maison, est de présenter une requête à la

Cour pour faire reviser l'ordonnance, en prouvant qu'il était de bonne foi, qu'il ignorait que la maison fût employée en contravention à la loi, ou que la maison n'a pas été employée pour les fins qu'on lui reproche.

L'appelant prétend que cette législation relève exclusivement du droit criminel, et qu'en conséquence, elle dépasse la compétence législative de l'autorité provinciale. Je m'accorderais volontiers avec lui, si la législature avait décrété que le communisme était un crime punissable par la loi, car il y aurait là clairement un empiétement dans le domaine fédéral, qui frapperait la législation d'illégalité et la rendrait *ultra vires* de la province. Mais tel n'est pas le cas qui se présente à nous. La législature, en effet, n'a érigé aucun acte au niveau d'un crime, et elle n'a nullement donné la caractère de criminalité à la doctrine communiste. Si la législature n'a pas le droit de créer des offenses criminelles, elle a le droit de légiférer pour prévenir les crimes, les désordres, comme la trahison, la sédition, les attroupements illégaux, déclarés des crimes par l'autorité fédérale, et pour faire disparaître les conditions qui sont de nature à favoriser le développement du crime. Pour atteindre ces buts, je n'entretiens pas de doute qu'elle peut validement légiférer sur la possession et l'usage d'un immeuble, car ceci est exclusivement du domaine du droit civil, et relève en vertu de l'art. 92 de l'Acte de l'Amérique britannique du Nord (s. 13) de l'autorité provinciale.

La cause de *Bédard* v. *Dawson et al., supra*, présente beaucoup de similitude avec le litige actuel. Là encore la validité d'une loi provinciale intitulée "Loi concernant les propriétaires de maisons employées comme maisons de désordre," 10 Geo. V (1920), c. 81, a été attaquée. Cette loi déclarait qu'il était illégal pour toute personne qui possède ou occupe une maison ou bâtisse de quelque nature que ce soit, de l'utiliser ou de permettre à une personne d'en faire usage comme maison de désordre. Une copie certifiée de tout jugement déclarant une personne coupable d'un acte criminel, ou d'une infraction en vertu des arts. 228, 228*a*, 229 ou 229*a* de l'ancien Code criminel, constituait une preuve à première vue que la maison avait servi aux fins pour lesquelles la condamnation a été obtenue. Après avis donné à la partie intéressée, si cette maison continuait d'être employée comme maison de désordre, une injonction pouvait être dirigée contre le propriétaire ou le locataire, leur défendant de s'en servir ou de tolérer l'usage de cette bâtisse pour les fins susdites. La Cour pouvait ordonner, après un délai de dix jours, *la fermeture de cette maison.*

La Cour Suprême du Canada, confirmant la Cour d'Appel de la province de Québec ((1921), 33 Que. K.B. 246), a décidé que cette loi était constitutionnelle, et bien que la loi criminelle et les règles de procédure qui s'y rapportent soient du ressort exclusif du Parlement fédéral, le Parlement provincial avait droit de légiférer sur toutes les matières civiles en rapport avec le droit criminel, et de sanctionner ses lois par une pénalité. Le jugé ([1923] S.C.R. at 681) de cette cause est le suivant:

The Quebec statute entitled "An Act respecting the owners of houses used as disorderly houses," 10 Geo. V, c. 81, authorizing a judge to order the closing of a disorderly house, is intra vires *the provincial legislature,* as it deals with matter of property and civil rights by providing for the suppression of a nuisance *and not with criminal law by aiming at the punishment of a crime....*

. . . Je suis clairement d'opinion que si une province peut validement légiférer sur toutes les matières civiles en rapport avec le droit criminel, si elle peut *adopter des lois destinées à supprimer les conditions qui favorisent le crime*, et contrôler les propriétés afin de protéger la société contre tout usage illégal qu'on peut en faire, si elle a le pouvoir incontestable de réglementer les courtiers dans leurs transactions financières pour protéger le public contre la fraude, si, enfin, elle a le droit d'imposer des incapacités civiles comme conséquence d'une offense criminelle, je ne vois pas pourquoi elle n'aurait pas également le pouvoir de décréter que ceux qui prêchent et écrivent des doctrines de nature à favoriser la trahison, la violation des secrets officiels, la sédition, etc., soient privés de la jouissance des immeubles d'où se propagent ces théories destinées à saper à ses bases, et renverser l'ordre établi.

L'expérience, il nous est permis d'en prendre une connaissance judiciaire, nous enseigne, en effet, que des Canadiens, il y a moins de dix ans, malgré les serments d'allégeance qu'ils avaient prêtés, n'ont pas hésité au nom du communisme à violer les secrets officiels, et à mettre en péril la sécurité de l'État. La suppression de la diffusion de ces doctrines subversives par des sanctions civiles, est sûrement aussi importante que la suppression des maisons de désordre. Je demeure convaincu que le domaine du droit criminel, exclusivement de la compétence fédérale, n'a pas été envahi par la législation en question, *et qu'il ne s'agit que de sanctions civiles établies pour la prévention des crimes et la sécurité du pays*.

On a aussi prétendu que cette législation constituait une entrave à la liberté de la presse et à la liberté de parole. Je crois à ces libertés: ce sont des droits indéniables dont bénéficient heureusement les gens de ce pays, mais ces libertés ne seraient plus un droit, et deviendraient un privilège, si on permettait à certains individus d'en abuser et de s'en servir pour diffuser des doctrines malsaines, qui conduisent nécessairement à de flagrantes violations des lois établies. Ces libertés, dont jouissent les citoyens et la presse, d'exprimer leurs croyances, leurs pensées et leurs doctrines, sans autorisation ou censure préalables, ne sont pas des droits absolus. Elles sont nécessairement limitées, et doivent s'exercer dans le cadre de la légalité. Quand les bornes sont dépassées, elles deviennent abusives, et la loi doit alors intervenir pour exercer une action répressive, et protéger les citoyens et la société.

La même raisonnement doit nécessairement servir à rencontrer l'objection soulevée par l'appelant à l'effet que la loi attaquée, est une entrave à la libre expression de pensée de tout individu, candidat à une élection. Les idées destructives de l'ordre social et de l'autorité établie, par des méthodes dictatoriales, n'ont pas plus de droits en temps électoraux qu'en aucun autre temps. Cette loi, dans l'esprit de certains, peut paraître sévère, il ne m'appartient pas d'en juger la sagesse, mais la sévérité d'une loi adoptée par le pouvoir compétent ne la marque pas du caractère d'inconstitutionnalité.

Pour toutes ces raisons, je suis d'avis que le présent appel doit être rejeté. . . .

RAND J.: By 1 Geo. VI, c. 11, passed by the Legislature of the Province of Quebec and entitled "An Act to Protect the Province against Communistic Propaganda" (now R.S.Q. 1941, c. 52), the following provisions are enacted:

3. *It shall be illegal for any person, who possesses or occupies a house within the Province, to use it or allow any person to make use of it to propagate communism or bolshevism by any means whatsoever. . . .*
12. *It shall be unlawful to print, to publish in any manner whatsoever or to distribute in the Province any newspaper, periodical, pamphlet, circular, document or writing whatsoever propagating or tending to propagate communism or bolshevism.*

The word "house" is defined to extend to any building or other construction whatever. By s. 4 the Attorney-General,

. . . *upon satisfactory proof that an infringement of section 3 has been committed, may order the closing of the house against its use for any purpose whatsoever for a period of not more than one year; the closing order shall be registered at the registry office of the registration division wherein is situated such house, upon production of a copy of such order certified by the Attorney-General.*

When a house is closed, an owner who has not been in possession may apply to the Superior Court to have the order revised upon proving that in good faith he was ignorant of the use being made in contravention of the Act or that the house has not been so used during the twelve months preceding the order. Conversely, after an order has been so modified or terminated, the Attorney-General may, on application to the same Court, obtain a decree reviving it. No remedy by resort to a Court is extended to the person in possession against whom the order has become effective. The Attorney-General may at any time permit reoccupation on any conditions thought proper for the protection of the property and its contents or he may revoke the order.

The action in this appeal was brought by an owner against a tenant to have a lease set aside and for damages on the ground of the use of the leased premises for the illegal purpose so defined and their closure under such an order. As the validity of the Act was challenged by the defence, the Attorney-General intervened and that issue became the substantial question in the proceedings. . . .

. . . The first ground on which the validity of s. 3 is supported is head 13 of s. 92 of the British North America Act, "Property in the Province," and Mr. Beaulieu's contention goes in this manner: by that head the Province is vested with unlimited legislative power over property; it may, for instance, take land without compensation and generally may act as amply as if it were a sovereign state, untrammelled by constitutional limitation. The power being absolute can be used as an instrument or means to effect any purpose or object. Since the objective accomplishment under the statute here is an Act on property, its validity is self-evident and the question is concluded.

I am unable to agree that in our federal organization power absolute in such a sense resides in either legislature. The detailed distribution made by ss. 91 and 92 places limits to direct and immediate purposes of provincial action. Under head 13 the purpose would, in general, be a "property" purpose either primary or subsidiary to another head of the same section. If such a purpose is foreign to powers vested in the Province by the Act, it will invade the field of the Dominion. For example, land could not be declared forfeited or descent destroyed by attainder on conviction of a crime, nor could the convicted person's right of access to provincial Courts be destroyed. These would trench upon both criminal law and citizenship status. The settled principle that calls for a determination of the "real character," the "pith and substance," of what purports to be enacted and whether it is "colourable" or is intended to effect its ostensible object, means that the true nature of the legislative act, its substance in purpose, must lie within s. 92 or some other endowment of provincial power. . . . The heads of ss. 91 and 92 are to be read and interpreted with each other and with the provisions of the statute as a whole; and what is then exhibited is a pattern of limitations, curtailments and modifications of legislative scope within a texture of interwoven and interacting powers.

In support of the legislation on this ground, *Bédard* v. *Dawson et al.* ([1923] S.C.R. 681) was relied on. In that case the statute provided that it should be illegal for the owner or occupier of any house or building to use it or allow it to be used as a disorderly house; and procedure was provided by which the Superior Court could, after a conviction under the Criminal Code, grant an injunction against the owner restraining that use of it. If the use continued, the Court could order the building to be closed for a period of not more than one year.

This power is seen to have been based upon a conviction for maintaining a public nuisance. Under the public law of England which underlies that of all the Provinces, such an act was not only a matter for indictment but in a civil aspect the Court could enjoin its continuance. The essence of this aspect is its repugnant or prejudicial effect upon the neighbouring inhabitants and properties.

On that view this Court proceeded in *Bédard*. . . .

. . . That the scene of study, discussion or dissemination of views or opinions on any matter has ever been brought under legal sanction in terms of nuisance is not suggested. For the past century and a half in both the United Kingdom and Canada, there has been a steady removal of restraints on this freedom, stopping only at perimeters where the foundation of the freedom itself is threatened. Apart from sedition, obscene writings and criminal libels, the public law leaves the literary, discursive and polemic use of language, in the broadest sense, free.

The object of the legislation here, as expressed by the title, is admittedly to prevent the propagation of communism and bolshevism, but it could just as properly have been the suppression of any other political, economic or social doctrine or theory; and the issue is whether that object is a matter "in relation to which" under s. 92 the Province may exclusively make laws. Two heads of the section are claimed to authorize it: head 13, as a matter of "Civil Rights," and head 16, "Local and Private Matters."

Mr. Tremblay in a lucid argument treated such a limitation of free discussion and the spread of ideas generally as in the same category as the ordinary civil restrictions of libel and slander. These obviously affect the matter and scope of discussion to the extent that it trenches upon the rights of individuals to reputation and standing in the community; and the line at which the restraint is drawn is that at which public concern for the discharge of legal or moral duties and government through rational persuasion, and that for private security, are found to be in rough balance.

But the analogy is not a true one. The ban is directed against the freedom or civil liberty of the actor; no civil right of anyone is affected nor is any civil remedy created. The aim of the statute is, by means of penalties, to prevent what is considered a poisoning of men's minds, to shield the individual from exposure to dangerous ideas, to protect him, in short, from his own thinking propensities. There is nothing of civil rights in this; it is to curtail or proscribe those freedoms which the majority so far consider to be the condition of social cohesion and its ultimate stabilizing force.

It is then said that the ban is a local matter under head 16; that the social situation in Quebec is such that safeguarding its intellectual and spiritual life against subversive doctrines becomes a special need in contrast with that for a general regulation by Parliament. A similar contention was made in *Re Section 6 of The Farm Security Act (1944) of Saskatchewan* ([1947] S.C.R. 394). What was dealt with there was the matter of interest on mortgages and a great deal of evidence to show the unique vicissitudes of farming in that Province was adduced. But there, as here, it was and is obvious that local conditions of that nature, assuming, for the purpose of the argument only, their existence, cannot extend legislation to matters which lie outside of s. 92.

Indicated by the opening words of the preamble in the Act of 1867, reciting the desire of the four Provinces to be united in a federal union with a constitution "similar in principle to that of the United Kingdom," the political theory which the Act embodies is that of parliamentary government, with all its social implications, and the provisions of the statute elaborate that principle in the institutional apparatus which they create or contemplate. Whatever the deficiencies in its workings, Canadian government is in substance the will of the majority expressed directly or indirectly through popular assemblies. This means ultimately government by the free public opinion of an open society, the effectiveness of which, as events have not infrequently demonstrated, is undoubted.

But public opinion, in order to meet such a responsibility, demands the condition of a virtually unobstructed access to and diffusion of ideas. Parliamentary government postulates a capacity in men, acting freely and under self-restraints, to govern themselves; and that advance is best served in the degree achieved of individual liberation from subjective as well as objective shackles. Under that government, the freedom of discussion in Canada, as a subject-matter of legislation, has a unity of interest and significance extending equally to every part of the Dominion. With such dimensions it is *ipso facto* excluded from head 16 as a local matter.

This constitutional fact is the political expression of the primary condition of social life, thought and its communication by language. Liberty in this is little less vital to man's mind and spirit than breathing is to his physical existence. As such an inherence in the individual it is embodied in his status of citizenship. Outlawry, for example, divesting civil standing and destroying citizenship, is a matter of Dominion concern. Of the fitness of this order of government to the Canadian organization, the words of Taschereau J. in *Brassard et al.* v. *Langevin* ((1877), 1 S.C.R. 145 at p. 195) should be recalled:

The object of the electoral law was to promote, by means of the ballot, and with the absence of all undue influence, the free and sincere expression of public opinion in the choice of members of the Parliament of Canada. This law is the just sequence to the excellent institutions which we have borrowed from England, institutions which, as regards civil and religious liberty, leave to Canadians nothing to envy in other countries.

Prohibition of any part of this activity as an evil would be within the scope of criminal law, as ss. 60, 61 and 62 of the Criminal Code dealing with sedition exemplify. Bearing in mind that the endowment of parliamentary institutions is one and entire for the Dominion, that Legislatures and Parliament are permanent features of our constitutional structure, and that the body of discussion is indivisible, apart from the incidence of criminal law and civil rights, and incidental effects of legislation in relation to other matters, the degree and nature of its regulation must await future consideration; for the purposes here it is sufficient to say that it is not a matter within the regulation of a Province. . . .

. . . I would, therefore, allow the appeal, set aside the judgments below, dismiss the action and direct a declaration on the intervention that the statute in its entirety is *ultra vires* of the Province. . . .

ABBOTT J.: The first question to be determined is whether the impugned legislation, in pith and substance, deals with the use of real property or with the propagation of ideas. As Mr. Scott put it to us in his very able argument: (1) the *motive* of this legislation is dislike of communism as being an evil and subversive doctrine, motive, of course, being something with which the Courts are not concerned; (2) the *purpose* is clearly the suppression of the propagation of communism in the Province, and (3) one *means* provided for effecting such suppression is denial of the use of a house.

In my opinion the Act does not create two illegalities which are separate and independent, as was suggested to us by Mr. Beaulieu, it creates only one, namely, the propagation of communism in the Province. Both s. 3 and s. 12 are directed to the same purpose, namely, the suppression of communism, although different means are provided to achieve that end. The whole Act constitutes one legislative scheme and in my opinion its provisions are not severable.

Since in my view the true nature and purpose of the Padlock Act is to suppress the propagation of communism in the Province, the next question which must be answered is whether such a measure, aimed at suppressing the propagation of ideas within a Province, is within the legislative competence of such Province.

The right of free expression of opinion and of criticism, upon matters of public policy and public administration, and the right to discuss and debate such matters, whether they be social, economic or political, are essential to the working of a parliamentary democracy such as ours. Moreover, it is not necessary to prohibit the discussion of such matters, in order to protect the personal reputation or the private rights of the citizen. That view was clearly expressed by Duff C.J. in *Re Alberta Statutes* ([1938] S.C.R. 100 at pp. 132-34). . . .

. . . The Canada Elections Act, the provisions of the British North America Act which provide for Parliament meeting at least once a year and for the election of a new parliament at least every five years, and the Senate and House of Commons Act, are examples of enactments which make specific statutory provision for ensuring the exercise of this right of public debate and public discussion. Implicit in all such legislation is the right of candidates for Parliament or for a Legislature, and of citizens generally, to explain, criticize, debate and discuss in the freest possible manner such matters as the qualifications, the policies, and the political, economic and social principles advocated by such candidates or by the political parties or groups of which they may be members.

This right cannot be abrogated by a Provincial Legislature, and the power of such Legislature to limit it, is restricted to what may be necessary to protect purely private rights, such as for example provincial laws of defamation. It is obvious that the impugned statute does not fall within that category. It does not, in substance, deal with matters of property and civil rights or with a local or private matter within the Province and in my opinion is clearly *ultra vires*. Although it is not necessary, of course, to determine this question for the purposes of the present appeal, the Canadian constitution being declared to be similar in principle to that of the United Kingdom, I am also of opinion that as our constitutional Act now stands, Parliament itself could not abrogate this right of discussion and debate. The power of Parliament to limit it is, in my view, restricted to such powers as may be exercisable under its exclusive legislative jurisdiction with respect to criminal law and to make laws for the peace, order and good government of the nation.

For the reasons which I have given, I would allow the appeal. . . .

~ Justices Cartwright, Fauteux and Nolan wrote judgments in which they held the Act *ultra vires* on the grounds that it was legislation in relation to criminal law and hence fell under head 27 of Section 91. Justice Locke concurred with Justice Nolan. Justice Kellock wrote a short judgment concurring with Justice Rand. ~

25. Oil, Chemical and Atomic Workers International Union v. Imperial Oil Ltd. and Attorney-General of British Columbia, *1963*

~ When the next major case involving an alleged infringement by a province of fundamental political rights came before the Supreme Court, the four judges, Rand, Locke, Kellock and Estey who along with Abbott formed the nucleus of the Court's "liberal bloc" in the 1950's had all left the Court. This change in the Court's membership may have had some bearing on the Court's decision in *The Oil, Chemical, and Atomic Workers* case. Here Justices Taschereau, Fauteux, Martland and Ritchie constituted the majority on a seven-judge panel which rejected an attack on a recent amendment to British Columbia's Labour Relations Act. Premier Bennett's administration had designed the amendment to prevent Trade Unions from using funds contributed through a check-off, or as a condition of union membership, for political purposes. The legislation was passed in 1961 following the 1960 election in which Premier Bennett had seen his majority reduced (from 38 to 32 in a 52-seat legislature) with corresponding gains realized by his socialist opposition, the New Democratic Party, drawing much of its support from organized labour.

In the majority's view the pith and substance of this legislation was "civil rights in the Province". The Province could as part of its legislative scheme governing labour relations confer rights and obligations on trade unions, and attach to such rights (in this case the right of check-off) conditions which affect participation in federal and provincial politics. Far from undermining fundamental political rights this legislation could be regarded as preventing trade unions from exploiting for partisan political purposes rights conferred on them by the province for the purpose of collective bargaining. Besides, this legislation left unions and their members free to support a political party on a voluntary basis and therefore in the majority's opinion did not "derogate from fundamental political freedoms" as had the provincial legislation under attack in the *Switzman* and *Alberta Press* cases.

On this last point Justice Cartwright in a dissenting opinion realistically recognized that organized labour derives virtually all of its income from moneys paid to unions as a condition of membership so that the B.C. legislation in effect amounted to a total ban on the trade unions' financial support of political parties. Justice Judson expressed the main constitutional grounds for the dissenters. He considered that the accurate way of characterizing this particular amendment to B.C.'s *Labour Relations Act* was not as legislation in relation to labour relations but as legislation in relation to the political activity of trade unions including their activity in federal elections. Such legislation fell outside any of the provincial powers. He did not, however, go as far as the third dissenter, Justice Abbott, who reiterated the position he had taken in the *Switzman* case and suggested that this type of legislation might also be beyond the federal Parliament's competence.

Two years later, in the *McKay* case,[1] the Supreme Court was once again confronted with a situation in which provincial legislation diminished the rights of participants in federal elections. Again the Court was very evenly split, 5 to 4, but this time the balance of power was reversed: the three dissenters in the *Oil, Chemical and Atomic Workers* case joined by Taschereau, who was now Chief Justice, and Justice Spence, a recent appointment to the Court, formed a majority which ruled against the province. The question in this case was whether a zoning by-law restricting the signs which could be posted in a Toronto suburb could validly prohibit the posting of signs for candidates in a federal election. As in the earlier case, the basic division of opinion hinged on whether or not the rights inherent in electoral activity, especially in federal elections, are regarded as constituting a distinct subject matter of legislation. The majority in the *McKay* case regarded federal electoral activity as a distinct constitutional value beyond the scope of otherwise valid provincial legislation. Justice Martland who wrote the dissenting judgment took the opposite view and concluded that provincial legislation in relation to property and civil rights in the province could apply "even though, incidentally, it may affect the means of propaganda used by an individual or by a political party during a federal election campaign."[2] ~

---

[1] *McKay et al.* v: *The Queen* [1965] S.C.R. 789.
[2] *Ibid.*, at p. 811.

OIL, CHEMICAL AND ATOMIC WORKERS INTER-
NATIONAL LTD. *v.* IMPERIAL OIL LTD. AND
ATTORNEY-GENERAL FOR BRITISH COLUMBIA

In the Supreme Court of Canada [1963] S.C.R. 584.

The judgment of Taschereau, Fauteux and Martland J.J.
was delivered by

MARTLAND J.: Prior to its amendment in 1961, s. 9 of the
Labour Relations Act, R.S.B.C. 1960, c. 205, contained, *inter
alia*, the following provisions:

9. *(1) Every employer shall honour a written assignment
of wages to a trade-union certified under this Act, except where
the assignment is declared null and void by a Judge or is
revoked by the assignor.*

. . .

*(3) Except where an assignor of wages revokes the assign-
ment by giving the employer written notice of the revocation,
or except where a Judge declares an assignment to be null and
void, the employer shall remit at least once each month, to the
trade-union certified under this Act and named in the assignment as assignee, the fees and dues deducted, together with a
written statement containing the names of the employees for
whom the deductions were made and the amount of each
deduction.*

On March 27, 1961, the *Labour Relations Act Amendment
Act, 1961*, (B.C.) c. 31, came into effect. It made a number
of amendments to provisions of the *Labour Relations Act*,
among which was the addition to s. 9 of a new subs. (6), which
provides as follows:

*(6) (a) No employer and no one acting on behalf of an
employer shall refuse to employ or to continue to employ a
person and no one shall discriminate against a person in regard
to employment only because that person refuses to make a
contribution or expenditure to or on behalf of any political
party or to or on behalf of a candidate for political office.*

*(b) No trade-union and no person acting on behalf of a
trade-union shall refuse membership to or refuse to continue
membership of a person in a trade-union, and no one shall
discriminate against a person in regard to membership in a
trade-union or in regard to employment only because that
person refuses to make or makes a contribution or expenditure,
directly or indirectly, to or on behalf of any political party or
to or on behalf of a candidate for political office.*

(c) (i) No trade-union and no person acting on behalf of a trade union shall directly or indirectly contribute to or expend on behalf of any political party or to or on behalf of any candidate for political office any moneys deducted from an employee's wages under subsection (1) or a collective agreement, or paid as a condition of membership in the trade-union.

(ii) Remuneration of a member of a trade-union for his services in an official union position held by him while seeking election or upon being elected to public office is not a violation of this clause.

(d) Notwithstanding any other provisions of this Act or the provisions of any collective agreement, unless the trade-union delivers to the employer who is in receipt of an assignment under subsection (1) or who is party to a collective agreement, a statutory declaration, made by an officer duly authorized in that behalf, that the trade-union is complying with and will continue to comply with clause (c) during the term of the assignment or during the term of the collective agreement, neither the employer nor a person acting on behalf of the employer shall make any deductions whatsoever from the wages of an employee on behalf of the trade-union.

(e) Any moneys deducted from the wages of an employee and paid to a trade-union that does not comply with this subsection are the property of the employee, and the trade-union is liable to the employee for any moneys so deducted.

The issue in the present case is as to the constitutional validity of paras. *(c)*, *(d)* and *(e)* of subs. (6), and primarily we are concerned with para. *(c)*, as paras. *(d)* and *(e)* must stand or fall with it.

The appellant is a local unit of the Oil, Chemical and Atomic Workers International Union and was certified under the provisions of the *Labour Relations Act*, as the bargaining agent for a group of employees of the respondent company at its refinery at Ioco, British Columbia. Under the provisions of the collective agreement between the appellant and the respondent company, the company had agreed to honour written assignments of wages given by employees in that group in favour of the appellant and to remit to the appellant each month the amount collected.

Following the enactment of subs. (6) of s. 9 of the Act, the respondent company advised the appellant that it could no longer honour the written assignments unless the appellant supplied it with the form of statutory declaration required by para. *(d)*. The appellant refused to supply this and sued the respondent company to compel it to honour the assignments, contending and seeking a declaration that paras. *(c)*, *(d)* and *(e)* of subs. (6) were *ultra vires* of the Legislature of the Province of British Columbia. Notice was given to the respondent the Attorney-General of British Columbia (hereinafter referred to as "the respondent"), who intervened in the proceedings. The position of the respondent company throughout the proceedings has been that it is precluded from honouring the assignments without having received the required statutory declaration, so long as the legislation in question remains in effect. It has taken the position that it is substantially in the position of a stakeholder, with no interest in the proceedings and prepared to abide by the result.

The learned trial judge held that the statutory provisions under attack were *intra vires* of the Legislature of the Province of British Columbia. This decision was affirmed by the unanimous judgment of the Court of Appeal of British Columbia ((1962) 38 WWR 533, 33 D.L.R. (2d) 732) and it is from that judgment that the present appeal is brought.

The appellant contends that the clauses in question are *ultra vires* of the Legislature of the Province of British Columbia, on the ground that the authority to enact them is not to be found within any of the subsections of s. 92 of the *British North America Act;* that they relate to the subject of federal elections and that they seek to curtail the fundamental rights of Canadian citizens essential to the proper functioning of parliamentary institutions. It is argued that they affect the political activity of trade unions, the right of which to engage in such activity is beyond the powers of a provincial legislature to curtail.

The submission of the respondent is that the legislation in question is a limitation only of the power to use certain specified funds for particular purposes by trade unions; that this limitation is valid legislation in respect of the field of labour relations and that the Legislature of British Columbia has the authority to enact it as being within the field of property and civil rights in the province, within s. 92(13) of the *British North America Act*.

That the field of legislation in relation to labour relations in a province is within the sphere of provincial legislative jurisdiction is established beyond doubt in the case of *Toronto Electric Commissioners* v. *Snider* ([1925] A.C. 396). This is not disputed by the appellant which, however, contends that the clauses in question are not in respect of labour relations at all.

In order to determine these issues it is necessary to consider the provisions of the *Labour Relations Act* as a whole and, in particular, to consider the true purpose and effect of those clauses which are under attack.

The object of this Act, which is similar to like statutes in other provinces of Canada, may be summarized in the words of MacDonald J., in *Re Labour Relations Board (Nova Scotia)* ((1952), 29 M.P.R. 377 at 396):

To my mind the object of the Act is to facilitate collective bargaining and stabilize industrial relations by enabling a union to establish before the Board its ability to represent a group of employees . . .

While it is theoretically possible for a collective agreement to be made with an uncertified trade union, it is only possible for a trade union to become the bargaining agent for a unit of employees who are not all members of the union by obtaining certification under the Act. It is clear that the Act is primarily concerned with the procedures necessary to obtain certification and for collective bargaining after certification has been obtained.

Those procedures materially affect the rights of employees in any unit suitable for collective bargaining and of their employer, who is compelled to bargain collectively with a certified trade union. The primary purpose of the Act is, therefore, to spell out the respective rights and obligations of the employer, the employee and the certified trade union, each of which is subject to its mandatory powers.

A trade union, as defined in the Act, may obtain certification for a group of employees, in accordance with the statutory requirements. It may apply for certification if it claims to have as members in good standing a majority of the employees in that group. . . .

The position is, therefore, that a trade union can, under the provisions of the Act, become the bargaining agent for all the employees within a particular unit, irrespective of the individual wishes of the minority of employees within that group, and that it can then bind each of such employees by the collective agreement which it makes. It is placed in a position to persuade those employees within the group, who were not members of the union, to seek membership, for it is now their bargaining agent, entering collective agreements on their behalf. In some instances the form of the collective agreement which it makes may compel their contribution to its funds, whether they are members or not. But this is not all. Section 8 of the Act provides as follows:

8. *Nothing in this Act shall be construed to preclude the parties to a collective agreement from inserting in the collective agreement a provision as a condition of employment, membership in a specified trade-union, or granting a preference of employment to members of a specified trade-union, or to preclude the carrying-out of such provisions.*

Where a collective agreement contains a provision of the kind contemplated in this section, membership in the trade union becomes a condition of employment within the group of employees in question and loss of membership automatically involves loss of employment. A person seeking employment in such a group, or desiring to remain as an employee within it, has no alternative but to obtain membership in the trade union which is its bargaining agent, and, for that purpose, to pay to it such dues as are imposed as a condition of membership in it.

I now propose to consider the provisions of the clauses in question in this case. The appellant's attack is mainly upon clause *(c) (i)*, which prohibits a trade union from contributing to, or expending on behalf of, a political party, or a candidate for political office, directly or indirectly, moneys deducted from an employee's wages under the check-off (whether statutory or pursuant to a collective agreement), or paid to it as a condition of membership in the trade union.

Clause *(c) (i)* deals first with funds obtained by the check-off, which is imposed under the statute by the provisions of s. 9(1). This right of check-off was created by the statute and granted as a statutory privilege to the trade union. The legislature which conferred that statutory right could also take it away again and, if the right can be eliminated entirely, in my opinion it is equally possible for the legislature to apply limitations in respect of the exercise of the power thus created.

The second method is by check-off authorized by a collective agreement. Again, as already pointed out, the right of a trade union to bind all employees in a specific group, whether members of the union or not, by the collective agrement which it negotiates is one which is conferred by the Act, and the legislature which conferred it could also eliminate it. It seems to me that if the legislature can eliminate that right entirely it can also impose limitations in respect of its use.

Finally, there is the provision as to membership dues paid

by an employee to a trade union as a condition of his membership in it. This is the point on which counsel for the appellant concentrated a good deal of his argument. Membership fees paid to a trade union were, he contended, its own property, which, as a voluntary association, it is entitled to disburse in such manner as its own constitution permits and as the majority of its membership decides; a trade union is entitled to engage in political activities as a free association of individuals and, therefore, within the limits previously mentioned, could disburse its funds for such purposes, and any attempted interference with such powers by a provincial legislature would be an interference with the democratic process in Canada and, therefore, beyond its powers.

This argument would have considerable force as applied to a purely voluntary association. However, the position of a trade union, which has been certified as a bargaining agent under the Act, is substantially different and every association within the definition of a trade union in the Act is empowered to seek certification. Such a union has, as a result of certification, ceased to be a purely voluntary association of individuals. It has become a legal entity, with the status of a bargaining agent for a group of employees, all of whom are thereby brought into association with it, whether as members, or as persons whom it can bind by a collective agreement, even though not members. It must, as their agent, deal with the members of the group which it represents equitably. It is clothed with a power to make binding agreements which can compel membership in it as a condition of employment. I find it difficult to regard as a free, voluntary association of individuals an entity which, by statute, is clothed with a power to require membership in it, and the consequent payment of dues to it as the price which must be paid by an individual for the right to be employed in a particular employment group.

The *Labour Relations Act* has materially affected the civil rights of individual employees by conferring upon certified trade unions the power to bind them by agreement and the power to make agreements which will compel membership in a union. Such legislation falls within the powers of the Legislature of the Province of British Columbia to enact, as being labour legislation, and, therefore, relating to property and civil rights in the province. The legislation which is under attack in the present proceedings, in my opinion, does nothing more than to provide that the fee paid as a condition of membership in such an entity by each individual employee cannot be expended for a political object which may not command his support. That individual, has been brought into association with the trade union by statutory requirement. The same legislature which requires this can protect his civil rights by providing that he cannot be compelled to assist in the financial promotion of political causes with which he disagrees. Such legislation is, in pith and substance, legislation in respect of civil rights in the province.

Considerable reliance was placed by the appellant on the judgment of Chief Justice Duff in respect of the Alberta *Act to Ensure the Publication of Accurate News and Information* ([1938] S.C.R. 100 at 132). In that judgment, which was concurred in by Davis J., Chief Justice Duff dealt with the right of public discussion under the constitution established by the *British North America Act* . . .

The test stated is as to whether legislation effects such a curtailment of the exercise of the right of public discussion as substantially to interfere with the working of the parliamentary institutions of Canada. The appellant, in this case, contends that the legislation in issue does affect such a curtailment in respect of the right of association for political purposes.

The legislation, however, does not affect the right of any individual to engage in any form of political activity which he may desire. It does not prevent a trade union from engaging in political activities. It does not prevent it from soliciting funds from its members for political purposes, or limit, in any way, the expenditure of funds so raised. It does prevent the use of funds, which are obtained in particular ways, from being used for political purposes.

The question in issue here is not as to the right to engage in political activity, but as to the existence of an unfettered right to use funds obtained in certain ways for the support of a political party or candidate. I think it is clear that, if such legislation were required, a provincial legislature could prevent the contribution of trust funds for such a purpose and that, equally, it could prevent the use by a corporation, created under provincial law, of funds derived from the sale of its bonds or shares for such a purpose. A trade union, when it becomes certified as a bargaining agent, becomes a legal entity (*International Brotherhood of Teamsters Etc., Local 213* v. *Therien* ([1960] S.C.R. 265)). When the legislature clothes that entity with wide powers for the exaction of membership fees, by methods which previously it did not, in law, possess, it can set limits to the objects for which funds so obtained may be applied.

Legislation of this kind is not, in my view, a substantial interference with the working of parliamentary institutions.

Reference was also made to the decision of this Court in *Switzman* v. *Elbling and Attorney-General of Quebec* ([1957] S.C.R. 285). In that case it was held that the *Act Respecting Communistic Propaganda* of the Province of Quebec was *ultra vires* of the Legislature of that Province. The majority of the Court decided the issue on the basis that the legislation in question was in respect of criminal law and, therefore, within the exclusive competence of the Parliament of Canada. Three members of the Court decided that the legislation was not within any of the powers ascribed to the provinces and that it constituted an unjustifiable interference with freedom of speech and expression essential to the democratic form of government established in Canada. . . .

In my opinion, the present situation is quite different. What the Legislature has provided here is that, though the civil rights of employees in the Province may be curtailed by enabling a trade union to bargain for them, to make agreements on their behalf, to enter collective agreements which may make union membership a condition of their employment and to collect membership fees by a system of check-off, they cannot be required, by the payment of union dues, to contribute to a political party or candidate selected for them by the trade union itself.

The appellant submitted that, even if the legislation were to be considered as, in pith and substance, designed to safeguard the fundamental right of an individual to support the party of his own choice, it would still be *ultra vires* of a provincial legislature. It was contended that only the Canadian Parliament could legislate in relation to individual political freedom. The submission was that, as a provincial legislature could not legislate to derogate from such rights, conversely it could not legislate for their protection.

I do not agree with this contention. It is the very fact that provincial legislation, in some instances, has apparently sought to derogate from fundamental political freedoms which has led to the expression of the view by some members of the Court, in cases such as the *Alberta Press* case and *Switzman* v. *Elbling and Attorney-General of Quebec*, that it could not be regarded as falling within the sphere of property and civil rights in the province, within s. 92 of the *British North America Act*. The same reasoning does not apply to legislation which seeks to protect certain civil rights of individuals in a province from interference by other persons also in that province. Legislation of that kind appears to me to be legislation in respect of civil rights within the province.

The appellant also contended that the enactment by the Parliament of Canada of s. 36 of c. 26, Statutes of Canada 1908, *An Act to amend the Dominion Elections Act*, which provision was repeated in s. 10 of the *Dominion Elections Act*, 1920 (Canada), c. 46, and again in s. 9 of the Dominion Elections Act, R.S.C. 1927, c. 53, but repealed in 1930, showed that the legislation in question here must have been an encroachment on the field reserved to the Parliament of Canada. That section provided:

36. No company or association other than one incorporated for political purposes alone shall, directly or indirectly, contribute, loan, advance, pay or promise or offer to pay any money or its equivalent to, or for, or in aid of, any candidate at an election, or to, or for, or in aid of, any political party, committee, or association, or to or for or in aid of any company incorporated for political purposes, or to, or for, or in furtherance of, any political purpose whatever, or for the indemnification or reimbursement of any person for moneys so used.

The argument was that this section clearly indicates that legislation regarding contributions to federal political parties is a matter outside the sphere of provincial legislation. But the section did not enable an association or company to make contributions for political purposes. It, in terms, forbade them. It does not follow that without that provision every association and company did have the legal right to make such contributions. The right of any association or company to do so would depend upon the scope of its lawful authority, which, in certain cases in any event, would depend upon the powers which had been conferred upon them by provincial legislation.

For these reasons, in my opinion, the appeal should be dismissed.

CARTWRIGHT J. (*dissenting*): I agree with the reasons and conclusion of my brother Judson and wish to add only a few words. . . .

The question to be decided is whether the enactment of clause (c) (i) of subs. 6 of s. 9 of the *Labour Relations Act* is within the powers of the provincial legislature. The clause is an absolute and unconditional prohibition of the contribution by a trade union to any political party or any candidate for political office of any moneys paid to the union as a condition of membership. It may well be that the Court could take judicial notice of the fact that moneys so paid make up practically the whole of the income of a trade union, but in the case before us there is uncontradicted evidence that, generally speaking, this is so as regards trade unions in British Columbia and that moneys so paid to the appellant union made up more than 99.8 per cent of its total revenue for the year 1960, the year preceding the issue of the writ.

The effect of the impugned legislation in the known circumstances to which it is to be applied is a virtually total prohibition of the expenditure by a trade union of any of its funds to further the interests of any political party or candidate in a federal election; it is the prohibition of, *inter alia*, a political activity in the federal field which prior to the enactment was lawful in Canada.

The prohibition, if valid, would be operative even if the forbidden contribution were approved and directed by a unanimous vote of all the members of the union concerned.

I find myself unable to accept the argument that this prohibition of an heretofore lawful and indeed normal political activity in regard to federal elections is ancillary, or necessarily incidental, to any of the provisions of the *Labour Relations Act* which are within the provincial power.

ABBOTT J. (*dissenting*): I am in agreement with the reasons of my brother Judson and I desire to add only a few brief comments. . . .

In the *Switzman* case, I expressed the view that the parliamentary institutions established in Canada by the *British North America Act* were those institutions as they existed in the United Kingdom in 1867. In the *Reference re Alberta Statutes* ([1938] S.C.R. 100) Sir Lyman Duff pointed out that those institutions contemplated a parliament and provincial legislatures working under the influence of public opinion and public discussion, and he expressed the opinion that any attempt to abrogate or suppress the exercise of such right of public debate and discussion was beyond the competence of a provincial legislature. With that view I am in agreement.

Parliamentary institutions as they existed in the United Kingdom in 1867 included the right of political parties to function as a means, whereby persons who broadly speaking share similar views as to what public policy should be, can seek to make those views prevail. It is common knowledge that political activities in general, and the conduct of elections in particular, involve legitimate and necessary expenditures by political parties and candidates, for the payment of which no provision is made out of public funds. That this is so is implicit in the terms of the *Canada Elections Act* 1960 (Canada), c. 39.

The right to join and to support a political party and the right of public debate and discussion fall within that class of rights categorized by Mr. Justice Mignault in his *Droit Civil Canadien*, vol. 1, p. 131, as *droits publics*, and in my opinion, under our constitution, any person or group of persons in Canada is entitled to promote the advancement of views on public questions by financial as well as by vocal or written means. It follows that any individual, corporation, or voluntary association such as a trade union, is entitled to contribute financially to support any political activity not prohibited by law.

Whatever power a provincial legislature may have to regulate expenditures for provincial political activities, in my opinion it cannot legislate to regulate or prohibit contributions made to assist in defraying the cost of federal political or electoral activities. Similarly, for the reasons which I expressed in the *Switzman* case, in my view Parliament itself cannot legislate to regulate or prohibit financial contributions for provincial political or electoral purposes except to the extent that such regulation or prohibition is necessarily incidental to the exercise of its powers under s. 91 of the *British North America Act*. . . .

JUDSON J. (*dissenting*): . . . The legislation has been held to be *intra vires* as legislation in relation to property and civil rights in the province under s. 92(13) of the *British North America Act*. The Attorney-General for British Columbia supports the judgment under appeal as a valid exercise of the provincial power on two grounds: (a) that it assures every individual who is a member of a trade union the right to refrain from supporting any political party without fear or discrimination; and (b) that it prevents money collected by check-off and as a condition of union membership being diverted from the support of normal union activity in the field of labour relations to the more remote field of political activity. He further submits that no intention to hinder the operations of any political party can be imputed to the legislature, that the legislation does not interfere with the right of an individual to engage in political activity either alone or in association with others, and that it is directed to freeing a union member from any obligation to make political contributions of which he disapproves.

On the other hand, the union attacks the legislation on 5 grounds:

1. The matters dealt with in these subsections do not fall within the field of labour relations but are in relation to the political activity of trade unions.

2. The legislation is legislation in relation to federal elections.

3. The legislation seeks to curtail fundamental rights of Canadian citizens guaranteed by the British North America Act *essential to the proper functioning of Parliamentary institutions.*

4. Even if the legislation should be considered in pith and substance legislation designed to safeguard "the fundamental right of the individual to give his support to the party of his choice", (as held in the Courts below), it is still ultra vires *the Province.*

5. A trade union, being formed by the voluntary association of its members, does not lose its freedom of choice in political matters by reason of the fact that certain of its activities may be validly regulated by provincial statutes.

The issues are not as clear-cut as might at first sight appear. The problem of the use of union funds is entangled with the machinery of the Act relating to collection of dues and with the powers of compulsory representation which the union acquires under the Act when it is certified as a unit that is appropriate for collective bargaining. But it also has a political aspect. The union constitution on file discloses that this local has financial obligations to the international union and also to the Canadian Labour Congress and the British Columbia Federation of Labour. The constitution of the New Democratic Party was also filed and it provides for affiliated membership open to trade unions and other groups. It follows from this that the local cannot take this statutory declaration even if it refrains itself from making any political contributions because the prohibition is against direct or indirect contributions. This leaves the only possible participation in political activity requiring financial contributions to the voluntary collection outside the framework of the Act and the collective agreement.

In my opinion, the union's submission that the matters dealt with in the questioned clauses do not fall within the field of labour relations but are in relation to the political activity of trade unions is an accurate characterization of this legislation.

The subject-matter of the legislation concerns political and constitutional rights, not property and civil rights. Section (c) has no relationship whatever to trade union action designed to promote collective bargaining, to change conditions of employment or the contract of employment. Its sole object and purpose is to prevent trade unions from making these contributions out of their own moneys. . . .

In my opinion, it would be a grave and unwarranted extension of principle to hold that the decision in *Toronto Electric Commissioners* v. *Snider* ([1925] A.C. 396) enables the province to control and curtail the political contributions of the trade union. Any such extension would be in direct conflict with the fundamental basis of the decision in this Court in *Switzman* v. *Elbling and Attorney-General of Quebec* ([1957] S.C.R. 285), where all the judges in the majority were of the opinion that the legislation there in question was outside the provincial power. Five members of the Court held that it was outside the provincial power because it was legislation in relation to criminal law. Three held that it was not within any of the powers specifically assigned to the provinces and that it constituted an unjustifiable interference with freedom of speech and expression essential under the democratic form of government established in Canada.

I am also of the opinion that this legislation is directly related to elections, including federal elections. Its purpose is not a general restriction on the disposition of funds of trade unions. The provincial legislature has no power to restrict the right of any person or organization within the province to make contributions at federal elections and to federal candidates. There was at one time such a restriction in the Dominion legislation. . . . This provincial legislation is really a re-enactment against trade unions in British Columbia of the former prohibition contained in the *Dominion Elections Act* and repealed in 1930. This is sufficient to characterize the legislation and to put it beyond provincial competence.

I am confining my reasons for judgment to the two first grounds put forward by the appellant, namely, that the control of political behaviour does not fall within the field of labour relations and is not within the provincial power, and secondly, that this legislation is legislation in relation to federal elections, a field exclusively within the Dominion power. . . .

~ Justice Ritchie wrote a short concurring opinion agreeing with Justice Martland. ~

26. The Queen *v.* Drybones
(The Canadian Bill of Rights), *1970*

~ A new chapter in Canadian civil liberties was inaugurated in 1960 with the enactment of the Canadian Bill of Rights. Technically the new Bill of Rights was not an addition to Canada's formal Constitution. It was passed as an ordinary Act of the federal Parliament. As such it did not apply to the provinces and could be set aside by subsequent federal legislation. The Act had two main clauses. Section 1 declared that in Canada certain fundamental rights and freedoms "have existed and shall continue to exist without discrimination by reason of race, national origin, colour, religion or sex." It listed as such fundamental rights the right to life, liberty, security of the person and property and the right not to be deprived thereof except by due process of law, the individual's right to equality before the law and protection of the law, freedom of religion, speech, assembly, association and the press. Section 2 provided that unless the Bill of Rights was explicitly set aside, every federal law shall "be so construed and applied as not to abrogate, abridge or infringe" the rights and freedoms set out in the Bill. It added to the rights listed in Section 1 a list of procedural rights, including the right of arrested persons to legal counsel, habeas corpus, the presumption of innocence, the right to an interpreter and the right to a fair hearing when a person's rights or duties are being determined. The final section of the Bill provided that all of these rights could be set aside when the War Measures Act was invoked by Parliament.

Following the passage of the Bill of Rights, there was a spate of cases in the lower courts of Canada testing the scope and meaning of the Act. But very few of these filtered up to the Supreme Court. The first two to do so elicited a very terse response from the Court.[1] They both involved appeals against deportation orders issued under the Immigration Act, and in both cases the Court considered that because the immigration officials had not exceeded their authority in issuing the deporta-

[1] *Rebrin* v. *Bird and the Minister of Citizenship and Immigration et al.* [1961] S.C.R. 376 and *Louie Yuet Sun* v. *The Queen* [1961] S.C.R. 70.

tion orders, the appellants had not been deprived of their liberty "except by due process of law."

The first real test of the Supreme Court's treatment of the Bill of Rights came in 1963 in the *Robertson and Rosetanni* case.[2] Robertson and Rosetanni had been charged with an offence under the federal Lord's Day Act, namely operating a bowling alley on Sunday. On appeal their main defence was that the Lord's Day Act conflicted with the Canadian Bill of Rights and was therefore inoperative. Justice Ritchie (supported by the three Quebec justices, Taschereau, Fauteux and Abbott) wrote the majority's opinion, dismissing the appeal. His approach to the Bill of Rights was basically conservative. He interpreted it not as a charter designed to enlarge the fundamental rights and freedoms of Canadians but as a means of conserving these rights in their 1960 form. The *Canadian Bill of Rights*, he argued, "is not concerned with 'human rights and fundamental freedoms' in any abstract sense, but rather with such 'rights and freedoms' as they existed in Canada immediately before the statute was enacted."[3] His review of Canadian history and jurisprudence revealed that the concept of religious freedom was well enshrined in Canadian law as was Lord's Day observance legislation long before 1960. Thus he concluded that the freedom of religion guaranteed by the Bill of Rights was not infringed by the Lord's Day Act. Somewhat illogically he went on to reason out the meaning of freedom of religion on his own without the aid of Canadian history and concluded that since the effect of the Act (whatever its purpose) was "purely secular and financial" it did not infringe religious freedom.

Justice Cartwright was the sole dissenter in this case. He rejected the majority's historical interpretation of the Bill and considered it "to apply to all laws of Canada already in existence at the time it came into force as well as to those thereafter enacted."[4] Further he held that legislation which compels under criminal sanctions the observance of Sunday as a religious holy day constitutes an infringement of religious freedom for Christians and non-Christians alike.

If Canadian civil libertarians were dismayed by the Court's decision in *Robertson and Rosetanni* they found new grounds for hope in the Court's next major decision on the Bill of

[2] *Robertson and Rosetanni* v. *The Queen* [1963] S.C.R. 651.
[3] *Ibid.*, 654.
[4] *Ibid.*, 662.

Rights. This did not occur until 1970 in the *Drybones* decision which concerned the compatibility of provisions in the Indian Act restricting the drinking rights of Indians with the egalitarian provisions of the Bill of Rights. Ironically, on this occasion the positions of Cartwright and Ritchie were completely reversed. Justice Ritchie still spoke for the majority, but this time it was an "activist" majority willing to use the Bill of Rights to invalidate a long established piece of federal legislation. Cartwright, now Chief Justice, along with Justices Abbott and Pigeon, refused to give the Bill such a wide-reaching effect.

Justice Ritchie's opinion removed the most conservative meaning of his judgment in the *Robertson and Rosetanni* case: the Bill of Rights could expand rights and freedoms beyond legislative restrictions which existed at the time of its enactment. But it is still not entirely clear what in his view is the precise role of historical data in interpreting the meaning of the rights and freedoms inscribed in the Bill. Still it is notable that a majority of the Court rejected the position adopted by a number of lower court judges that the Bill of Rights was nothing more than an interpretation Act. According to this view, the Bill simply sets out some guidelines for the interpretation of statutes: statutes should be interpreted so far as possible in a manner consistent with the Bill of Rights but where no such interpretation is possible the Bill of Rights must be ignored. This was the most conservative approach the courts could have taken to the Bill. The three justices (Abbott, Pigeon and Chief Justice Cartwright) who did accept this conservative approach were clearly troubled by the implications of a more activist approach and did not want to enlarge the judiciary's opportunities for overruling Parliament. The Chief Justice frankly acknowledged that he had arrived at this position after a reconsideration of the position he had taken in *Rosetanni and Robertson*.

The majority's position on the meaning of "equality before the law" was also much more liberal than the understanding of this concept which had prevailed in some of the lower courts. Justice Tysoe of British Columbia had advanced the view that this egalitarian ideal simply required that there must be no discrimination amongst the particular category of people to whom a law applies. This would mean that it would be perfectly in accord with equality before the law to have laws restricting the rights of women, or Indians, or Catholics, so long as all who belong to a particular category were equally discriminated against. The six judge majority (and the three dissenters did not dissent on this point) rejected this view and held that Canadians cannot have their rights limited by federal law solely on the basis of race. ~

THE QUEEN v. DRYBONES
In the Supreme Court of Canada [1970] S.C.R. 282.

CHIEF JUSTICE CARTWRIGHT (*dissenting*): . . .

In approaching this question I will assume the correctness of the view that s. 94(*b*) infringes the right of the respondent to equality before the law declared by clause (b) of s. 1 of the *Bill*, in that because he is an Indian it renders him guilty of a punishable offence by reason of conduct which would not have been punishable if indulged in by any person who was not an Indian. . . .

In *Robertson and Rosetanni* v. *The Queen, supra,* I had to deal with a similar question as in my view *The Lord's Day Act* did infringe the freedom of religion. At pages 661 and 662 I used the following words:

It remains to consider the reasons for judgment of Davey J.A. in Regina v. Gonzales *(1962) 32 D.L.R. (2d) 290. At page 239 of the C.C.C. Reports the learned Justice of Appeal says:*

In so far as existing legislation does not offend against any of the matters specifically mentioned in clauses (a) to (g) of s. 2, but is said to otherwise infringe upon some of the human rights and fundamental freedoms declared in s. 1, in my opinion the section does not repeal such legislation either expressly or by implication. On the contrary, it expressly recognizes the continued existence of such legislation, but provides that it shall be construed and applied so as not to derogate from those rights and freedoms. By that it seems merely to provide a canon or rule of interpretation for such legislation. The very language of s. 2 "be so construed and applied as not to abrogate" assumes that the prior Act may be sensibly construed and applied in a way that will avoid derogating from the rights and freedoms declared in s. 1. If the prior legislation cannot be so construed and applied sensibly, then the effect of s. 2 is exhausted, and the prior legislation must prevail according to its plain meaning.

With the greatest respect I find myself unable to agree with this view. The imperative words of s. 2 of the Canadian Bill of Rights, *quoted above, appear to me to require the courts to refuse to apply any law, coming within the legislative authority of Parliament, which infringes freedom of religion unless it is expressly declared by an Act of Parliament that the law which does so infringe shall operate notwithstanding the* Canadian Bill of Rights. *As already pointed out s. 5(2), quoted above, makes it plain that the* Canadian Bill of Rights *is to apply to all laws of Canada already in existence at the time it came into force as well as to those thereafter enacted. In my opinion where there is irreconcilable conflict between another Act of Parliament and the* Canadian Bill of Rights *the latter must prevail.* . . . .

After a most anxious reconsideration of the whole question, in the light of the able arguments addressed to us by counsel, I have reached the conclusion that the view expressed by Davey J.A., as he then was, in the words quoted above is the better one.

The question is whether or not it is the intension of Parliament to confer the power and impose the responsibility upon the courts of declaring inoperative any provision in a Statute of Canada although expressed in clear and unequivocal terms, the meaning of which after calling in aid every rule of construction including that prescribed by s. 2 of the *Bill* is perfectly plain, if in the view of the court it infringes any of the rights or freedoms declared by s. 1 of the *Bill*.

In approaching this question it must not be forgotten that the responsibility mentioned above, if imposed at all, is imposed upon every justice of the peace, magistrate and judge of any court in the country who is called upon to apply a Statute of Canada or any order, rule or regulation made thereunder.

If it were intended that the question should be answered in the affirmative there would, in my opinion, have been added after the word "declared" in the seventh line of the opening paragraph of s. 2 of the *Bill* some such words as the following "and if any law of Canada cannot be so construed and applied it shall be regarded as inoperative or *pro tanto* repealed."

What now appears to me to have been the error in my reasoning in the passage from *Robertson and Rosetanni* v. *The Queen* quoted above is found in the statement that the *Bill* requires the courts to refuse to apply any law of Canada which is successfully impugned as infringing one of the declared rights or freedoms whereas on the contrary, as Davey J.A. had pointed out, the *Bill* directs the courts to apply such a law not to refuse to apply it.

For these reasons I would dispose of the appeal as proposed by my brother Pigeon.

The judgment of Fauteux, Martland, Judson, Ritchie and Spence J.J. was delivered by

RITCHIE J.: This is an appeal brought with leave of this Court from a judgment of the Court of Appeal for the North-west Territories ((1967), 61 W.W.R. 370) dismissing an appeal by the Crown from a judgment of Mr. Justice W. G. Morrow of the Territorial Court of the Northwest Territories by which he had acquitted Joseph Drybones of being "unlawfully intoxicated off a reserve" contrary to s. 94(b) of the *Indian Act*, R.S.C. 1952, c. 149, after having heard an appeal by way of trial *de novo* from a judgment of Magistrate Anderson-Thompson who had convicted the respondent of this offence and sentenced him to be fined $10 and costs and in default to spend three days in custody. The full charge against Drybones was that he, *On or about the 8th day of April, 1967 at Yellow-knife in the Northwest Territories, being an Indian, was unlawfully intoxicated off a reserve, contrary to s. 94(b) of the Indian Act.*

The respondent is an Indian and he was indeed intoxicated on the evening of April 8, 1967, on the premises of the Old Stope Hotel in Yellowknife in the Northwest Territories where there is no "reserve" within the meaning of the *Indian Act*.

When he was first arraigned before Magistrate Anderson-Thompson, Drybones, who spoke no English, pleaded guilty to this offence, but on appeal to the Territorial Court, Mr. Justice Morrow found that there was some serious doubt as to whether he fully appreciated his plea in the lower court and he was allowed to withdraw that plea whereafter the appeal proceeded as a trial *de novo* with a plea of not guilty. Section 94 of the *Indian Act* reads as follows:

94. *An Indian who*
(a) *has intoxicants in his possession,*
(b) *is intoxicated, or*
(c) *makes or manufactures intoxicants off a reserve, is guilty of an offence and is liable on summary conviction to a fine of not less than ten dollars and not more than fifty dollars or to imprisonment for a term not exceeding three months or to both fine and imprisonment.*

I agree with the Court of Appeal that the use of the words "off a reserve" creates

. . . an essential element to be proved in any charge laid under section 94. But once it is proved, as it was in the present case, that the offence was not committed upon a reserve, the requirement of the section was satisfied. The fact that there are no reserves in the Territories is quite irrelevant.

The important question raised by this appeal has its origin in the fact that in the Northwest Territories it is not an offence for anyone except an Indian to be intoxicated otherwise than in a public place. The Liquor Ordinance which is of general application in the Territories, (R.O.N.W.T. 1957, c. 60, s. 19(1)) provides that: *No person shall be in an intoxicated condition in a public place* . . . but unlike s. 94 of the *Indian Act*, there is no provision for a minimum fine and the maximum term of imprisonment is only 30 days as opposed to 3 months under the *Indian Act*.

The result is that an Indian who is intoxicated in his own home "off a reserve" is guilty of an offence and subject to a minimum fine of not less than $10 or a term of imprisonment not exceeding 3 months or both, whereas all other citizens in the Territories may, if they see fit, become intoxicated otherwise than in a public place without committing any offence at all. And even if any such other citizen is convicted of being intoxicated in a public place, the only penalty provided by the Ordinance is "a fine not exceeding $50 or . . . imprisonment for a term not exceeding 30 days or . . . both fine and imprisonment.

The argument which was successfully advanced by the respondent before Mr. Justice Morrow and before the Court of Appeal was that because of this legislation, Indians in the Northwest Territories, by reason of their race, are denied "equality before the law" with their fellow Canadians, and that s. 94(*b*) of the *Indian Act* therefore authorizes the abrogation, abridgement or infringement of one of the human rights and fundamental freedoms recognized and declared as existing in Canada without discrimination by reason of race, pursuant to the provisions of the *Canadian Bill of Rights* . . . which provides, *inter alia*:

1. It is hereby recognized and declared that in Canada there have existed and shall continue to exist without discrimination by reason of race, national origin, colour, religion or sex, the following human rights and fundamental freedoms, namely

. . .

(b) the right of the individual to equality before the law and the protection of the law;

. . .

2. *Every law of Canada shall, unless it is expressly declared by an Act of the Parliament of Canada that it shall operate notwithstanding the Canadian Bill of Rights, be so construed and applied as not to abrogate, abridge or infringe, or to authorize the abrogation, abridgement or infringement of any of the rights or freedoms herein recognized and declared.*

5.(2) *The expression 'law of Canada' in Part I means an Act of the Parliament of Canada enacted before or after the coming into force of this Act, any order, rule or regulation thereunder, and any law in force in Canada or in any part of Canada at the commencement of this Act that is subject to be repealed, abolished or altered by the Parliament of Canada.*

The Court of Appeal agreed with Mr. Justice Morrow that s. 94(b) of the *Indian Act* is rendered inoperative by reason of this legislation and the Notice of appeal to this Court is limited to the single ground

That the Court of Appeal in the Northwest Territories in upholding the decision of the Territorial Court of the Northwest Territories erred in acquitting the respondent of "an offence contrary to s. 94 (b) of the Indian Act, R.S.C. 1952 Ch. 149 on the ground that s. 94 of the Indian Act is rendered inoperative by reason of the Canadian Bill of Rights, Stat. Can. 1960 Ch. 44."

It was contended on behalf of the appellant that the reasoning and conclusion of the courts below make the question of whether s. 94 has been rendered inoperative by the *Bill of Rights* dependent upon whether or not the law of any province or territory makes it an offence to be intoxicated otherwise than in a public place and that its operation could therefore not only vary from place to place in Canada but also from time to time, depending upon amendments which might be made to the provincial or territorial legislation. I can, however, find no room for the application of this argument in the present case as the ordinance in question is a law of Canada within the meaning of s. 5(2) of the *Bill of Rights* (see *Northwest Territories Act*, R.S.C. 1952, c. 195, s. 17) and it is a law of general application in the Territories, whereas the *Indian Act* is, of course, also a law of Canada although it has special application to Indians alone.

The question of whether s. 94 of the *Indian Act* is rendered inoperative by reason of the provisions of the *Bill of Rights* on the ground that it abrogates, abridges or infringes the right of Canadians of the Indian race to "equality before the law" was considered by the Court of Appeal of British Columbia in *Regina* v. *Gonzales* ((1962), 37 W.W.R. 257) where Tysoe J.A., speaking for the majority of the Court, concluded that: *Sec. 94*(a) *of the* Indian Act *does not abrogate or infringe the right of the appellant to 'equality before the law' as I understand it. Sec. 2 of the* Canadian Bill of Rights *does not therefore affect it.*

In reaching the same conclusion, Davey J.A., (as he then was) who wrote separate reasons for judgment from the other two members of the Court, took the view that s. 1 of the *Bill of Rights* should be treated as merely providing a canon of construction for the interpretation of legislation existing at the time when the statute was enacted.

~ Justice Ritchie then quotes at length from the same judgment quoted by the Chief Justice above. ~

This proposition appears to me to strike at the very foundations of the *Bill of Rights* and to convert it from its apparent character as a statutory declaration of the fundamental human rights and freedoms which it recognizes, into being little more than a rule for the construction of federal statutes, but as this approach has found favour with some eminent legal commentators, it seems to me to be important that priority should be given to a consideration of it.

I will hereafter refer to the case of *Robertson and Rosetanni* v. *The Queen* ([1963] S.C.R. 651), but in the present context I mention it only to say that like the courts below I agree with what was said by the present Chief Justice in his dissenting reasons for judgment when commenting on the above view expressed by Mr. Justice Davey. . . . I do not find that this expression of opinion in any way conflicts with the reasoning of the majority of this Court in *Robertson and Rosetanni* v. *The Queen, supra,* which held that there was no conflict between the impugned section of the *Lord's Day Act* and the *Bill of Rights*.

I am, however, with respect, of the opinion that Mr. Justice Davey's reasoning is untenable on another ground. The result of that reasoning is to conclude that any law of Canada which can only be "construed and applied sensibly" so that it offends against the *Bill of Rights*, is to operate notwithstanding the provisions of the Bill. I am unable to reconcile this interpretation with the opening words of s. 2 where it is provided that:

Every law of Canada shall, unless it is expressly declared by an Act of the Parliament of Canada that it shall operate notwithstanding the Canadian Bill of Rights, *be so construed and applied as not to abrogate* . . .

(The italics are my own.)

If Mr. Justice Davey's reasoning were correct and the *Bill of Rights* were to be construed as meaning that all laws of Canada which clearly offend the Bill were to operate notwithstanding its provisions, then the words which I have italicized in s. 2 would be superfluous unless it be suggested that Parliament intended to reserve unto itself the right to exclude from the effect of the *Bill of Rights* only such statutes as are unclear in their meaning.

It seems to me that a more realistic meaning must be given to the words in question and they afford, in my view, the clearest indication that s. 2 is intended to mean and does mean that if a law of Canada cannot be "sensibly construed and applied" so that it does not abrogate, abridge or infringe one of the rights and freedoms recognized and declared by the Bill, then such law is inoperative "unless it is expressly declared by an Act of the Parliament of Canada that it shall operate notwithstanding the *Canadian bill of Rights*".

I think a declaration by the courts that a section or portion of a section of a statute is inoperative is to be distinguished from the repeal of such a section and is to be confined to the particular circumstances of the case in which the declaration is made. The situation appears to me to be somewhat analogous to a case where valid provincial legislation in an otherwise unoccupied field ceases to be operative by reason of conflicting federal legislation.

I think it is desirable at this stage to deal with the submission made on behalf of the appellant to the effect that the rights and freedoms recognized and declared by the *Bill of Rights* must have reference to *and be circumscribed by* the laws of Canada as they existed on the 10th of August, 1960, when the Bill was passed, which laws included s. 94 of the *Indian Act*. This submission is based in large measure on the following paragraph from the reasons for judgment of this Court in *Robertson and Rosetanni* v. *The Queen, supra*, where it said:

It is to be noted at the outset that the Canadian Bill of Rights *is not concerned with 'human rights and fundamental freedoms' in any abstract sense but rather with such rights and freedoms as existed in Canada immediately before the statute was enacted (see also s. 5(1)). It is therefore the "religious freedom" then existing in this country that is safeguarded by the provisions of s. 2 . . .*

What was at issue in that case was whether the *Lord's Day Act*, in providing that "it shall be unlawful for any person on the Lord's Day . . . to carry on or transact any business of his ordinary calling . . ." abrogated, abridged or infringed the right to "freedom of religion", and it was contended on behalf of the appellant that the phrase "freedom of religion" as used in the *Bill of Rights* meant "freedom to enjoy the freedom which my own religion allows without being confined by restrictions imposed by Parliament for the purpose of enforcing the tenets of a faith to which I do not subscribe." In considering this contention, it became necessary to examine the decided cases in order to determine what was the accepted meaning of "freedom of religion" as it existed in Canada immediately before the *Bill of Rights* was enacted and the last-quoted excerpt from the reasons for justment must, in my view, be read in this sense. This appears to me to be confirmed by the succeeding paragraph of these reasons where it is said:

It is accordingly of first importance to understand the concept of religious freedom which was recognized in this country before the enactment of the Bill of Rights *and after the enactment of the* Lord's Day Act *in its present form.*

If it had been accepted that the right to "freedom of religion" as declared in the *Bill of Rights* was circumscribed by the provisions of the Canadian statutes in force at the date of its enactment, there would have been no need, in determining the validity of the *Lord's Day Act* to consider the authorities in order to examine the situation in light of the concept of religious freedom which was recognized in Canada at the time of the enactment of the *Bill of Rights*. It would have been enough to say that "freedom of religion" as used in the Bill must mean freedom of religion subject to the provisions of the *Lord's Day Act*. This construction would, however, have run contrary to the provisions of s. 5(2) of the Bill which makes it applicable to every "Act of Parliament of Canada enacted before or after the coming into force of this Act."

In any event, it was not necessary to decide this question in *Robertson and Rosetanni* because it was found that the impugned provisions of the *Lord's Day Act* and the *Bill of Rights* were not in conflict, and I accordingly do not consider that case to be any authority for the suggestion that the *Bill of Rights* is to be treated as being subject to federal legislation existing at the time of its enactment, and more particularly I do not consider that the provisions of s. 1(b) of the *Bill of Rights* are to be treated as being in any way limited or affected by the terms of s. 94(b) of the *Indian Act*.

The right which is here at issue is "the right of the individual to equality before the law and the protection of the law". Mr. Justice Tysoe, who wrote the reasons for judgment on behalf of the majority of the Court of Appeal of British Columbia in the *Gonzales* case, *supra*, expressed the opinion that as these words occur in the *Bill of Rights* they mean

A right of every person to whom a particular law relates or extends, no matter what may be a person's race, national origin, colour, religion or sex, to stand on an equal footing with every other person to whom a particular law relates or extends and a right to the protection of the law.

(The italics are Mr. Justice Tysoe's.)

Like the members of the courts below, I cannot agree with this interpretation pursuant to which it seems to me that the most glaring discriminatory legislation against a racial group would have to be construed as recognizing the right of each of its individual members "to equality before the law", so long as all the other members are being discriminated against in the same way.

I think that the word "law" as used in s. 1(b) of the *Bill of Rights* is to be construed as meaning "the law of Canada" as defined in s. 5(2) (i.e. Acts of the Parliament of Canada and any orders, rules or regulations thereunder) and without attempting any exhaustive definition of "equality before the law" . I think that s. 1(b) means at least that no individual or group of individuals is to be treated more harshly than another under that law, and I am therefore of the opinion that an individual is denied equality before the law if it is made an offence punishable at law, on account of his race, for him to do something which his fellow Canadians are free to do without having committed any offence of having been made subject to any penalty.

It is only necessary for the purpose of deciding this case for me to say that in my opinion s. 94(b) of the *Indian Act* is a law of Canada which creates such an offence and that it can only be construed in such manner that its application would operate so as to abrogate, abridge or infringe one of the rights declared and recognized by the *Bill of Rights*. For the reasons which I have indicated, I am therefore of opinion that s. 94(b) is inoperative. . . .

260 - LEADING CONSTITUTIONAL DECISIONS

It may well be that the implementation of the *Canadian Bill of Rights* by the courts can give rise to great difficulties, but in my view full effect must be given to the terms of s. 2 thereof.

The present case discloses laws of Canada which abrogate, abridge and infringe the right of an individual Indian to equality before the law and in my opinion if those laws are to be applied in accordance with the express language used by Parliament in s. 2 of the *Bill of Rights*, then s. 94(*b*) of the *Indian Act* must be declared to be inoperative.

It appears to me to be desirable to make it plain that these reasons for judgment are limited to a situation in which, under the laws of Canada, it is made an offence punishable at law on account of race; for a person to do something which all Canadians who are not members of that race may do with impunity; in my opinion the same considerations do not by any means apply to all the provisions of the *Indian Act*.

HALL J.: I agree with the reasons of my brother Ritchie and wish only to add some observations regarding the decision in *Regina* v. *Gonzales* ((1962), 37 W.W.R. 257).

The concept that the Canadian Bill of Rights is operative in the face of a law of Canada only when that law does not give equality to all persons within the class to whom that particular law extends or relates, as it was expressed by Tysoe J.A. at p. 264:

Coming now to sec. 1(b) *of the* Canadian Bill of Rights. *The meaning of the word "equality" is well known. In my opinion, the word "before" in the expression "equality before the law," in the sense in which that expression is used in sec. 1*(b) *means "in the presence of." It seems to me this is the key to the correct interpretation of the expression and makes it clear that "equality before the law" has nothing to do with the application of the law equally to everyone and equal laws for everyone in the sense for which appellant's counsel contends, namely, the same laws for all persons, but to the position occupied by persons to whom a law relates or extends. They shall be entitled to have the law as it exists applied equally and without fear or favour to all persons to whom it relates or extends.*

is analogous to the position taken by the Supreme Court of the United States in *Plessy* v. *Ferguson* ((1896), 163 U.S. 537) and which was wholly rejected by the same Court in its historic desegregation judgment *Brown* v. *Board of Education* ((1953), 347 U.S. 483).

In *Plessy* v. *Ferguson*, the Court had held that under the "separate but equal" doctrine equality of treatment is accorded when the races are provided substantially equal facilities even though these facilities be separate. In *Brown* v. *Board of Education*, the Court held the "separate but equal" doctrine to be totally invalid.

The social situations in *Brown* v. *Board of Education* and in the instant case are, of course, very different, but the basic philosophic concept is the same. The Canadian Bill of Rights is not fulfilled if it merely equates Indians with Indians in terms of equality before the law, but can have validity and meaning only when subject to the single exception set out in s. 2 it is seen to repudiate discrimination in every law of Canada by reason of race, national origin, colour, religion or sex in respect of human rights and fundamental freedoms set out in s. 1 in whatever way that discrimination may manifest itself not only as between Indian and Indian but as between all Canadians whether Indian or non-Indian.

PIGEON J. (*dissenting*): . . . one must observe that the *Bill* itself begins by a solemn declaration by Parliament in the form of an enactment that, in Canada, the enumerated rights and freedoms "have existed and shall continue to exist . . .". This statement is the essential element of the very first provision of the *Bill* and it is absolutely unqualified. It is the starting point of that legislation and I have great difficulty in reconciling it with the contention that in fact those rights and freedoms were not wholly and completely existing but were restricted by any number of statutory and other provisions infringing thereon. . . .

In the instant case, the question whether all existing legislation should be considered as in accordance with the non-discrimination principle cannot fail to come immediately to mind seeing that it arises directly out of head 24 of s. 91 of the *B.N.A. Act* whereby Parliament has exclusive legislative authority over "Indians, and Lands reserved for Indians". As was pointed out by Riddell J. in *Rex* v. *Martin* ((1917), 29 C.C.C. 189 at 192), this provision confers legislative authority over the Indians *quâ* Indians and not otherwise. Its very object in so far as it relates to Indians, as opposed to Lands reserved for the Indians, is to enable the Parliament of Canada to make legislation applicable only to Indians as such and therefore not applicable to Canadian citizens generally. This legislative authority is obviously intended to be exercised over matters that are, as regards persons other than Indians, within the exclusive authority of the Provinces. Complete uniformity in provincial legislation is clearly not to be expected, not to mention the fact that further diversity must also result from special legislation for the territories. Equality before the law in the sense in which it was understood in the Courts below would require the Indians to be subject in every province to the same rules of law as all others in every particular not merely on the question of drunkenness. Outside the territories, provincial jurisdiction over education and health facilities would make it very difficult for federal authorities to provide such facilities to Indians without "discrimination" as understood in the Courts below.

If one of the effects of the *Canadian Bill of Rights* is to render inoperative all legal provisions whereby Indians as such are not dealt with in the same way as the general public, the conclusion is inescapable that Parliament, by the enactment of the Bill, has not only fundamentally altered the status of the Indians in that indirect fashion but has also made any future use of federal legislative authority over them subject to the requirement of expressly declaring every time "that the law shall operate notwithstanding the *Canadian Bill of Rights*". I find it very difficult to believe that Parliament so intended when enacting the *Bill*. If a virtual suppression of federal legislation over Indians as such was meant, one would have expected this important change to be made explicitly not surreptitiously so to speak.

In s. 2, the crucial words are that every law of Canada shall, subject to the exception just noted, "be so construed and applied as not to abrogate, abridge or infringe" any of the rights and freedoms recognized and declared in the *Bill*. The question is whether those words enact something more than a rule of construction. Of themselves, it seems to me that they do not. Certainly the word "construed" implies nothing else. Does the word "applied" express a different intention? I do not think so and, even if this may appear a trite saying, I must point out that what respondent asks the Court to do and what the Courts below have effectively done is not to apply the statute, the *Indian Act*, but to decline to apply it.

The strongest argument against viewing s. 2 as a canon of construction is undoubtedly that the exception "unless it is expressly declared by an Act of Parliament of Canada that it shall operate notwithstanding the *Canadian Bill of Rights*" is thereby deprived of any practical meaning. It cannot be denied that the operation of a rule of construction is not normally subject to such a qualification. On the contrary, that principle is that it has no effect against the clearly expressed will of Parliament in whatever form it is put.

On the other hand, in seeking to give effect to some words

in s. 2 that cannot for obvious reasons be applicable to any existing law, one must always bear in mind the very starting point of the *Bill*, namely that the rights and freedoms therein recognized are declared as existing, not as being introduced or expanded. If in s. 1 the act means what it says and recognizes and declares *existing* rights and freedoms only, nothing more than proper construction of existing laws in accordance with the *Bill* is required to accomplish the intended result. There can never be any necessity for declaring any of them inoperative as coming in conflict with the rights and freedoms defined in the *Bill* seeing that these are declared as existing in them. Thus, it appears to me that s. 1 cannot be construed as suggested by respondent without coming in conflict with s. 1.

If, with respect to existing legislation, we had to choose between reading s. 1 as written and failing to adopt a construction of s. 2 that gives some meaningful effect to the exception, it seems to me that the choice should be in favour of giving paramount effect to s. 1. It is the provision establishing the principle on which the whole act rests.

Another compelling reason is the presumption against implicit alteration of the law, Parliament must not be presumed to have intended to depart from the existing law any further than expressly stated (*Maxwell, On Interpretation of Statutes*, 9th ed., p. 84, cited in *Duchesneau* v. *Cook* ([1955] S.C.R. 207 at 215). . . .

The meaning of such expressions as "due process of law", "equality before the law", "freedom of religion", "freedom of speech", is in truth largely unlimited and undefined. According to individual views and the evolution of current ideas, the actual content of such legal concepts is apt to expand and to vary as is strikingly apparent in other countries. In the traditional British system that is our own by virtue of the *B.N.A. Act*, the responsibility for updating the statutes in this changing world rests exclusively upon Parliament. If the Parliament of Canada intended to depart from that principle in enacting the *Bill*, one would expect to find clear language expressing that intention. On the contrary, what do we find in s. 1 but an apparent desire to adhere to the traditional principle and to avoid the uncertainties inherent in broadly worded enactments by tying the broad words to the large body of existing law and in effect declaring the recognized human rights and fundamental freedoms to be as existing in the laws of Canada.

~ Justice Abbott also wrote a short dissenting opinion. ~

27. Attorney-General for Nova Scotia *v.*
Attorney-General for Canada
(Nova Scotia Interdelegation Case), *1951*

~ Since the 1930's the federal and provincial governments had been seeking methods of legislative co-operation which would enable them together to act effectively in fields where, largely as a result of judicial review, neither level of government could legislate adequately alone. One of the devices most often canvassed was the delegation of legislative power either by the Dominion to a province or by a province to the Dominion. This device had been recommended by the Rowell-Sirois Royal Commission on Dominion-Provincial Relations as a way of overcoming the rigidities which the division of powers imposed on some important areas of policy-making. Because of doubts as to whether it was constitutionally valid for the federal Parliament and the provincial legislatures to transfer legislative functions to one another the Royal Commission called for a constitutional amendment to establish such a power of delegation.

It was precisely this technique of voluntary interdelegation which was embodied in the Nova Scotia statute challenged before the Supreme Court in this case. This Bill would have authorized the provincial government to delegate to the federal Parliament the power to legislate with respect to employment in areas under provincial jurisdiction. It also anticipated the Nova Scotia Legislature receiving from the national Parliament the power to make laws in relation to employment in industries under federal jurisdiction as well as legislative authority in the indirect tax field. Before proceeding with its enactment the government of Nova Scotia first submitted the question of the constitutional validity of this delegation procedure to the Supreme Court of Nova Scotia. A majority of that Court ruled that it was unconstitutional for either Parliament or the legislatures to employ the delegation device contemplated in the Nova Scotia legislation.

The appeal from this judgment was dismissed by the Supreme Court of Canada in a unanimous decision. The various members of the Court who wrote opinions insisted upon a fundamental distinction between delegations of power by Parliament or the legislatures to subordinate agencies, and delegations of power from one legislative level to the other. There was ample authority to justify the former type of delegation but the latter was, in their view, clearly unconstitutional. Interdelegation between the national and provincial legislatures would have the effect of altering the basic scheme of Canadian federalism and neither Parliament nor the legislatures were authorized by the B.N.A. Act to make what in the Court's opinion would be tantamount to *ad hoc* amendments to the division of legislative powers. In reaching this conclusion the Supreme Court pledged its allegiance to the water-tight compartments approach to the division of powers: Sections 91 and 92 established an unbreachable barrier between the powers assigned *exclusively* to each level of government.

Although the Supreme Court's decision in this case put the interdelegation of power between Parliament and the provincial legislatures beyond the pale of the Constitution it left intact other possibe forms of legislative collaboration. Referential and conditional legislation are two such techniques which have been frequently employed in the past and which, in principle, were not affected by this case. In referential legislation either Parliament or a provincial legislature referentially incorporates in a statute the valid enactments of the other; in conditional legislation a legislature make the carrying out of the policy stated in a statute conditional upon the act of another governmental agency. But an additional and far more useful avenue for the advancement of co-operative federalism was to be opened up by the Supreme Court two years after this case in the Willis[1] case. ~

ATTORNEY-GENERAL FOR NOVA SCOTIA
v. ATTORNEY-GENERAL FOR CANADA
In the Supreme Court of Canada. [1951] S.C.R. 31.

RINFRET C.J.: This is a reference by the Lieutenant-Governor in Council of the Province of Nova Scotia, submitting to the Supreme Court of that Province the question of the constitu-

[1] *P.E.I. Potato Marketing Board* v. *H. B. Willis Inc.*, [1952] 2 S.C.R. 392. See below pp. 223-29.

tional validity of a Bill, Number 136, entitled "An Act respecting the delegation of jurisdiction from the Parliament of Canada to the Legislature of Nova Scotia and *vice versa*."

By virtue of this Bill, if it should come into force, by proclamation, as therein provided, the Lieutenant-Governor in Council, may from time to time delegate to and withdraw from the Parliament of Canada authority to make laws in relation to any matter relating to employment in any industry, work or undertaking in respect of which such matter is, by section 92 of The British North America Act, 1867, exclusively within the jurisdiction of the Legislature of Nova Scotia. It provides that any laws so made by the Parliament of Canada shall, while such delegation is in force, have the same effect as if enacted by the Legislature.

The Bill also provides that if and when the Parliament of Canada shall have delegated to the Legislature of the Province of Nova Scotia authority to make laws in relation to any matter relating to employment in any industry, work or undertaking in respect of which such matter is, under the provisions of The British North America Act, 1867, exclusively within the legislative jurisdiction of such Parliament, the Lieutenant-Governor in Council, while such delegation is in force, may, by proclamation, from time to time apply any or all of the provisions of any Act in relation to a matter relating to employment in force in the Province of Nova Scotia to any such industry, work, or undertaking.

Finally, the Bill enacts that if and when the Parliament of Canada shall have delegated to the Legislature of the Province of Nova Scotia authority to make laws in relation to the raising of a revenue for provincial purposes by the imposing of a retail sales tax of the nature of indirect taxation, the Lieutenant-Governor in Council, while such delegation is in force, may impose such a tax of such amount not exceeding 3 per cent of the retail price as he deems necessary, in respect of any commodity to which such delegation extends and may make regulations providing for the method of collecting any such tax.

The provisions of the Bill, therefore, deal with employment in industries, works, or undertakings, exclusively within the legislative jurisdiction in the one case of the Legislature of the Province of Nova Scotia and in the other case within the exclusive legislative jurisdiction of the Parliament of Canada, and it also deals with the raising of revenue for provincial purposes by means of indirect taxation.

In each of the supposed cases either the Parliament of

Canada, or the Legislature of Nova Scotia, would be adopting legislation concerning matters which have not been attributed to it but to the other by the constitution of the country.

The Supreme Court of Nova Scotia *en banc*, to which the matter was submitted, answered that such legislation was not within the competence of the Legislature of Nova Scotia, except that Doull J. dissented and expressed the opinion that the Bill was constitutionally valid, subject to the limitations stated in his answers. I agree with the answers given by the majority of the Judges in the Supreme Court *en banc*.

The Parliament of Canada and the Legislatures of the several Provinces are sovereign within their sphere defined by The British North America Act, but none of them has the unlimited capacity of an individual. They can exercise only the legislative powers respectively given to them by sections 91 and 92 of the Act, and these powers must be found in either of these sections.

The constitution of Canada does not belong either to Parliament, or to the Legislatures; it belongs to the country and it is there that the citizens of the country will find the protection of the rights to which they are entitled. It is part of the protection that Parliament can legislate only on the subject matters referred to it by section 91 and that each Province can legislate exclusively on the subject matters referred to it by section 92. The country is entitled to insist that legislation adopted under section 91 should be passed exclusively by the Parliament of Canada in the same way as the people of each Province are entitled to insist that legislation concerning the matters enumerated in section 92 should come exclusively from their respective Legislatures. In each case the Members elected to Parliament or to the Legislatures are the only ones entrusted with the power and the duty to legislate concerning the subjects exclusively distributed by the constitutional Act to each of them.

No power of delegation is expressed either in section 91 or in section 92, nor, indeed, is there to be found the power of accepting delegation from one body to the other; and I have no doubt that if it had been the intention to give such powers it would have been expressed in clear and unequivocal language. Under the scheme of the British North America Act there were to be, in the words of Lord Atkin in *The Labour Conventions Reference* ([1937] A.C. 326), "water-tight compartments which are an essential part of the original structure."

Neither legislative bodies, federal or provincial, possess any portion of the powers respectively vested in the other and they cannot receive it by delegation. In that connection the word "exclusively" used both in section 91 and in section 92 indicates a settled line of demarcation and it does not belong to either Parliament, or the Legislatures, to confer powers upon the other. . . .

TASCHEREAU J.: These questions, although limited to indirect taxation and to laws in relation to employment matters, cover a much wider field. For if it is within the powers of Parliament and of the Legislatures to confer upon each other by consent, a legislative authority which they do not otherwise possess, to deal with the subject matters found in the questions submitted, the same powers would naturally exist to enact laws affecting all the classes of subjects enumerated in Section 91 and 92 of the B.N.A. Act. I may say at the outset that I am of the opinion that the conclusion arrived at by the Supreme Court of Nova Scotia is right.

The British North America Act, 1867, and amendments has defined the powers that are to be exercised by the Dominion Parliament and by the Legislatures of the various provinces. There are fields where the Dominion has exclusive jurisdiction, while others are reserved to the provinces. This division of powers has received the sanction of the Imperial Parliament, which was then and is still the sole competent authority to make any alterations to its own laws. If Bill 136 were *intra vires*, the Dominion Parliament could delegate its powers to any or all the provinces, to legislate on commerce, banking, bankruptcy, militia and defence, issue of paper money, patents, copyrights, indirect taxation, and all other matters enumerated in Section 91; and on the other hand, the Legislatures could authorize the Dominion to pass laws in relation to property and civil rights, municipal institutions, education, etc. etc., all matters outside the jurisdiction reserved to the Dominion Parliament. The powers of Parliament and of the Legislatures strictly limited by the B.N.A. Act, would thus be considerably enlarged, and I have no doubt that this cannot be done, even with the joint consent of Parliament and of the Legislatures.

It is a well settled proposition of law that jurisdiction cannot be conferred by consent. None of these bodies can be vested directly or indirectly with powers which have been denied them by the B.N.A. Act, and which therefore are not within their constitutional jurisdiction.

This question has often been the subject of comments by eminent text writers, and has also been definitely settled by numerous authoritative judicial pronouncements.

Lefroy's *Canada's Federal System* (1913 at p. 70) cites the words of Lord Watson on the argument in *C.P.R.* v. *Bonsecours* ([1899] A.C. 367):

> *The Dominion cannot give jurisdiction, or leave jurisdiction, with the province. The provincial parliament cannot give legislative jurisdiction to the Dominion parliament. If they have it, either one or the other of them, they have it by virtue of the Act of 1867. I think we must get rid of the idea that either one or the other can enlarge the jurisdiction of the other or surrender jurisdiction. . . .*

. . . Lefroy in *Legislative Power in Canada* at page 242, expresses the view with which I agree, that the Federal Parliament cannot amend the British North America Act, nor either expressly or impliedly take away from, or give to, the provincial Legislatures a power which the Imperial Act does, or does not give them; and he adds that the same is the case, *mutatis mutandis*, with the Provincial Legislatures. At page 689, the same author adds that within the area and limits of subjects mentioned in Section 92 of the British North American Act, the provincial Legislatures are supreme and have the same authority as the Imperial Parliament or the Dominion would have under like circumstances, to confide to a municipal institution or body of its own creation, authority to make by-laws or regulations as to subjects specified in the enactment and with the object of carrying the enactment into operation and effect. This proposition rests upon the language and decision of the Judicial Committee of the Privy Council in *Hodge* v. *The Queen* (9 App. Cas. 117).

It will be seen therefore that as a result of all these authorities and pronouncements, Parliament or the Legislatures may delegate in certain cases their powers to subordinate agencies, but that it has never been held that the Parliament of Canada or any of the Legislatures can abdicate their powers and invest for the purpose of legislation, bodies which by the very terms of the B.N.A. Act are not empowered to accept such delegation, and to legislate on such matters.

It has been further argued that as a result of the delegation made by the Federal government to the Provinces, the laws enacted by the Provinces as delegates would be federal laws and that they would, therefore, be constitutionally valid. With this proposition I cannot agree. These laws would not then be enacted "with the advice and consent of the Senate and House of Commons," and would not be assented to by the Governor-General, but by the Lieutenant-Governor, who has no power to do so. Moreover, as already stated, such a right has been denied the Provinces by the B.N.A. Act.

If the proposed legislation were held to be valid, the whole scheme of the Canadian Constitution would be entirely defeated. The framers of the B.N.A. Act thought wisely that Canada should not be a unitary state, but it would be converted into one, as Mr. Justice Hall says, if all the Provinces empowered Parliament to make laws with respect to *all matters* exclusively assigned to them. Moreover, it is clear that the delegation of legislative powers by Parliament to the ten Provinces on matters enumerated in Section 91 of the B.N.A. Act could bring about different criminal laws, different banking and bankruptcy laws, different military laws, different postal laws, different currency laws, all subjects in relation to which it has been thought imperative that uniformity should prevail throughout Canada.

For the above reasons, I have come to the conclusion that this appeal should be dismissed.

~ Justices Kerwin, Rand, Kellock, Estey, and Fauteux all wrote opinions holding that Bill No. 136 was unconstitutional. ~

28. P.E.I. Potato Marketing Board v. H. B. Willis Inc., *1952*

~ In this case the Supreme Court was asked to determine the constitutional validity of a slightly modified version of the delegation device which the Court had ruled unconstitutional in the *Nova Scotia Interdelegation* case. Here it was a question of whether the federal Parliament could validly delegate legislative powers not to a provincial legislature but to an administrative board created by a provincial legislature. This question arose out of another joint effort by the legislature of a province and the Dominion to arm a single provincial marketing board with the power of regulating both intra-provincial and extra-provincial aspects of trade in natural produce. The Prince Edward Island Legislature had passed the Agricultural Products Marketing Act in 1940 authorizing the Lieutenant-Governor in Council to establish a board for regulating various aspects of trade in natural products within the province. The Act also provided that such a board could, with the approval of the Lieutenant-Governor in Council, perform any functions delegated to it by the Dominion. In September, 1950, the government of P.E.I., exercising its power under this Act, established a Potato Marketing Board to administer a scheme for regulating local trade in potatoes. Meanwhile, at the federal level, Parliament had enacted in 1949 the Agricultural Products Marketing Act, the crucial section of which authorized the Governor in Council to delegate the Dominion's jurisdiction over interprovincial and export trade to a provincial board. Following this, the federal government by order in council in October, 1950, delegated to the P.E.I. Potato Marketing Board the power to regulate the extra-provincial marketing of potatoes from the province.

The validity of this device of Dominion delegation to a provincial board was first challenged successfully before the Supreme Court of Prince Edward Island. The provincial Supreme Court simply followed the Supreme Court of Canada's earlier decision in the *Nova Scotia Interdelegation* case and reasoned that if the B.N.A. Act prohibited Parliament from delegating legislative power to a provincial legislature it must also prohibit Parliament from delegating power to a creature of such a legislature. But the federal Supreme Court was able to find a distinction of kind between the type of delegation at issue in this case and that which it had found invalid the year before. Delegation from Parliament to a provincial board did not, apparently, involve a transfer of power across the sacrosanct wall dividing provincial from federal powers. A provincial board, although it might be a thoroughly subordinate offspring of a provincial legislature could still exist, at least in thought, as an autonomous unit entirely distinct from the provincial legislature which created it. Justice Rand rationalized this point of view by suggesting that it could be regarded as simply a coincidence that both the Dominion and a province had decided to bestow their regulatory powers on the same group of men.

Devious as the Court's logic in this case might seem, its decision to uphold this form of delegation did, in large measure, reverse the consequences of its earlier decision. The power which Parliament could not delegate directly to a provincial legislature could be indirectly delegated to an agency established by such a legislature.

The first application of this valid form of delegation had the ironical purpose of reversing the Privy Council's last decision on the B.N.A. Act – a decision which had had an expansionary effect on the Dominion's powers. In the *Winner*[1] case the Privy Council had ruled that an interprovincial bus line, even though one phase of its operation was completed entirely within a province, was, for purposes of licensing regulations, entirely within the jurisdiction of the federal Parliament. Shortly after this decision was brought down, the Dominion agreed to enact legislation which would return to the individual provincial transport boards the power of licensing interprovincial carriers. Thus while the type of delegation validated in the *Willis* case might facilitate greater decentralization in the operation of Canadian federalism, it is doubtful whether it could work in the opposite direction to promote greater administrative uniformity or simplification. On this point it must be noted that the Supreme Court in the *Willis* case declined to determine whether the indirect delegation procedure could be validly reversed and the provinces delegate regulatory powers to federal agencies.

In 1968 the Supreme Court by a 5 to 2 majority turned back a challenge to the federal Motor Transport Vehicle Act which delegated regulatory power over extra-provincial carriers

[1] *A.-G. Ont.* v. *Winner* [1954] A.C. 541.

to provincial boards.[2] The legislation challenged in this case went even further than that at issue in the *Willis* case towards a delegation of legislative power from federal to provincial authorities. Here Parliament had delegated authority directly to the provincial boards, authorizing them to apply to extra-provincial carriers not simply existing provincial licensing regulations but also any subsequent changes provincial legislatures might make in provincial regulations. By validating this form of delegation the Supreme Court further reduced the impact of the *Nova Scotia Interdelegation* case and by the same token increased the opportunities for a more flexible working of the Canadian federal system. ～

P.E.I. POTATO MARKETING BOARD
v. H. B. WILLIS INC.
In the Supreme Court of Canada. [*1952*] *2 S.C.R. 392.*

RINFRET C.J.: In my opinion the appeal of the Prince Edward Island Potato Marketing Board should be upheld.

The judgment of the Supreme Court of Prince Edward Island *in banco* was delivered on the 31st of January, 1952. The Lieutenant-Governor in Council had referred to that Court for hearing and consideration the following questions:

(1) Is it within the jurisdiction and competence of the Parliament of Canada to enact The Agricultural Products Marketing Act, (1949) 13 George VI, (1st Session) c. 16?

(2) If the answer to question No. 1 is yes, is it within the jurisdiction and competence of the Governor-General in Council to pass P.C. 5159?

(3) Is it within the jurisdiction and competence of the Lieutenant-Governor in Council to establish the said Scheme and in particular s. 16 thereof?

(4) Is it within the jurisdiction and competence of the Prince Edward Island Potato Marketing Board to make the Orders made under the said Scheme or any of the Orders so made?

Tweedy J. wrote the main judgment, in which the Chief Justice and MacGuigan J. concurred, the Chief Justice simply adding a few additional reasons.

[2] *Coughlin* v. *Ontario Highway Transport Board et al.* [1968] S.C.R. 569.

The main ground of the judgment of Tweedy J. appears to have been that the Supreme Court of Canada in *A.-G. of N.S.* v. *A.-G. of Can.* ([1951] S.C.R. 31) which held that the Parliament of Canada and each provincial legislature were not capable of delegating one to the other the powers with which it had been vested, nor of receiving from the other the powers with which the other has been vested. In the opinion of the Supreme Court *in banco* of Prince Edward Island that judgment was really decisive with respect to the first two questions in the reference under appeal.

With deference, such is not the effect of the judgment of this Court in the Nova Scotia reference. It was made quite clear in our reasons for judgment that they only applied to the questions as put and which had to deal only with an Act respecting the delegation from Parliament of Canada to the Legislature of Nova Scotia and *vice versa*. The unanimous opinion of this Court was that each legislature could only exercise the legislative powers respectively given to them by ss. 91 and 92 of the Act, that these sections indicated a settled line of demarcation and it did not belong to the Parliament of Canada or the Legislatures to confer their powers upon the other. At the same time it was pointed out that *In re Gray* ((1918) 57 Can. S.C.R. 150) and *The Chemical Reference* ([1943] S.C.R. 1), the delegations there dealt with were delegations to a body subordinate to Parliament and were, therefore, of a character different from the delegation meant by the Bill submitted to the Court in the Nova Scotia reference.

But, on the other hand, the delegations passed upon by this Court *In re Gray* and *The Chemical Reference* were along the same lines as those with which we are concerned in the present appeal. It follows that our judgment in the Nova Scotia reference can be no authority for the decision which we have to give in the present instance. It may be added that at bar counsel did not rely upon that ground in this Court.

The first question submitted to the Supreme Court *in banco* of Prince Edward Island had to do with the jurisdiction and competence of the Parliament of Canada to enact The Agricultural Products Marketing Act (1949), 13 George VI, (1st Session) c. 16. That Act was assented to on the 30th of April, 1949. The preamble, among other things, stated that it was "desirable to co-operate with the provinces and to enact a measure respecting the marketing of agricultural products in interprovincial and export trade." S. (2) of the Act reads as follows:

2. *(1) The Governor in Council may by order grant author-*
ity to any board or agency authorized under the law of any
province to exercise powers of regulation in relation to the
marketing of any agricultural product locally within the prov-
ince, to regulate the marketing of such agricultural product
outside the province in interprovincial and export trade and for
such purposes to exercise all or any powers like the powers
exercisable by such board or agency in relation to the marketing
of such agricultural product locally within the province.

(2) The Governor in Council may by order revoke any
authority granted under subsection one.

The effect of that enactment is for the Governor in Council
to adopt as its own a board, or agency already authorized under
the law of a province, to exercise powers of regulation outside
the province in interprovincial and export trade, and for such
purposes to exercise all or any powers exercisable by such board,
or agency, in relation to the marketing of such agricultural
products locally within the province. I cannot see any objection
to federal legislation of this nature. Ever since *Valin* v. *Langlois*
((1879) 5 App. Cas. 115), when the Privy Council refused leave
to appeal from the decision of this Court ((1879) 3 Can. S.C.R.
1), the principle has been consistently admitted that it was
competent for Parliament to "employ its own executive officers
for the purpose of carrying out legislation which is within its
constitutional authority, as it does regularly in the case of
revenue officials and other matters which need not be enumerated." The latter are the words of Lord Atkin, who delivered
the judgment of the Judicial Committee in *Proprietary Articles*
Trade Association et al v. *A.-G. for Canada et al* ([1931] A.C.
310).

In The Agricultural Products Marketing Act of 1949 that is
precisely what Parliament has done. Parliament has granted
authority to the Governor in Council to employ as its own a
board, or agency, for the purpose of carrying out its own
legislation for the marketing of agricultural products outside
the province in interprovincial and export trade, two subject-
matters which are undoubtedly within its constitutional authority. Moreover, it may be added, that in doing so Parliament was
following the advice of the Judicial Committee in the several
judgments which it rendered on similar Acts and, more particularly, on the Reference concerning the Natural Products Marketing Act ([1937] 1 D.L.R. 691), adopted by Parliament in
1934 (S. of C. 24 and 25 George V, c. 57), (1937), that the

proper way to carry out legislation of that character in Canada, in view of the distribution of legislative powers under the British North America Act, was for Parliament and the Legislatures to act by co-operation.

I would, therefore, answer question (1) in the affirmative. . . .

RAND J.: The validity of the provincial legislation generally was not impugned since its provisions are virtually identical with those of the Act of British Columbia which was approved by the Judicial Committee in *Shannon* v. *Lower Mainland Dairy Products Board* ([1938] A.C. 708). The Committee there construed the Act as a whole to be limited to transactions strictly within the field of local or provincial trade. The administration of the Act so circumscribed, apart from co-operative Dominion legislation, may encounter serious practical difficulties if not insuperable obstacles; but that cannot affect its constitutional validity nor its administration conjointly with Dominion powers.

The principal point of attack was the efficacy of the Dominion delegation. Mr. Farris argued that the province was incompetent to confer on the Board capacity to accept such powers from the Governor in Council. This question was not involved in Shannon, *supra*, as the administration there was provincial only and s. 7 of the Act was not expressly considered. The Potato Board is not, under the statute, a corporation, and the contention is this: the power to create such an entity and to clothe it with jural attributes and capacities is derived from head 13 of s. 92 of the Act of 1867 which deals with property and civil rights within the province; as the incorporation of companies under head 11 has its source in the prerogative, a body so created may have unlimited "capacities"; the prerogative is not drawn on for a body created under any other head than 11; a board created as here can have, then, only a capacity in relation to local law. From this it follows that the purported grant of authority from the Dominion in inoperative.

The central feature of this argument is the notion of the creation of an "entity." That a group of human beings acting jointly in a certain manner, with certain scope and authority and for certain objects, can be conceived as an entirety, different from that of the sum of the individuals and their actions in severalty, is undoubted; and it is the joint action so conceived that is primarily the external counterpart of the mental concept.

But to imagine that total counterpart as an organic creation fashioned after the nature of a human being with faculties called "capacities" and to pursue a development of it logically, can lead us into absurdities. We might just as logically conceive it as a split personality with co-ordinate creators investing it with two orders of capacities. These metaphors and symbolisms are convenient devices to enable us to aggregate incidents or characteristics but carried too far they may threaten common sense.

What the law in this case has done has been to give legal significance called incidents to certain group actions of five men. That to the same men, acting in the same formality, another co-ordinate jurisdiction in a federal constitution cannot give other legal incidents to other joint actions is negated by the admission that the Dominion by appropriate words could create a similar board, composed of the same persons, bearing the same name, and with a similar formal organization, to execute the same Dominion functions. Twin phantoms of this nature must, for practical purposes, give way to realistic necessities. As related to courts, the matter was disposed of in *Valin* v. *Langlois*. No question of disruption of constitutive provincial, features or frustration of provincial powers arises: both legislatures have recognized the value of a single body to carry out one joint, though limited, administration of trade. At any time the Province could withdraw the whole or any part of its authority. The delegation was, then, effective. . . .

~ Justice Kerwin (Justice Fauteux concurring), Justices Taschereau, Kellock (Justice Locke concurring) and Justice Estey (Justice Cartwright concurring) all wrote opinions in which they held that The Agricultural Products Marketing Act, 1949, was *intra vires*. The answers to the other questions in the reference are not included here as they were not directly concerned with the constitutional question of delegation. ~

SUGGESTIONS FOR
FURTHER READING

General:

LASKIN, BORA. *Canadian Constitutional Law.* Toronto: Carswell, 1960.

LEDERMAN, W. R. (ed.) *The Courts and the Canadian Constitution.* The Carleton Library, McClelland and Stewart Limited, 1964.

LYON, NOEL J. and ATKEY, RONALD G. (eds.) *Canadian Constitutional Law in a Modern Perspective.* Toronto: University of Toronto Press, 1970.

MCWHINNEY, EDWARD. *Judicial Review in the English-Speaking World.* Toronto: University of Toronto Press, 1960.

QUEBEC. *Royal Commission of Inquiry on Constitutional Problems, 1956.* Report. Volume II, Fourth Part: "Federalism." Quebec, 1956.

✔ THE SENATE OF CANADA. *Report to the Honourable the Speaker Relating to the Enactment of the B.N.A. Act, 1867.* (O'Connor Report) Ottawa: Queen's Printer, 1939.

STRAYER, B. L. *Judicial Review of Legislation in Canada.* Toronto: University of Toronto Press, 1968.

*The Role of Judicial Review in Federal Politics
and Government:*

CREPEAU, P.-A. and MACPHERSON, C. B. (eds.) *The Future of Canadian Federalism.* Toronto: University of Toronto Press, 1965.

FREUND, PAUL A. "A Supreme Court in a Federation: Some Lessons from Legal History." (1953) 53 *Columbia Law Review,* 597.

————. "Umpiring the Federal System," in A. W. MacMahon, (ed.), *Federalism: Mature and Emergent.* New York: Russell & Russell, 1962.

MACDONALD, V. C. "The Constitution in a Changing World," (1948) 26 *Canadian Bar Review,* 22.

MACKINNON, VICTOR S. *Comparative Federalism.* The Hague: Martinus Nyhoff, 1964.

MALLORY, J. R. *Social Credit and The Federal Power in Canada.* Toronto: University of Toronto Press, 1954 (Esp. Chs. III and X).

————. "The Courts and The Sovereignty of The Canadian Parliament," (1944) 10 *Canadian Journal of Economics and Political Science,* 165.

MCWHINNEY, EDWARD. *Comparative Federalism.* Toronto: University of Toronto Press, 1962.

PELTASON, J. W. *Federal Courts in the Political Process.* New York: Doubleday & Co., 1955.

The Judicial Committee of the Privy Council:

BROWNE, G. P. *The Judicial Committee and the British North America Act.* Toronto: University of Toronto Press, 1967.

CANNON, L. A. "Leave to Appeal," (1925) 3 *Canadian Bar Review,* 473.

————. "Some Data Relating to Appeals to The Privy Council: (1925) 3 *Canadian Bar Review,* 455.

HALDANE, VISCOUNT. "The Work for the Empire of the Judicial Committee of the Privy Council," (1922) 1 *Cambridge Law Journal,* 143.

HUGHES, HECTOR. *National Sovereignty and Judicial Antonomy in the British Commonwealth of Nations.* London: King, 1931.

JENNINGS, W. IVOR, "Constitutional Interpretation – The Experience of Canada," (1937) 51 *Harvard Law Review,* 1.

KEITH, A. B. *Responsible Government in the Dominions.* Oxford: Clarendon Press, 1928. Volume II, 1087-1109.

The Supreme Court of Canada:

LASKIN, BORA. "The Supreme Court of Canada; a Final Court of Appeal of and for Canadians," (1951) 29 *Canadian Bar Review,* 1038. Also in W. R. LEDERMAN (ed.), *The Courts and the Canadian Constitution.*

MACKINNON, FRANK. "The Establishment of the Supreme Court of Canada," (1946) 26 *Canadian Historical Review*, 258. Also in W. R. LEDERMAN (ed.), *The Courts and the Canadian Constitution*.

MORIN, JACQUES-YVAN. "A Constitutional Court for Canada," (1965) 43 *Canadian Bar Review*, 545.

OSGOODE HALL LAW JOURNAL. "Supreme Court Review," (1964) Volume 3.

RUSSELL, PETER H. *The Supreme Court of Canada as a Bilingual and Bicultural Institution*. Ottawa: Queen's Printer, 1969.

SANDWELL, B. K. "The Supreme Court and the Constitution," *Saturday Night,* August 23, 1952.

UNDERHILL, FRANK H. "Edward Blake, The Supreme Court Act and the Appeal to the Privy Council, 1875-76," (1938) 19 *Canadian Historical Review*, 245.

Trends in Judicial Review:

FLETCHER, MARTHA. "Judicial Review and the Division of Powers," in J. PETER MEEKISON (ed.), *Canadian Federalism: Myth or Reality*. Toronto: Methuen, 1968.

FOUTS, DONALD F. "Policy-Making in the Supreme Court of Canada, 1950-1960" in GLENDON SCHUBERT and DAVID J. DANELSKI (eds.), *Comparative Judicial Behaviour*. Oxford University Press, 1969.

MACDONALD, V. C. "The Privy Council and The Canadian Constitution," (1951) 29 *Canadian Bar Review*, 1024.

MCCONNELL, W. H. "The Judicial Review of Prime Minister Bennett's 'New Deal'," (1968) 6 *Osgoode Hall Law Journal*, 39.

PECK, SIDNEY R. "A Scalogram Analysis of the Supreme Court of Canada, 1958-1967," in GLENDON SCHUBERT and DAVID J. DANELSKI (eds.), *Comparative Judicial Behaviour*. Oxford University Press, 1969.

PIGEON, LOUIS-PHILIPPE. "The Meaning of Provincial Autonomy," (1951) 29 *Canadian Bar Review*, 1135. Also in W. R. LEDERMAN (ed.) *The Courts and the Canadian Constitution*.

RUSSELL, P. H. "The Supreme Court's Interpretation of the Constitution Since 1949," in PAUL FOX (ed.), *Politics: Canada*. McGraw-Hill of Canada, 1962.

SCOTT, F. R. "The Consequences of the Privy Council Decisions," (1937) 15 *Canadian Bar Review*, 485.

————. "Centralization and Decentralization in Canadian Federation," (1951) 29 *Canadian Bar Review*, 1095.

Problems and Procedures of Constitutional Interpretation:

GRANT, J. A. C. "Judicial Review in Canada: Procedural Aspects," (1964) 42 *Canadian Bar Review*, 195.

JOANES, A. "Stare Decisis in the Supreme Court of Canada," (1958) 35 *Canadian Bar Review*, 175.

LABRIE, F. E. "Canadian Constitutional Interpretation and Legislative Review," (1949-50) 8 *University of Toronto Law Journal*, 298.

LASKIN, BORA. "Tests for the Validity of Legislation: What Is The Matter?", (1955-56) 11 *University of Toronto Law Journal*, 14.

LEDERMAN, W. R. "The Concurrent Operation of Federal and Provincial Law in Canada," (1963) 9 *McGill Law Journal*, 155. Also in W. R. LEDERMAN (ed.), *The Courts and the Canadian Constitution*.

MUNDELL, D. W. "Tests for the Validity of Legislation Under the B.N.A. Act" (1954) 32 *Canadian Bar Review*, 813.

————. "A Reply to Professor Laskin," (1955) 33 *Canadian Bar Review*, 915.

RUBIN, G. "The Nature, Use and Effect of Reference Cases in Canadian Constitutional Law," (1959-60) 6 *McGill Law Journal*, 168. Also in W. R. LEDERMAN (ed.), *The Courts and the Canadian Constitution*.

Peace, Order and Good Government:

KENNEDY, W. P. M. "Interpretation of the British North America Act," (1943) 8 *Cambridge Law Journal*, 146.

LASKIN, BORA. "Peace, Order and Good Government Reexamined." (1947) 25 *Canadian Bar Review*, 1054. Also in W.

R. LEDERMAN (ed.), *The Courts and the Canadian Constitution.*

RICHARD, E. R. "Peace, Order and Good Government," (1940) 18 *Canadian Bar Review*, 243.

Trade and Commerce:

BALLEM, J. B. "The Trade and Commerce Power – Sleeping Giant or Empty Facade?", (1956) 34 *Canadian Bar Review*, 482.

DEXTER, GRANT. "Commerce and The Canadian Constitution," (1932) 33 *Queen's Quarterly*, 250.

SMITH, ALEXANDER. *The Commerce Power in Canada and the United States.* Toronto: Butterworth & Co. (Canada) Limited, 1963.

Treaty Implementation:

HEAD, IVAN L. "The Canadian Offshore Mineral Rights Reference: The Application of International Law to a Federal Constitution," (1968) 18 *University of Toronto Law Journal*, 131.

HENDRY, J. M. *Treaties and Federal Constitutions.* Washington: Public Affairs Press, 1955.

LEDERMAN, W. R. "Legislative Power to Implement Treaty Obligations in Canada," in J. H. AITCHISON (ed.), *The Political Process in Canada.* Toronto: University of Toronto Press, 1963.

SOWARD, F. H. "External Affairs and Canadian Federalism," in A. R. M. LOWER, F. R. SCOTT, *et al.*, *Evolving Canadian Federalism.* Durham, N.C.: Duke University Press, 1958.

Taxation:

MACDONALD, V. C. "Taxation Powers in Canada," (1939) 19 *Canadian Bar Review*, 79.

PERRY, J. H. *Taxation in Canada.* Toronto: University of Toronto Press, 1953. (Ch. 8.)

SCOTT, F. R. "The Constitutional Background of Taxation Agreements," (1955) 2 *McGill Law Journal*, 1.

Civil Liberties:

CAVALLUZZO, PAUL. "Judicial Review and the Bill of Rights: Drybones and Its Aftermath," (1971) 9 *Osgoode Hall Law Journal*, 511.

LASKIN, BORA. "Our Civil Liberties – The Role of the Supreme Court," (1955) 41 *Queen's Quarterly*, 455.

————. "An Inquiry into the Diefenbaker Bill of Rights (1959) 37 *Canadian Bar Review*, 77.

SCHMEISER, D. A. *Civil Liberties in Canada*. Oxford University Press, 1964.

SCOTT, F. R. *Civil Liberties and Canadian Federalism*. Toronto: University of Toronto Press, 1959.

TARNOPOLSKY, W. S. *The Canadian Bill of Rights*. Toronto: The Carleton Library No. 83, 1975.

Delegation:

BALLEM, J. B. "Note on Marketing Legislation – Delegation by the Dominion Parliament to a Provincial Board," (1952) 30 *Canadian Bar Review*, 1050.

COMANS, C. K. "Co-operation Between Legislatures in a Federation – Delegation – The Australian Experience," (1953) 33 *Canadian Bar Review*, 814.

CORRY, J. A. "Difficulties of Divided Jurisdiction; Appendix: The Delegation of Power by Dominion to Province or by Province to Dominion," *Appendix 7 to Report of Royal Commission on Dominion-Provincial Relations*. 1940. Ottawa: Queen's Printer, 1940.

LYSYK, K. "Constitutional Law – The Inter-Delegation Doctrine: A Constitutional Paper Tiger?" (1969) 47 *Canadian Bar Review*, 271.

NOTE ON THE EDITOR

Peter H. Russell graduated from the University of Toronto in philosophy and history in 1955. He received a Rhodes scholarship and obtained his B.A. from Oxford University in philosophy, politics and economics. He joined the staff of the University of Toronto in 1958 where he is now a Professor of Political Economy and Principal of Innis College. Professor Russell has published a number of articles and books relating to the Supreme Court of Canada, constitutional law and political theory. He recently spent two years teaching in East Africa where he carried out a study of the administration of justice in Uganda.